Healthy Martial Arts

Winner
Eastern USA International Martial Arts Association
Readers Choice Award

Dr. Jolie Bookspan

ISBN: 0-9721214-4-7

Foreword
by Grandmaster Sean Elliot Martin

First of all, congratulations. By picking up this book, you show that you approach the martial arts with seriousness and wisdom. There are various reasons why people study martial arts. Students pursue physical health, mental discipline, spiritual enlightenment, friendly (or not-so-friendly) competition, artistic expression, cultural preservation, and/or self-defense through martial arts training. No matter your interest in the martial arts, this book is an absolutely invaluable tool, and there is no one more qualified to write it than Dr. Jolie Bookspan. Dr. Bookspan's achievements in the fields of sports medicine, exercise physiology, and martial arts are too many to be easily listed, and I am among the many who believe her to be the greatest fitness expert alive. She is a tireless researcher and teacher who has traveled the world in the pursuit of knowledge and better ways to communicate that knowledge. She is a student who has the patience and the humility to continually learn from others. She is a martial artist of astonishing discipline and physical ability. Perhaps most importantly, she is a strong and dedicated person who has seen and experienced physical suffering first-hand and has healed herself and others. I have literally seen tears of gratitude in the eyes of individuals who returned to thank Dr. Bookspan for stopping their pain.

Although I did not realize the true significance at the time, I came to a full appreciation of Dr. Bookspan's miracles when I recalled the afternoon that two of my advanced students, Christopher Michael Emmolo and Elizabeth Pallack, and I spent at the Philadelphia museum. We joined Dr. Bookspan and her associates to take photographs for this very book. Between shots, Christopher and I slung each other around like rag dolls as usual (our idea of having a good time). Elizabeth turned handsprings and back flips with one of Dr. Bookspan's students. We had fun, but I thought nothing of it at the time. It was only later that I realized the importance of that afternoon. Less than a year before, Christopher believed that he would never be able to train as a martial artist again due to crippling arthritis. Elizabeth had been told that any kind of gymnastics would be impossible for the rest of her life due to a very severe ankle injury she suffered as a teen. These conditions had robbed them of their lives. That was before they began to work with Dr. Bookspan.

Perhaps the key to Dr. Bookspan's miracles lies in her ability to demystify the methods of healthy living, and to empower the individual to take control over his or her own well-being. You just need the knowledge to do the job right. Depending upon your own background, you may already be aware of certain principles of healthy martial arts practice that are covered in this book. However, I believe that every reader, no matter how educated, will learn crucial information from this work. The benefits of such knowledge are numerous: personal health, avoidance of injury for one's self and one's students, increased efficiency of particular techniques, and perhaps even (dare I say it?) avoidance of lawsuits. Whatever your motivation, your choice to study this book is a sign that you are ready to take personal control of your own life and health in the martial arts and begin a new phase of your journey. May this journey bring you more than you ever hoped for.

Grandmaster Sean Elliot Martin, Soke (Founder) and Shihan (Senior Master, 6th degree black belt) of the Kage Essensu (Shadow Essence) martial arts system,
Godan (5th degree black belt) Jiu-jitsu,
Godan (5th degree black belt) freestyle karate,
Multiple award winner in the EUSA International Black Belt Hall of Fame

Healthy Martial Arts
Table of Contents

When the student is ready,
the lesson appears
—Buddhist proverb

"No matter how you may excel in the art of karate,
and in your scholastic endeavors,
nothing is more important than your behavior
and your humanity as observed in daily life."
—Master Gichin Funakoshi, founder of Shotokan karate

What is a Martial Arts Lifestyle?

Training in the martial arts is more than interrupting your day at specific times to change clothes, and bow, do strange exercise, then return to sedentary behavior, poor posture, and undisciplined actions. Martial arts is not only what you do in the training hall. It is designed as a system of learning how to live your regular life.

A martial arts lifestyle is thinking and acting in healthy patterns throughout daily life. It is seeking out knowledge. It is living a life of strong body and mind through cheerful, healthy movement in daily activities of cleaning the house, and lifting and carrying groceries. A martial arts lifestyles is interacting with people, animals, and objects in kind and honorable ways.

"Master the divine techniques of the Art of Peace
and no enemy will dare to challenge you."
—Morihei Ueshiba, creator of Aikido, who sought to transform violence and destruction to techniques of harmony

This book shows ways to transfer all the various martial arts training to daily life. Time to begin.

"Indeed, man wishes to be happy
even when he so lives as to make happiness impossible."
—St. Augustine

Specificity

Specificity is a training term. It means that skills like strength, speed, awareness, and courage need specific practice. Practicing one skill does not automatically or directly transfer ability to another. This chapter tells how specificity works so that you can train better. Each chapter in this book shows how to develop another part of the whole and how to make them all work together.

Physical Specificity

To develop a skill you need to practice the skill. To become fast, you must train fast. To develop jumps, you must jump. Strength, power, endurance, agility, focus, and mental stability are different body systems. Each develops through different training. Exercising one part, such as arms or legs, or one ability like strength, flexibility, or patience does little to develop the others.

Long runs give you cardiovascular improvement specific to running, not sustained combat with many punches. Strength athletes do not look like body builders, even though they often can lift more weight and are stronger. Strength athletes train differently than body builders and get different results. Slow weight lifting or slow forms practice does not train the rapid joint movement needed in quick fighting moves, or to catch a falling child. Slow lifting may build strength, like any other weight lifting, but not the power that depends on speed, or the injury prevention from training rapid stabilization.

The martial arts asks you to look for all the different parts, practice them, and use them in all their forms. Skills do not work in isolation for real life. Instead of exercising by isolating and separating each ability or body part, this book shows how to use each to augment the others.

Mental Specificity

You practice respect in a training hall, dojo, kwoon, and dojang. You bow to the space before entering, and thank it when leaving. You do this to deliberately put in your mind that you are entering a special place where you will benefit. Then your actions follow. Mentally do the same with all the spaces you enter and leave. The market, the school, the theater. When you do that you will not litter. You will not stick gum, or do other things that show you do not understand respect.

You must train goodness to achieve goodness. Just practicing forms and punches will not do this. You must practice happiness to be happy.

"Men acquire a particular quality by constantly acting a particular way—you become just by performing just actions, temperate by performing temperate actions, brave by performing brave actions."
—Aristotle, Greek philosopher, 384-322 B.C., pupil of Plato

Specificity in Life Skills

In the martial arts, sometimes you learn things but don't know why. In school and life, you have to do many things that you don't know when or how you will use them. Sometimes sad things happen and you wonder why they happen at all. The martial artist will use all the many experiences to learn how to make everything better that comes after.

A long time ago, far away, in Morocco, a little girl was born to a family of spinners. She learned the craft of spinning. It was a hard life. One day her father sold her to weavers. Afraid and abandoned, she learned the craft of weaving. It was a hard life.

Pirates swept through the village and captured her. They took her on their boat. In the jail cell where they kept her, worms crawled the walls.

She was taken to the island of Java and taught to make masts. She was taken to forests to cut down trees and saw wood. It was a terrible and hard life. One night aboard the ship a storm came and broke the ship apart. Everyone was thrown into the water. She began to swim, past the others drowning. It was a terrible night. She swam until she got to the only landfall—China. She wandered the coast, thinking of the hard life she had. "What was that all for? I don't even know who I am anymore."

In China, legend foretold that a foreign woman would come and make a wondrous tent for the Emperor. She was brought to the emperor. He said to her, "Make me a wondrous tent."

She said, "Make you a wondrous tent?" "How can I make you a tent? If you want a tent, bring me cloth." They told her they didn't have such materials.

She said, "I was once a spinner. Bring me a certain kind of worm." These were the worms of her jail cell–silk worms. She spun wondrous silk for them. They had never seen such thread.

She said, "Here is the thread for your material." They said, "We don't know how to make cloth from such thread." She told them, "I was once a weaver. I will weave this."

With the incredible silk cloth, she said, "You have your tent." But they didn't know how to make it stand. They said it was soft. How will it stand?" She said, "You must make tent poles. They didn't understand, and she said, "I was a mast maker, I will carve the wood for you and show you."

She made the most wondrous tent. All the misfortunes of her life were the skills she needed to survive and to serve her.

"You may train for a long time,
but if you merely move your hands and feet and jump up and down like a puppet, learning
karate is not very different from learning a dance. You will never have reached the heart of
the matter; you will have failed to grasp the quintessence of karate-do."
—Master Gichin Funakoshi

Healthy Strength, Endurance, and Power Training
Joint and Muscle Stabilization

Strength, endurance, and power training are more than doing separate exercises to work
separate muscles. Many common exercises do not train your muscles in ways they need to
work in real life. Strengthening, by itself, does not decrease risk of injury or increase skill and
ability. Some exercises train the body to move in ways that are not healthy. The effective, fun
skills in this chapter strengthen while retraining healthy movement patterns for health and
joint stability. This chapter shows how to train your muscles the way they need to move and
work together both in martial arts and daily life.

Functional Conditioning

Exercising the body in ways used for real activity is called functional exercise. Long ago,
traditional martial arts used training exercises similar to fighting technique. Different areas of
the body were taught to work together, not exercised as separate parts. Later, exercises
changed and became isolated from their purpose.

You do not fight by lifting weights overhead slowly and carefully. Lifting weights to isolate
specific muscles does not train the multi-function movement that strengthens the body and
stabilizes joints during daily life or fighting moves. You do not fight bent over. Doing
crunches will not train abdominal muscles the way they work to hold your torso in position,
or power your moves in martial arts when standing up. You do not move in sparring and
fighting by taking even steps on a level surface. Running on a treadmill or other machine
does not train ability to run, jump, and pivot with agility, to judge uneven terrain, and move
with the changing balance and stabilization that prevents ankle sprain and leg injury.

A main function of muscles is to pull with enough tension to hold bones in a specific position, or keep them from moving to unhealthy positions. When you don't use muscles to do this, slouching and unstable joint positions result. A more effective way of training is to change the practice of exercise "for each body part" or "large muscle groups and small muscle groups" to natural motion and joint stabilization. Working muscle groups often promotes poor function, which is missing the point of strength training. The functional exercises in this chapter train effective martial arts technique, strengthen the body as a whole, and retrain your muscles to position your joints for stability, injury prevention, and healthy movement prevent injuries—all at the same time.

"Hoping to see karate included in the universal physical education taught in our public schools, I set about revising the kata so as to make them as simple as possible. Times change, the world changes, and obviously the martial arts must change too. The karate that high school students practice today is not the same karate that was practiced even as recently as ten years ago, and it is a long way indeed from the karate I learned when I was a child in Okinawa."
— Gichin Funakoshi, *Karate-do: My Way of Life* (1956)

How Muscles Work

What do muscles do? How do they move you? When you make a picture in your mind of muscles working, what do you see? To train wisely, you need to see. Picture muscles like marionette strings. They pull. When they pull, they move the bone they connect to. All skeletal muscles work by pulling bones. Look at the back of your hand and move your fingers. The moving "strings" are the tendons of your arm muscles that connect to your fingers to pull your fingers back. Turn your hand over to see the strings in your wrist. They are the tendons of the muscles that bend your hand and fingers. Feel at the back of your knees. On each side, you can feel the strings that are the tendons of the hamstring muscles. Hamstrings connect upper leg to lower leg and pull to bend your knee. Hamstrings also attach to the bottom of your hip bone to help pull your leg back.

Figure 3-1. The biceps muscle connects to the lower arm bone at the inner elbow. When your biceps contracts, it pulls your lower arm upward, bending your elbow.

Lunge and Front Stances

Done properly, lunges and stances strengthen leg and knee muscles, and train healthy knee position you can transfer to daily life to use for healthy bending. Torso and knee position are key to getting the most strengthening, stretch, and effective use from stances and lunges.

Figure 3-2. Good front knee placement over foot. Torso upright, back straight, not arched.

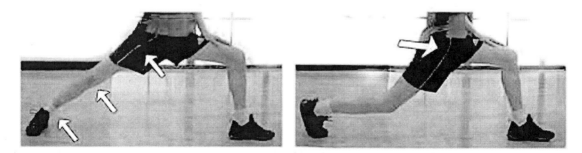

Figure 3-3. Left—For stances press the back leg in line with leg muscles to keep weight from pushing down and inward on the knee joint and arch of the foot. Lifting force to safeguard knee is indicated by arrows. Right—For lunges turn the back foot straight. Tuck your hip to stretch the front of the hip of the rear leg. Upright pelvis begins at arrow.

Front Leg Position. Keep the front knee over the front foot, not forward of the foot, or swaying inward.

Back Leg Position. Some front and side stances are done with the back foot turned out. Use your leg muscles to keep the leg from sagging downward and inward on the inside knee. Press outward enough to keep your weight on muscles and off the knee and ankle joints. Don't increase the arch of the lower back. Keep your torso upright. In the lunge, the back foot is straight, not toe-outward. Keeping the foot straight adds stretch to the rear leg, foot, and hip. The lunge is a multi-muscle exercise that should be used for daily life bending during household activity, giving exercise and stretch while it trains martial arts skills. The lunge strengthens and accustoms the body to functional movement for stronger smoother stances and natural movement for the martial arts.

Strengthening Using the Lunge. To get a functional moving stretch and strengthening exercise, lower and raise the body in lunge position without moving the feet. Start by standing in lunge position with the back foot straight, not turned. Center your weight between both legs, not leaning on the front leg. Lift the rear heel. Bend both knees to lower your body straight down without moving the feet. Don't let the front knee come forward when lowering; keep the front knee over the front foot. Keep your torso straight and upright. Don't lean forward or arch the lower back. Start with ten lunges, and increase. Practice lunges first slowly, then more quickly to train functional speed and power.

To increase the strength and function of the lunge, hold hand weights. Lift the weights upward as you rise from each lunge. Lower the weight as you lower into a low lunge. Use a variety of curls, overhead presses, shrugs, lifts to the side and front. You don't need expensive weights or equipment. Lift buckets, furniture, household items, spare auto parts, bicycles, and children. Involve children in learning healthy fun movement.

Do not lean back or let your lower back arch when lifting the weights upward. Leaning and arching shift the load off your muscles and onto your low back. Tuck your hip and use torso muscles to hold your body straight. Don't let your front knee sag inward or forward as you bend. Press your body weight toward your heel and use thigh muscles to position the knee over the foot.

To progress, lunge with your front foot on a bench. Keep your weight centered on both legs. Keep weight on your entire front foot, not just toes. Then, turn around, putting the rear foot on the bench. Center your weight, keeping your back foot straight, not turned outward. Keep your knee over the foot as you lower. Don't let the knee come forward under the weight of lowering. Hold your body weight upward on your leg muscles to keep body weight from pressing downward on the joint, making the knee hurt.

Squat and Horse Stances

The squat is a functional strengthener. Done properly, squats strengthen hip, legs and knees while training good bending position to use for all daily bending for objects on floor and low areas. Use partial squats for household lifting to train whole body movement that combines balance, posture, strength, and flexibility, and protects the back from bad bending.

Done incorrectly, squats and stances shift your weight to the joints of your lower spine and knees. Practice with a mirror to see knee and back position. The idea is to use your leg and hip muscles, not shift body weight onto your knee.

Keep your weight back toward your heels. Move your hips back without arching the low back. Keep your hips tucked under. Keep your knees over your feet, not forward or inward. Keep your kneecaps in the same direction as the feet. Keep your weight on the sole of the foot, not the arch. Feel the stance in your thigh and hip muscles, not the knee joints.

Figure 3-4. For healthy squatting and horse stances, keep lower leg upright, knee over foot (middle and right). Tuck hip under so that the back is straight, not arched. Don't let the hip stick out in back or knee come forward (left).

To progress, lift weights when rising with each squat. Try a variety of curls, presses, shrugs, lifts, and other movements used in martial arts. Do one-legged half squats. Keep the standing leg from wobbling or turning in at the knee to develop healthy leg positioning while increasing strength.

To sit in a full squat, keep heels on the floor, a customary sitting posture in much of the world. Sitting on heels—not toes—reduces pressure on the knees and is a built-in functional Achilles tendon stretch. Avoid squatting on the ball of the feet. It pressures the knees. Keep body weight back toward the heels and the heels down on the ground. Maintain feet and knees in the same direction to avoid twisting knee. Avoid pressing body weight inward on the knees or arches. Keep knees over feet, not drooping inward.

Figure 3-5. When sitting in a squat (left), keep heels down, with your weight on your heels for better strengthening and stretch while protecting your knees.

Pushups and Planks

Pushups and planks (holding a pushup position without pushing up and down) functionally strengthen many areas at once. Done properly they train holding healthy spine and other joint position that transfers to standing movement, and improve endurance and skill in maneuvering body weight.

Another benefit of pushups and planks, which put body weight on the arms, is to strengthen bones of the forearms, wrist, and hands. One of three main sites of osteoporosis is the wrist.

The main training benefit of pushups for health in the martial arts is to train holding the spine in position against load. Learn to hold straight position, without letting your spine sag into an arch. You will feel your abdominal muscles working strongly.

Figure 3-6. Don't let the back arch or sway (left), or hike up (right). Both poor postures shift the exercise away from the back and abdominal muscles.

Push-ups done without preventing low back sway are not effective exercise, do not train stabilization, and hammock the lower spine under body weight. The resulting back pain is often a mystery to people who think they are exercising to prevent back pain.

Hold your head up straight in line with your back. Keep the upper back from rounding. Keep elbows slightly bent, not locked straight. If arms are too weak to support body weight, strengthen them, but don't injure elbow joints by locking. Keep body weight distributed over the entire hand, not only the heel of the hand, to strengthen the wrist without compressing the joint. Use a mirror or training partner to help determine positioning.

Figure 3-7. When you pull your torso to straight position, you will work abdominal muscles

You use back, hip, and abdominal muscles to prevent the lower back from swaying into an arch. This same repositioning knowledge is critical for healthy positioning in life, the martial arts, and back pain control.

If holding a tucked pushup position even for a few seconds without arching is difficult, it becomes clear why posture sags under body weight throughout the day, pressuring the low back. Use pushups and planks, holding straight position to train for real-life posture and martial arts movement. If you can't do many pushups, don't be discouraged or do them on knees. Hold a real pushup position to functionally train your abdominal and back muscles at the same time. The point is to learn how to hold your own body weight in healthy position. You don't train this on your knees. Try one pushup, then two, then more. When your core muscles are strong enough to hold spine posture without arching during slow pushups, increase power with increasingly fast pushups. When strength increases so that body weight is not enough resistance, put weights, children, or training partners on your back, without letting your low back arch or sag. Chapter 4 on core and abdominal training explains using muscles to strengthen and stabilize the torso during movement.

Strength and Stability Pushups and Planks
For all the stability planks and pushups that follow, prevent your low back from arching, not by tightening the abdominal muscles, but using them to move the spine into healthy position. Transfer the knowledge of how to use abdominal muscles to change hip and spine angles to hold a straight body position when you are standing and moving.

Plank With One Arm Lifted. Hold a straight plank and lift one arm straight in line with your body. Relax your shoulder and straighten your upper body, instead of straining to lift your arm against a rounded upper back. Keep your body flat, not turned to the lifted side. Hold for increasing amounts of time, without letting your back sway downward under the load.

Figure 3-8. Pushup position with one arm lifted. Upper back straight, not rounded.

Extended Pushup. Hold your arms far in front of your body. Hold a straight position without letting your lower back sway down toward the floor.

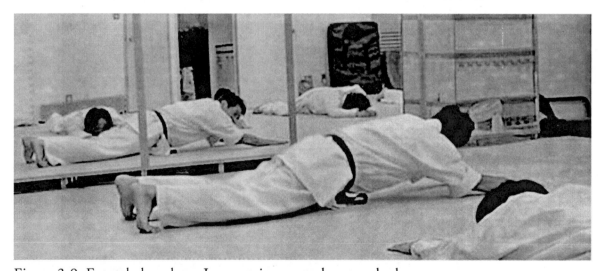

Figure 3-9. Extended pushup. Lower spine neutral, not arched.

Pushups and Planks With Feet Raised. Prop your feet on any support at various heights. Hold a straight position without letting your back sag into an arch. If you let your lower back sag under your body weight, you are missing the benefit and purpose of this exercise.

Figure 3-10. Pushups with feet raised. Train straight position without lumbar sagging.

More Strength and Stability Pushups. Do pushups and planks with both hands on a medicine ball or larger ball that rolls. Use abdominal and core muscles to keep your body straight. If you let your lower back sag downward under your body weight, you are missing the benefit and purpose of this exercise. Sagging is not the natural lumbar curve.

Try pushups or holding a pushup position on one arm without letting the lower back arch, or turning your body to the side. Use core muscles to keep body straight. Try balancing with each hand on a separate ball. Try pushups with hands on one ball and feet on another ball or other rolling or unstable object. Switch hands in the air, and other inventive variations.

Figure 3-11. One-handed pushups are one of many training moves on a ball or rolling object. Face the ground, not tilting to the side. Keep your back straight using torso muscles.

Handstand

The handstand trains several strength and balance abilities at once, and increases bone density in the arms and wrists, helpful for osteoporosis prevention and martial arts. Denser arm bones benefits arts like capoeira that use arm balancing techniques, striking arts that hit with and receive strikes on the forearms, all forms that deliver punches and hand strikes, and grappling arts using bone locks. Following are two ways to do handstands.

To get started with a quick handstand, stand with your back to a wall, standing one to two feet away. Crouch down to put both hands on the floor. Step one foot high up on the wall behind you. The front of your body now faces the wall. Lift the other foot to pull yourself to a handstand with both feet on the wall. Keep your hip tucked to prevent arching and to hold your body straight. The handstand is a great opportunity to train neutral hip position.

Add a leg stretch to the handstand by leaving one foot against the wall and bringing the other leg as far away from the wall as you can, to an overhead split. Increase the stretch by bringing the foot that is against the wall lower, closer to hip height. Use a hand position far enough from the wall that you can extend both legs.

The second handstand method springs onto the hands from a stand. Face a wall about two feet away. Quickly and lightly step forward onto one leg. Lean over, placing both hands on the floor about a foot away from the wall. Immediately swing your back leg high and let the other leg quickly follow upward. Put both feet against the wall and hold, Figure 3-12.

Increase strength and function from handstands with dips—small pushups down toward the floor and back up to the handstand position. Increase arm strength and balance by shifting your weight from arm to arm. Work up to holding a handstand without a support, and walking on hands. When coming down from the handstand, either forward or backward, land lightly to prevent injury.

Figure 3-12. Handstands strengthen the upper body and help balance, even when done against a support. Left—avoid arching the back. Right—Get better balance training and practice using core muscles to maintain straight body position.

Pull-ups and Hangs

Pull-ups are functional training for strengthening and hauling yourself up or others down. Hang from a bar, doorjamb, or tree limb. Tuck hips under, as described for pushups. Tucking specifically trains core muscles in a functional manner to hold healthy positioning.

If you cannot yet do full pull-ups, just hang to train grip, arm strength, and body posture. Make increasing efforts to pull. Use a step to boost the initial lift, then lower body weight unassisted. Avoid relying on machines that allow using less than body weight. These machines prevent needed training of hanging against full body weight. Do functional pulling up by climbing trees and ropes. Hang from chinning bars or tree limbs and "walk" your hands to move side to side. For those who feel that body weight is not enough to build strength, add more weight—a knapsack, a friend, or hang and pull up with one arm.

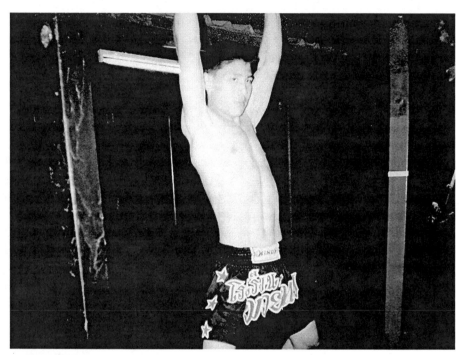

Figure 3-13. Strengthen upper body and grip with pull-ups. In this photo, the lower back is arching. Increase functional training by straightening body position. Tuck the hip as if starting a partial crunch to pull the body straight.

Back Strengthening and Stabilizing

A tightened, forward-bent posture occurs frequently from a daily life of sitting, slouching, and then exercising by bending forward for crunches, leg lifts, and touching toes. If you spend much time bending forward, your body will obey. It will become bent like an old person. It is important to exercise the back to both straighten out and extend backward. Chapter 5 on flexibility covers how to retrain your back to healthy straight position. The following exercises strengthen and retrain your back for healthy, stable position in daily activities and martial arts.

Upper Body Extension. Lie face down, hands under chin or to the sides. Lift and lower your upper body without using hands. Don't force or pinch. Keep your neck straight and lift with the upper body, instead of bending back at the neck. Strengthening back muscles though movement that extends the spine is different from the injurious process of arching or hyperlordosis. In arching, the weight of the upper body compresses the bent lower spine. In extension, muscles contract to strengthen without folding and pinching the low back under body weight. If done by lengthening the spine, extension unloads the discs, which are compressed and loaded with forward bending. It is a more effective strengthener and retraining exercise than standing on hands and knees and lifting one arm and leg.

Figure 3-14. Upper body extension functionally strengthens the back. Done right, you learn upper body straightening rather than craning the neck and lower back to raise the head.

Lower Body Extension. Lie face down, hands under chin or to the sides. Keep knees straight to lift legs a few inches then lower several times. Or start with one leg at a time then progress to both. Learning to use muscles to stretch the front of hip while extending the leg helps counter the shortened, bent-forward hip that contributes to tight, painful posture. Lower back extension exercises back muscles without loading the discs, which occurs with forward bending.

Figure 3-15. Lower body extension functionally strengthens, stretches, and extends the hip

Rowing Pushup. Although lifting weights bent over can strengthen muscles, over time, the discs may degenerate and push out of place, which is called disc herniation. Instead of bending over to lift weights for strengthening, use rowing pushups. You will train straight stable spine position while getting the benefits of lifting weights to the back.

Figure 3-16. Hold a tucked pushup position. Lift weights to strengthen back and arms while training stabilized straight torso position using core muscles. Stay flat, not turned.

Back Bends and Back Bend Pushups. It is important to strengthen back muscles by moving them away from the overstretched, bent-forward position. Back bends can be helpful for this, and good as a multi-joint stretch and strengthener.

Lie on your back with knees bent, feet on the floor. Bend both hands overhead with fingers facing back toward your shoulders. Push your hands and feet against the floor to lift hips and shoulders from the floor. Don't strain or over-tighten your back while lifting. Hold the lifted position briefly then lower. Work up to at least 10 to 20 back bend pushups, up and down.

Figure 3-17. Use back bends for multi-segment strengthening, stabilization, and stretch. Do back bend pushups by pushing up and down from the ground many times. Don't force up, or land on your head on the way down. Learn to extend the entire spine, not only pinch and bend from one or two hyper-mobile segments.

Hands, Wrists, and Elbows

Traditional equipment to train the hand and wrist in the different martial arts were just available heavy objects, usually farming tools, to carry, grip, swing, hold during forms practice, and lift for exercise and contests.

Eventually specific tools developed. Goju-ryu karate and others use chishi (strength stones) and nigiri game (gripping jars) for grip training. Chashi (or chishi), originating in China, are five to fifteen pound round cement blocks with a stick handle about the length of the user's shin. Chikairashi are ten pound stones originally used in Okinawa. Sashi are stone or iron weights with a handle, held like dumbbells by the hands or feet during technique training. Tetsugeka iron boots were worn for kicking training. Some Okinawan styles use the tan, a barbell-like weight, in various stances for twisting moves and rolling on forearms to toughen. The 70-80 pound (approximately 35 kg) Goju style konguken is a large oval ring of iron pushed, pulled and twisted by one or more training partners for arm and body strengthening. India clubs are like weighted bowling pins, thrown, juggled, and swung for wrist, hand, and arm strengthening. The Kwan-tao (General Kwan's knife) is a heavy kung-fu ax swung to strengthen wrists and forearms. Various bolos and ropes with weighted ends were adapted from hunting tools in many cultures, and swung for entertainment and exercise.

Figure 3-18. Many well-known weapons were originally farming tools. Nunchaku were used for rice harvesting.

There is no need to buy training tools. Use household items to strengthen hands and wrists. Carry suitcases, buckets, grocery bags, and other items with handles, arms by your sides, holding with finger grip (farmer's carry). Carry heavy dumbbells or any heavy item across the room, lifting and setting down properly, using legs, not bending forward. Use the farmer's carry for unwieldy items like plate weights, phone books, logs, and encyclopedias, as if they were suitcases, to train finger and hand grip. Train pinch-grip and holding-grip strength by finger-carrying and palm-carrying partially inflated medicine balls of different weights, full laundry bags, bags of sand and gardening soils and mulch, rubber balls filled with water and any hard to grip objects. Practice swings with pipe, lengths of rebar, tire irons, brooms, and garden tools.

Figure 3-19. Gears, brake drums, axels, and machine parts make handy weight training

Dangle a weighty item from a rope tied to the middle of a stick or pipe. Hold the stick horizontally in both hands with the weight hanging between the hands. Roll the weight up, twisting one hand at a time toward the body like a motorcycle throttle, until the weight winds up the stick. Then roll hands the other way to lower the weight. Change grip to an underhand grip and repeat. Then move both hands to one side of the rope so that the stick is unevenly weighted. Try to maintain the stick horizontal while winding and unwinding the weight up and down the rope. Strengthen hands and wrists in a similar and simple way by driving screws in a block of wood using a screwdriver. Then reverse each screw back out. Repeat with the other hand.

Use daily life for natural hand training: Open jars. Wring wet clothes. Work with clay. Give massages. Scrub floors. Use pliers, hand tools. Snap sticks. Squeeze things. Saw wood. Shuck corn. Chop vegetables. Husk coconuts.

Carry groceries and children with hands, not a cart. Don't lean back when carrying. Stand straight, torso tucked using core muscles. Chapter 4 on abdominal and core training explains how leaning back shifts weight to the low back, and how standing straight using torso muscles reduces back pain and gives better training when lifting and carrying.

For pushups and handstands, keep body weight distributed over the entire hand and fingers, not concentrated on the wrists. Distributing weight increases hand strength while uncompressing the wrist joint. Do pushups on fists, on fingertips, then fewer fingers, and groupings of fingers. Start by holding the pushup position, then progress to pushups.

Figure 3-20. Train wrist, hand, and finger strength with a variety of pushups and planks

Hang from a bar or tree limb to strengthen grip. Increase time held. Hang from fingers, then fewer fingers, and groupings of fingers. Perhaps eventually to hang from one finger. Hang from door jams and oddly shaped overhead structures for finger grip training.

Jump up to hang from fingers, instead of carefully grasping a bar, to practice unexpected situations requiring quick, sure grasp. Instead of hanging from a pull-up bar, loop a towel over the bar. Grip the towel at each end and hang to train grip. When practicing handstands, practice on fists and fingertips too.

Wrap rubber bands and other thick stretchy bands around fingers. Open, close, and twist fingers against the tension of the bends. Hold one hand closed with the other and try to open. Regularly stretch fingers back gently, and open fingers as wide as possible. Get days of rest between intense periods of training finger and handgrip to prevent tendon overuse.

Figure 3-21. Train finger and wrist by resisting rubber bands, webs, or your other hand wrapped around fingers, and gripping and opening against clay, sand, and other substances. Use opening, closing, diagonal, and twisting moves.

Feet and Ankles

Feet and ankles need exercise. Tight, weak feet and ankles are more likely to cramp, hurt, strain, and develop plantar fasciitis and deformed toes. Weak, unused toes easily deform and curl. Toes must be straight and strong for balance and healthy gait. Weak, overly stretched ankles are prone to recurrent sprains. Feet are easy to condition since they routinely bear body weight and movement forces greater than body weight.

Exercise feet by increasing general exercise with attention to using foot muscles to hold foot posture instead of letting muscles atrophy in "supportive" shoes. Use ankle and thigh muscles to keep weight off arches. Don't let feet roll inward on arches when standing and moving. Many cases of "flat feet" are bad posture, not a structural problem.

Rise up and down on toes. Keep weight over the big toe and second toe, not teetering ankles outward. Work up to at least 20 raises on both feet together, then try the same on one foot at a time.

Pick up increasingly heavy things with toes and pass them to your hand while standing and sitting.

Put toes under something heavy like a door, your other foot, or a friend, and lift toes.

Put your heel on the floor and push a heavy object sideways with the outside of the forefoot swiveling from the heel. Then pull the object back the other way with the inside of the foot. Push and pull ten times, change feet, and repeat.

Sit on the floor in front of a heavy object. Push it away with the bottom of your toes. Push at least 20 times on each foot. Carefully try pushing only with the tips of the toes.

Play hopscotch. Hopscotch is a game possibly developed for Roman soldiers to exercise their feet and ankles. Do other fun combination balancing, jumping, and hopping games. Jump rope with shock absorption, so that you cannot hear each landing.

Stand on one foot. Move the other leg in all directions at varying speeds. Try this while on the phone or other activity.

Hold your own foot and ankle in healthy position without slumping downward on the arches. Don't wear a tight shoe to do what your own muscles should. Foot muscles atrophy from the disuse caused by a tight, "supportive" shoe.

Neck

A strong neck reduces chances of a knock out punch and other head and neck injury from strikes. Use functional strengthening techniques that strengthen while retraining healthy neck positioning. One built-in exercise is the daily practice of not allowing your head and neck to tilt and slouch forward during ordinary life and exercise.

Keep head in line with the shoulder. To determine straight placement, stand with your back against a wall, touching the heels, hip, upper back, and head. If standing straight is not comfortable, see Chapter 5 on flexibility for stretches to restore normal resting length so that you can stand straight and still be comfortable (Figure 5-5, 5-7, and hip stretches).

Done properly, neck bridges, can strengthen your neck safely. To do the back neck bridge, lie on your back, knees bent, feet on the floor. Press feet against the floor to lift hips. Press against the back of your head to raise shoulders from the floor. Lift from the shoulders, keeping the neck straight (Figure 3-22). Don't bend your neck back. Bending the neck at high angles compresses the spine and does not train neck muscles to hold you straight, as needed for daily health and martial arts safety. Raise and lower the hips slowly to train positioning, until quicker movements can be done to simulate various martial arts moves.

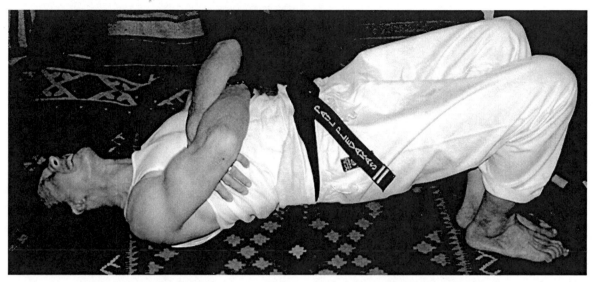

Figure 3-22. Neck bridge, done functionally to strengthen muscles that hold the neck in line

The front neck bridge can be done face down, starting from a pushup position. Lower to balance on your feet and crown of the forehead. Keep your neck in a straight line. For side neck bridges, keep the neck straight. Do not let the neck bend or twist under your body weight. Omit neck bridges with neck injury, and if you have a habitual bad posture of overly pressing chin inward, or head backward, causing neck pain.

Progress to doing neck bridges with feet raised on a ledge, bench, or other surface. Keep the neck straight so that you do not injure it in the name of strengthening it.

Another way to strengthen the neck is carrying loads using a rucksack with a forehead strap. This is a common practice in many areas of the world where people carry large, heavy burdens. Keep the neck and upper body straight, not craning forward against the load.

Headstands can strengthen the neck and body while retraining straight positioning. Done improperly the headstand can compress the neck vertebrae and the discs between them. Positioning is important. Don't allow your neck to bend or compress under body weight. Maintain neck length using muscular effort.

To get started, put the top of your head down on the floor. Place hands on the floor far enough in front of your face that you can see the entire hand. Put each knee on each elbow to begin to balance. Then pull your legs up into a headstand. Practice until you can keep torso position straight, not arched. Don't allow your neck to bend greatly, or compress under body weight.

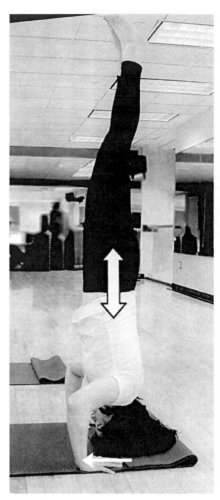

Figure 3-23. Done properly, the headstand strengthens the body and trains healthy neck position. Left—Don't let your low back sag into an arch. Right—Use core muscles to keep hip level and spine neutral. Balance is easier with hands several inches forward of the head (bottom arrows). Do not allow your neck to crane, or body weight to compress your neck. Maintain neck length and position with neck and shoulder muscles.

Wheelchair Athletes

Not exercising or moving enough weakens and predisposes to further pain and disability. This is called secondary injury. Secondary injury can be more debilitating than the initial injury. People with injury or disability, whether using a wheelchair or not, need exercise and effort against conditions that hinder function. Many conditions lead to use of a wheelchair. Goals for wheelchair athletes include restoring function, muscle length, and ability to move independently of the chair, whether for transfers to bed, car, or bathroom, or to gain an increasing portion of time in standing and independent movement. This section explains principles for martial artists who use a wheelchair, and anyone with reduced function who spends long periods sitting.

Time spent out of the chair each day, to stand, lean, hang, use a tilt board, swim or do other exercise, helps restore resting muscle length, reduce pain, prevent skin breakdown and pressure sores, strengthen bones, and helps many aspects of health. In anyone who sits for extended periods, muscles of the front of the shoulder, chest, torso, and hip, and back of the knees become shortened. Back muscles become overstretched, rounded, and weak.

Chronic forward bending from sitting is a factor in round shoulders, tight front (anterior) muscles that prevent comfortable straightening, and can degenerate and herniate discs in the neck and low back by squeezing them backward between vertebrae as they bend forward.

Functional exercise is needed to straighten, not further bend the body forward. Unfortunately, most people stretch and exercise by more forward bending. This is also a critical issue for those with spinal osteoporosis. Curling the upper back forward for conventional abdominal training can pressure the vertebrae into crush fractures. Rethink abdominal exercise as challenging the abs to hold healthy upright torso position against gravity and body weight, and to restore functional posture.

Isometric Abs. Lie flat on your back. Stretch arms up next to your head, hands resting on the floor, elbows near ears. Use abdominal muscles to press your lower back and ribs downward without letting knees bend. Straighten the crease of your hip. Many people become too tight in the front hip and shoulder to straighten their body and lie flat. This is an important therapeutic exercise to prevent muscle shortening and strain, and train straighter standing.

To progress, lie flat, arms next to ears. Hold light dumbbells in each hand about an inch from the floor. Use abdominal muscles to prevent the low back from arching from the floor. Raise and lower the dumbbells about an inch without touching the floor, as many times as you can. Use abs to keep the lower back from rising off the floor, particularly when lowering the weights. Don't allow your ribs to stick up or your back to arch. This functional abdominal exercise simulates daily life activities where you need abs to properly position your back when lifting and carrying overhead.

There are some who say you must bend your knees to "protect the back" from arching. But it is your own abdominal and core muscles that can and should hold your back in position. Keeping knees bent promotes the original problem—bent hip and lack of use of abs. How could you stand up and go about your life if the way to "protect your back" were to keep knees bent? It is not knees that control the angle of the spine. It is your own torso muscles.

Many people let their back arch when standing and sitting, and keep their hip bent all the time, even when standing, then exercise that way, feeding a negative cycle of tight, bent hip, pain, and an arched back. Their hip can becomes so tight that they even need a pillow under their knees to sleep on their back. What they need is to stretch the front of their hip so their hip and legs can extend without pulling the back into an arch. Use the isometric ab exercise to strengthen abdominal muscles at the same time as retraining posture, and to reduce stretch-weakness of the back and tightness of the anterior hip.

Functional Abs. Exercise training is best done in ways that restore healthy body use for daily life, and promote healthy joint position without pressure on the discs of the neck and back. Forward bending exercises like crunches work the abdominal muscles, but are not functional or healthy. After sitting all day, more forward bending only adds to bent forward posture and pressure on the discs of the back and neck. Instead, learn to use muscles in ways that increase health, ability to straighten out, and function for real life. Functional exercise is easy to challenging depending on degree of weakness and overall movement ability.

Sit away from the back of the chair. Reach arms straight and high overhead, pulling biceps back to your ears. Many people arch their back when raising arms and weights overhead. Arching back shifts holding the weight of the upper body off the muscles and onto the low back joints. To shift effort back to the abdominal muscles, tuck the hip to straighten your torso, as if starting a crunch, enough to straighten without curling forward. Don't tighten, just move your torso out of an overly-arched position. Keep arms stretched overhead. Use this changed way of reaching for healthier overhead activities from combing and washing hair, to getting shirts on and off, to putting away groceries.

To progress, face backward to a stretchy band tied to a support at shoulder to head height. Sit (or stand where possible) far enough away for desired tension on the band. Hold the band overhead, not allowing your torso to be pulled back into an arch by the band. Breathe normally. Don't tighten muscles, or allow the hip to tip, or the back to arch. Experiment with small repetitions, pulling the band a few inches forward and back while maintaining straighter torso position, as needed for healthy posture without arching.

Holding a Pushup Position. A key concept to better training is that merely strengthening muscles will not change poor posture or ergonomics that lead to injurious pressures on joints. People often work their abs, believing stronger abs will automatically support the back or help daily activities. However, many people with strong muscles still have back pain from overarching their back when standing and sitting. For this reason, crunches and forward bending has not been as effective as hoped in alleviating back pain and helping life activities. Instead, use abdominal exercise to strengthen while you retrain body mechanics. One example is holding a pushup position (plank).

With as much weight as possible on hands and feet (or lowest limb segment), tuck your hips as if starting a crunch. Do not hike your hips up in the air or drop your head. Use your abs to keep your back straight without even a small arch, to remove the pressure of body weight from the lower back and work the abs to a high degree. Use this exercise to challenge and raise function of the body as a whole, working to support your body weight.

Lifting Weights During Wheel Chair Sitting. Lifting weights while sitting is hard on the back, whether in a wheelchair, exercise ball, or weight bench. The highest forces on the vertebral discs occur when sitting leaning forward—more than any other posture, even more than standing and bending wrong to pick up something. Don't do lifts sitting bent forward. Even for overhead lifts with straight sitting, it is better to transfer to the floor. Practice a variety of arm moves in all directions, speeds, and movements.

Practicing transfer skills of getting back and forth from the chair to other devices is good exercise. Pushing your own wheelchair, when possible, is more good exercise. Most important is to get out of the chair as much as possible, reducing stress on the spine from sitting. Many who are not confined to a chair, already sit much of the day, then sit to exercise. They would also be better served not sitting. Get out of the chair in any way possible to straighten the body, increase mobility, and ability to support body weight.

Power and Plyometrics

Power is how fast you can be strong. Power is speed times strength. By learning to move faster, you increase the power of your moves.

Plyometrics are exercises designed to train muscles for quick, powerful moves. The muscle is first quickly stretched under load then immediately, forcefully contracted. Examples of plyometric training are pushups with a clap in-between each, and rapidly jumping over things or people with quick crouches between each.

Plyometric exercises stress muscles and associated attachments more than other kinds of exercise. Learn and use healthy joint positioning and shock absorption for safe plyometric training.

Plyometric Throwing. Throw and catch a heavy medicine ball against a sturdy wall or in the air in a quick succession of forceful throws and quick deceleration catches, fully bending arms. Many small children love being thrown in the air and safely caught. Remember safety.

Do not arch the low back when throwing or catching. Keep hips tucked. Don't lean back when standing and throwing overhead. Use torso muscles to handle the load, not the low back. The chapter on core and abdominal training explains how to use the core to position and stabilize the torso.

Plyometric Leg Presses and Jumps. From low stances, repeatedly jump high in the air. Land by coming down to low stance. Land lightly on toes, and bend knees when landing. Let the heels come completely down for the next push-off. Land softly. Use the leg and hip muscles for shock absorption. Concentrate on healthy foot, ankle, knee, and hip positioning. Don't let body weight sag inward on the joints. Hold straight positioning.

Plyometric Pushups. Do pushups, pushing off powerfully. Clap hands in the air in between each. Start with lifting hands from the floor, then hands and feet. Land with shock absorption without allowing your low back to arch and sag downward when landing. Land lightly, not heavily or stiffly. Keep hips tucked so that your torso and low back are straight, not arched or bent at the hip.

Do jumping pushups, pushing off powerfully enough to lift hands and feet from the floor. Jump sideways to cross the room, then jump back.

Do jumping pushups, rotating a quarter turn with each jump so that you face the next cardinal compass point each jump—north, east, south, west. Push off powerfully enough to lift hands and feet from the floor. Do four quarter-turn jumps to return to starting position. Then try to jump enough to turn from facing north to south in one jump.

Add balance to plyometric training with pushups on a ball. Push off powerfully to lift hands from the ball and clap in air.

Figure 3-24. Plyometric pushups can be done from the ground or on a ball to add balance. Lower and jump up strongly. Clap in the air. Do many, as quickly as you can.

Partner Strength, Power, and Stability Drills

Partner Pushing Punch. This partner drill trains strong stable shoulder, arm, wrist, hand, and fist position during strikes. Partners stand facing each other. Each partner presses each fist or open hand strongly against the other partner's fist or open hand. Each partner moves through the full range of the strike, back and forth, slowly, pressing at full strength to resist each other. One partner presses one arm forward, the other resists backward while pressing the opposite arm forward against the first partner's resistance.

Maintain straight back position, not arched. Maintain healthy joint angles of all segments.

Figure 3-25. Left and Right—Push each other's arm with strength through the full range of a strike, back and forth. Choose a variety of open and closed hand strikes. Keep hands, wrists, elbows, shoulders, and back in healthy position.

Partner Squats. Back-to-back squats train leg strength and balance during functional movement. Stand back-to-back. Each partner places feet far away from the other partner. Lower with knees over feet, not forward. Keep the back straight and upright, not arched or bent forward. Start with at least ten squats up and down, and work to increase the number.

Figure 3-26. Fun partner squat training for multi-segment strength and balance. Left—Start back-to-back. Don't link arms, just stand far apart and lean against each other. Right—Rise and lower many times, keeping knees over heels. Practice slowly and rapidly.

Figure 3-27. Unhealthy knee positioning. Pushing the knees forward shifts body weight to the knee joints and reduces exercise in the leg muscles. Don't allow the back and head to curl forward (left) or the back to arch (right).

Partner Leg Press. This partner drill trains three skills: leg strength and stability, core, and balance. Lie on your back with feet up. Your training partner puts their chest or back on your feet and assumes straight stable torso position while you press them up and down. When pressing with your legs, don't let hips curl, which stresses the discs. Keep hips on the floor. The partner being pressed maintains straight back position using abdominal muscles.

Figure 3-28. The partner leg press trains multi-function strength, balance, joint stability, and positioning. Keep body and neck straight to train the muscles for healthy positioning and better exercise.

Partner Leg and Arm Press. This partner drill trains arm strength, leg strength, core, and balance. Lie on the back with feet up. Your training partner does pushups on your feet. The partner keeps straight stable torso position while you press them up and down. Both partners move at once and need to balance. When pressing with your legs, don't let hips curl upward and round the back, which stresses the discs. Keep both hips on the floor. The partner being pressed maintains straight back position using abdominal muscles.

Figure 3-29. The partner leg and arm press trains multi-function strength, balance, joint stability, and positioning.

Working in partners is a fun way to train strength, balance, power, cooperation, and team spirit.

Plyometric Arm Press, Standing. The partner plyometric arm press trains arm punching power and recoiling ability of both partners at once. Stand facing a heavy wall, tree, or makiwara (striking) board. Your training partner stands behind you. You powerfully push off the wall, throwing yourself backward. Your training partner catches you by decelerating with their arms. Using this coiled energy, the partner immediately tosses you forward against the wall. Catch yourself by decelerating with your arms. Keep pushing off powerfully back and forth for many rapid repetitions. Switch positions and continue.

Keep your torso position stable, not letting your low back arch under the load of deceleration. Don't let your neck flop. Hold it stable. Don't bang your face against the wall when thrown forward. Practice contacting the wall with open hands and fists in a variety of striking positions.

Figure 3-30. This fun partner plyometric drill trains powerful punches and stable torso positioning under high movement and load. Push off the wall quickly and powerfully. Partner catches and immediately pushed forward strongly. Continue quickly, for many pushes, then switch positions.

Plyometric Arm Press, Reclining. Sit against a wall, or lie back on an incline or sofa, with arms extended, feet on the floor. Have a friend stand between your legs, their back to you, holding their body strongly and straight so they can lie backward with their back on your hands. Fling the partner to an upright stand. When they fall back to you, catch them on your hands, then fling them forward again. This partner reclining arm press can also be done with your partner face down, lying their chest on your hands.

Progress until you can generate enough power to toss your partner upward while you are lying flat without the aid of a wall or other support, Figure 3-31.

Figure 3-31. The reclining plyometric partner arm press trains powerful arms, cooperation, and straight body positioning. Push away and catch the partner quickly, many times.

Plyometric Leg Press. This drill is the same as the previous, but uses feet instead of hands to push and catch. The partner doing the leg presses must use shock absorption with each catch, bending knees and hips. Keep healthy knee positioning. Don't let your knees sway in (knock-knee) under load. The partner being tossed faces either toward or away from the catching partner's feet, and maintains straight body positioning, not letting the upper body bend forward from momentum or gravity.

Figure 3-32. The plyometric partner leg press uses legs to powerfully press away and catch the training partner. The partner holds the body straight and uses muscles for shock absorption.

Effective Strength Training Using a Ball

Two of the least effective uses of an exercise ball are to sit on it to lift weights, and to do crunches. Sitting puts the greatest load on the discs of the low back. Adding weight while sitting further compresses the spine longitudinally. Sitting on a ball does little for strength and balance. You can sit with poor posture and almost no stabilization. The ball does not automatically give posture or exercise. Crunches do not work your abdominal muscles the way you need for martial arts, or almost any other sport or function. Most people stand all day with their hip bent and their back arched, then drape over a ball with their hip bent and back arched. It does not add to health or function. Instead, work abdominal and core muscles during exercise on the ball by using all the principles described in this chapter and Chapter 4 on core training. Use your core muscles to prevent your body from arching under your body weight. Holding position without sagging trains you how to hold your spine in position when standing and doing martial arts. Extending backward over a ball to get a back or hip extension stretch is one thing. Doing exercises while allowing the spine to sag is missing the point and the benefit of core conditioning using the ball.

Do pushups and planks with hands on the exercise ball and feet on the floor, or on another exercise ball. Do pushups with hands on the floor and feet up on an exercise ball or one foot on each of two. In all cases, use core muscles to prevent the low back from sinking into an arch like a hammock under your body weight.

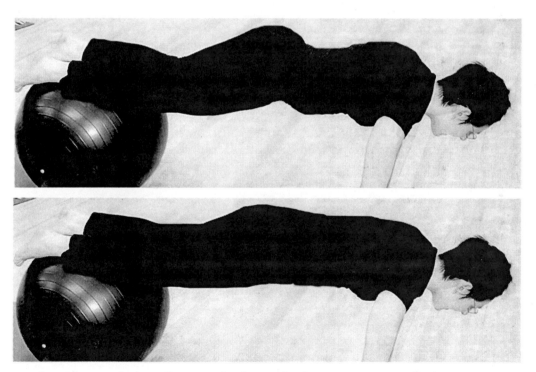

Figure 3-33. Upper photo—Letting the lower back sag into an arch does not strengthen muscles. Arching transfers body weight to lumbar joints. Lower photo—Instead, use torso muscles to move the spine and hip to straight neutral position against loads.

Once you can hold a pushup position with hands on the floor and feet on the ball, lift one leg from the ball without arching your back. Keep your hip tucked under to hold your back straight. The lift will then come from your leg muscles, not by arching your spine. Hold, and repeat many times on each leg. Do pushups with the leg lifted and the body straight.

Figure 3-34. Use muscles to hold neutral and prevent low back arch when lifting the leg. You will feel the effort shift from the low back joints to the abdominal and leg muscles.

Hold a pushup position, one leg on the ball and the other one leg 90 degrees out to the side in the air. Hold and do pushups. Switch legs and repeat.

Hold a pushup position and lift one arm straight up in front. Don't tilt to the side. Keep the arm lifted high and straight in line with the body. Hold your body flat over the floor, not tilted. Once you can balance in good straight position with one arm lifted, add lifting the opposite leg. Hold and repeat many times on each side.

Do side planks by turning to one side to lift one arm upward. Start with feet on the ball and both hands on the floor. Turn your body and raise one arm straight to the ceiling. Hold as long as you can. Do both sides. Then try the side plank with both feet on the floor, and both hands on the ball, pushup style. Turn your body to the side and balance on one hand, lifting the other arm to point straight to the ceiling. Hold as long as you can. Do both sides.

Some people are told to only use the ball on a non-slip surface or to not use it while sweating. While it makes sense not to thoughtlessly slip off, balance challenge is the point. Use muscles to prevent slipping and to maintain position. To train more balance, kneel on the ball. Eventually, learn to stand on it.

The ball can be a helpful tool. Don't waste training by doing crunches or sitting on it. Most people bend forward and sit much of the day. Instead of more forward bending and sitting, use the ball to strengthen in functional ways that transfers to standing and moving skills.

Change Bad Strength Training Moves to New Healthy Ones

There are martial arts practitioners who use traditional techniques, no matter how injurious, because they feel that traditional style must be preserved. It isn't sacrilege or unusual to change traditional moves. Battlefield styles without ground components added ground and grappling techniques when they moved from using long weapons on horseback to personal and police fighting. As some styles of the martial arts spread, developers wanted to appeal to more educated classes. Moves associated with peasants were avoided. Emphasis on techniques for national and personal defense was reduced. Competition styles and aesthetically pleasing forms evolved (katas in Japan and Okinawa, kuen in China, and hyung in Korea) whether useful for actual fighting or not, even if tough on the body. It was an art form. When the martial arts were developed, survival itself took priority. Many techniques that were effective were also unhealthy. The fighting classes were expendable. Their aches and pains were their own problem. Now things can change. You don't have to choose between damaging your body and being able to train. Change is part of martial arts. Change moves that pressure joints to better ones that train you while improving your body and daily life.

Transfer Strength and Power to Real Life

Certain moves that are often used to work out in a gym do not train the body in ways you need for health, daily life, or martial arts. Gym bodies often look artificial and do not have the look, agility, and healthy function of someone who moves in natural real life. Get out of the gym and change the idea of exercise as being "for each body part" or stopping daily life routine to go "work-out," to natural movement the way the whole body needs for real life. Use the real world as your playground. Lift and haul house and garden supplies. Learn to easily walk and move over uneven ground so that when you need to defend yourself, you won't sprain your ankle on a cracked sidewalk. Use muscles to keep healthy joint positioning all the time to get free exercise, to avoid neck, back, and knee pain, and for a stronger look, rather than appear an "easy mark" with unconfident, tight, slumped posture. Take the stairs to train your legs to move you easily when needed. Use lunges and squats every time you bend and lift, not just something to do in a gym then bend over wrong to put down the weights. You will keep your legs strong, and your body accustomed to easy movement. You will save your back and get free exercise. Walk, sit, move, and lift for built-in exercise all day, every day to better prepare you to move, run, and deflect an attack.

Who is Strong? Who is Weak?

It is the weak who are cruel. Gentleness can only be expected from the strong.

Strengthen Discipline

Don't obsess and train to exclusion of living. But don't worry that it takes years to train. As Chinese proverb says, "Talk does not cook rice." Don't fret about missing movies and parties and vice. You are not missing your youth to develop intelligence, skill, discipline, and art.

"For everything you have missed, you have gained something else."
—Ralph Waldo Emerson

Practice Strength of Character

"A champion is someone who gets up when he can't."
—Jack Dempsey

Practice True Power

"Power is the ability to do good things for others."
—Brooke Astor, Presidential Medal of Freedom recipient

Use Strength to Remove Mental Obstacles

In ancient times, a king placed a boulder on a roadway. He hid himself and watched to see if anyone would remove the rock. Some of the king's wealthiest merchants and courtiers came by and loudly blamed the king for not keeping the roads clear. None did anything about getting the big stone out of the way. A peasant came along carrying a load of vegetables. He tried to move the stone to the side of the road. After much pushing and straining, he succeeded. As the peasant picked up his load of vegetables, he noticed a purse lying where the boulder had been. The purse contained gold coins and a note from the king saying that the gold was for the person who removed the boulder from the road. The peasant knew what many never understand. Do something. Improve your condition.

"A man who has attained mastery of an art
reveals it in his every action."
—Samurai adage

Abdominal and Core Conditioning

Some of the martial arts have the concept that power stems from abdomen below the navel, called the hara in Japanese, the tan-joon in Korean martial arts, and the tantien in Chinese. Other styles, like Burmese Bando, Khmer boxing (Pradal Serey), and the Thai styles of Muay Thai, Ling Lom ground fighting, and Thaiyuth, don't have a belief structure about force coming from the torng (abdomen) or any other single area. Thai fighters are among the highest conditioned athletes of any style.

Long ago, martial arts strength training worked the abdominal muscles in the way they are used in martial arts and other real movement. Later, abdominal training grew away from function and became isolated exercise. The drawback of that approach is that, by itself, stronger abdominal musculature does not automatically move the spine into healthy position, enhance athletic ability, or fix back pain. Many strong athletes have back pain. Another frequent issue is the back pain common from conventional abdominal exercises. This chapter shows how abdominal muscles work in the martial arts and daily life. It gives fun, effective exercises that strengthen the core at the same time as they retrain the spine and hip positioning needed to prevent back pain and injury and increase ability.

How Abdominal and Core Muscles Work for Daily Activity and Standing

Using Core and Abdominal Muscles When Standing. You do not fight or stand bent over. Training the core must be in the way it is used. Common exercises for the abdominal muscles bend the body forward (flexion). However, the way you need abdominal muscles to work is to stand straight - pulling forward only enough to prevent backward lean, and hold your spine upright in neutral. A small inward curve belongs in the lower spine. The injurious posture of a large inward curve comes from not using abdominal muscles enough. Doing flexion and core strengthening exercise does not stop this bad posture.

Abdominal muscles run between ribs and hipbone. Without their use, ribs lift up and the front of the pelvis tilts down and forward. The normal small inward lumbar curve exaggerates. This arching pinches the lower spine backward at an angle, squeezing the joints of the vertebrae and surrounding soft tissue. A "swayback" is not just the way you are made. The mastery of using abdominal muscles is to prevent letting the lower back overarch during all daily actions.

Figure 4-1. Left—Upper body lean-back, overarching the lumbar spine. Right—Abdominal muscles pull torso forward enough to reduce the overarch and restore neutral spine.

To feel what abdominal muscles do to support your back, stand up. Lean your shoulders and upper body backward to arch your lower back. Push your abdomen forward. Stick your behind out in back. Feel your upper body weight shift backward as you arch. You may feel a familiar discomfort in your lower back. The exaggerated arch is called hyper-lordosis (often used interchangeably with lordosis).

Hyperlordosis is not healthy and not attractive. It is the source of much lower back pain, usually after long standing, running, and overhead lifting. Hyperlordosis occurs when the abdominal muscles are not deliberately used to reposition the spine to prevent it. Reduce the hyperlordosis by tucking your hip under and pulling ribs downward, as if starting a crunch just enough to reduce the arch in the lower back, level the hip, restore neutral spine, and stand upright. Do not push the hip forward. Do not bend or round the upper body forward. When done properly, posture straightens, and pressure in the low back will be gone.

Abdominal muscles work like all other skeletal muscles. They move the bones they attach to. Don't tighten or clench. Just move the lower spine to restore healthy neutral position. Use abdominal muscles in this way all the time, when standing and reaching during daily life and martial arts training. This use of abdominal muscles exercises the core functionally - the way needed for back pain control during real life, and stronger, safer positioning for all movement.

Tightening Abdominal Muscles is Not the Same as Using Them. It is not useful to tighten muscles when moving. See for yourself. Tighten your legs and run. Tighten your abdomen, press navel inward, and try to breathe in. Tightening prevents full breathing. Try moving around with the area held tightly. If you know healthy movement, you see that tightening stops smooth movement. Tightening also does not correct arched, injurious positioning. Tightening does not move you out of bad posture into good position. It is not tightening that trains the core, powers martial arts moves, or protects the back, it is using core muscles to deliberately reposition your spine, described next.

Using Abdominal Muscles to Punch and Push. Increased core activation during punching comes from positioning the lower spine so that it does not over-arch. Arching (increasing lordosis) reduces the force you can generate and transfers body weight and force of a strike off the abdominal muscles to the lower back. Striking or receiving a strike while arched is injurious. Reducing the arch is done by moving the torso using abdominal muscles.

To feel core muscles at work to reposition, stand near a wall (or surface). Extend your arm forward in strike position. Push your knuckles strongly against the wall, without bending your elbow. Allow the push of your arm to push your back into an arch, Figure 4-2 below left. Push increasingly hard. You may feel the pressure in your lower back.

Figure 4-2. Left—non-neutral hip. To feel how abdominal muscles are needed in punching, press fist, letting upper body lean back and hip tilt forward, arching the lower back. You may feel pressure in your low back. Right—Tuck hip and bring upper body forward until neutral. Feel the pressure in the low back disappear, with greater strength in the punching arm.

Fix your spine positioning by tilting the bottom of your hip under you until straight, Figure 4-2, right. The motion is like beginning a crunch, without rounding the upper body. Pressure in the low back should disappear. You will feel effort shift to the abdominal muscles and strength shift to the punching arm. For all strikes, generate more force and protect your back by using abdominal muscles to move the hip and spine to prevent over-arching.

Figure 4-3. Neutral spine when punching or pushing (right). Neutral position gives a better abdominal workout, a better punch, and shifts the counterforce of the push from the lower back onto abdominal muscles.

Practice the new neutral spine position for all standing and striking. Don't allow your lower back to increase arch at any point. Tuck the hip only enough to prevent overarching and restore neutral spine Don't round forward. Hunching the upper body and head forward is uncomfortable for your neck and back, and puts your chin closer for your opponent to hit.

Using the Core With Overhead Weapons. Weapons, throws, and several blocks and strikes use overhead arm movement. A common error is to lean the upper body backward when raising the arms. Leaning back and lifting the ribs in front increases the lower back arch. Upper body weight presses on the lower back. In some cases, it also increases injurious forces on the shoulder.

Check if you increase the lumbar arch when raising arms overhead. Notice if you lean your upper body backward. Arching the lower back to raise arms is a bad habit.

Instead of arching, maintain neutral spine position, which better powers movement from the abdominal muscles. Tuck the bottom of your hip under to make the line vertical from center hip crest down to the top of the upper leg bone, as in Figure 4-2. Pull ribs down to level. Hip and spinal repositioning to reduce the lower back arch is done by using, not tightening, your abdominal muscles. Reducing the lower back arch will reduce compressive force on the lower back caused by overarching. When using abs to properly position, you will feel immediate improvement in stance, and greater arm power during overhead tactics.

Figure 4-4. Left—Prevent leaning back and lumbar overarching to raise arms for overhead strikes. Right—Use abdominal muscles to tuck the hip to vertical, repositioning the spine. The move will be more powerful and body weight shifts from lower spine onto core muscles.

Figure 4-5. Left—Don't arch your back or lean back to reach overhead. Right—Use abdominal muscles to reduce the lumbar arch and reposition the spine and hip. Note the change in the hip from downward tilt in front to level, seen in the belt.

Using Abdominal Muscles for Overhead Lifting. A common bad habit is allowing the lower spine to increase in arch when lifting weight overhead instead of using abdominal muscles to hold the spine in healthy position.

Figure 4-6. Prevent lower back arching when lifting weight overhead. Arching may occur from leaning the upper body backward (left) or tilting the hip down in front (middle). Keep hip level and upper body upright, reducing lower back arch to neutral (right).

Using Abdominal Muscles to Break Boards. When breaking or holding boards, stop the lower spine from over-arching using abdominal muscles. The hip tuck moves the spine away from pinching backward, reducing force transmitted upon impact.

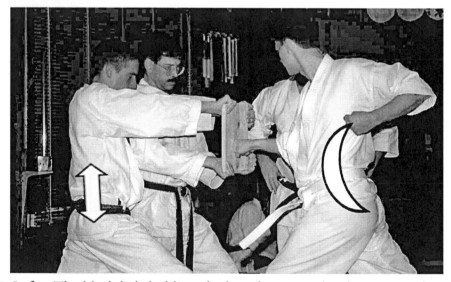

Figure 4-7. Left—The black belt holding the board prevents lumbar over-arch. Right—The white belt has not learned this yet. He arches to draw back the fist (chamber the arm). Note the downward tilt to the front of the white belt compared to the more level black belt.

Using Abdominal Muscles for Elbow Strikes. An arched lower back shifts the leverage of the strike off the abdominal muscles and onto to the lower back. Tucking the hip to restore neutral spine increases the strength of the strike and stops painful low back compression.

Figure 4-8. Right—over-arch. Left—restoring neutral spine for more effective strike. The back of the hip tucks under and the front pulls upward to neutral.

Using Abdominal Muscles to Kick. Stand facing a wall at a distance to swing a side kick. Put your foot against the wall as if you just kicked it. Let your back arch. Begin pushing the wall with your foot without allowing your knee to give way. You will feel pressure, maybe a familiar ache in your low back from daily bad posture habits. Fix your positioning by using abs. Keep hip tucked under. Feel the reduction in pressure on the low back, and a new strength in the kicking leg.

Using Abdominal Muscles for Throws. Arching the low back transfers weight of both your upper body and your opponent to your low back, and makes the throw less effective. Use abdominal muscles to tuck your hip and keep ribs from lifting, to reduce low back arch.

Figure 4-9. Throws/bars with low back improperly arched (left) and straightened (right)

Using Abdominal and Core Muscles for Carrying Gear

Prevent allowing your body to sag under the weight of gear and bags, whether arching your back (left), hunching forward (center), or sagging to the side (right, Figure 4-10). Use muscles to hold your body straight against the load, to exercise muscles in functional ways, and reduce pressure on your joints (Figure 4-11).

Figure 4-10. Leaning with unhealthful posture to offset a load. Shifts effort from muscles to joints. Feels easier, but reduces exercise and increases strain.

Figure 4-11. Use your muscles to hold upright position against load, for functional exercise and health of your joints

Effective Core Training

The exercises in this section strengthen back and abdominal musculature at the same time, and consciously retrain healthy spine position for all standing and moving. These exercises replace conventional forward bending abdominal exercises, which pressure lumbar and neck discs outward, encouraging disc herniation, and rounded posture habits.

Isometric Abs. A major purpose of abdominal muscles is to hold the low back in position without overarching in any activity. The isometric ab exercise strengthens the abdominal and back muscles at the same time, while retraining how to hold the back without arching.

Lie face up, arms overhead on floor, biceps by ears. Hold hand weights an inch above the floor without lifting ribs or arching your lower back. Press the low back toward the floor to reduce the arch. Don't tighten, just use abdominal muscles to move the back to healthy straight position. Transfer this training to control the posture of the spine when standing. Pulse the hand weights up and down a few inches. Don't allow the back to arch at any point.

Figure 4-12. Isometric ab exercise done incorrectly. Don't allow the lower back to arch upward or ribs to lift. Arching loses the purpose and benefit of this exercise.

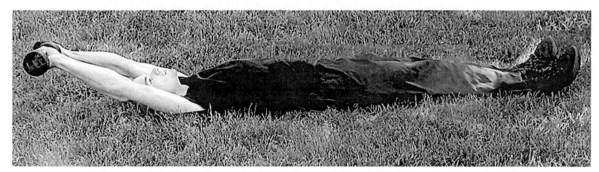

Figure 4-13. Press ribs and lower back down to reduce the lumbar arch. Done correctly, you will feel the load transfer to abdominal muscles, off lower spine and shoulder. Transfer this knowledge to how to prevent overarching when you stand, reach, and lift overhead.

Pushups and Planks. The plank is done by holding a pushup position, usually in the upper position with elbows slightly bent (not locked straight). Done correctly, by not allowing the lumbar spine to arch, the plank is an effective way to retrain core muscles to hold healthy spine position. Much back, hip, and abdominal muscle use is needed to prevent the lower back from swaying into an arch (hyperlordosis) under body weight. The same stabilization repositioning knowledge is critical for neutral spine positioning in life, in the martial arts, and for back pain control.

Pushups and planks done without preventing lower back sway are not effective exercise, do not train stabilization, and reinforce injurious ergonomics. Arching transfers body weight off your core muscles and onto your vertebrae, making the low back hurt. Use a mirror or training partner, where possible, to determine positioning.

Figure 4-14. Don't let your low back arch (left) or hip lift up (right). Arching transmits the pressure of body weight to the low back joints (facets) and does not exercise core muscles.

Figure 4-15. Straight neutral position. Uses abdominal muscles to straighten spine and hip,

Pushup Position With One Arm Lifted. Prevent your back from arching. Hold the body straight and the arm straight in line with the body. Keep breathing.

Figure 4-16. Train straight positioning. Relax shoulder down to hold arm straight in line.

One Hand and Opposite Foot Lifted. Hold a pushup position. Lift the opposite arm and leg and hold. Keep breathing with upper body relaxed. Prevent arching at any point. Switch sides, working up to switching sides by jumping.

Figure 4-17. Upper—Don't arch lower back to lift your leg. Lower—Use muscles to hold neutral spine to lift opposite arm and leg in line with your body. Effort shifts off spine joints, onto hip and leg muscles. Keep shoulder down and upper back straight to lift arm.

Side Plank. Hold a pushup position. Turn to one side and balance on one arm and foot. Use oblique abdominal muscles to prevent your body from sagging. Keep breathing. Practice both sides.

Figure 4-18. Side plank. Hold straight without sagging. Breathe and smile.

Lift the top leg while balancing on one hand and foot. Use oblique abdominal muscles to prevent your body from sagging under its own weight. Lift your leg up to your arm at least ten times. Keep breathing. Practice both sides.

Figure 4-19. Side plank and top leg lifted, training core muscles to hold straight position

Pushups and Planks With Leg Out—The Peeing Dog. Hold a plank position with your body parallel to the floor (flat, not tilted) and one leg held in the air straight out to the side. You will feel core muscles working strongly to hold your body straight. Work up to doing pushups with the leg held to the side. Don't let your back arch. When you can lower and raise in a pushup, rise all the way back to downward dog with your leg still held straight out to the side. Lower to flat pushup position, lower and rise to a pushup, then push back to downward dog, always keeping the leg out to the side. Work up to at least ten. Then more.

Figure 4-20. Fondly called the "peeing dog." Holding straight spine highly works core.

Pushups and Planks With Opposite Arm and Leg Out. Hold a straight pushup position (plank) with one leg straight to the side. Hold the opposite arm straight out to the other side. Use abdominal and back muscles to hold body flat and straight. Work up to pushups.

Figure 4-21. Pushups with opposite arm and leg held directly out to each side

Roman Chair. Sit on a high support. Hook feet under anything secure. Hold your upper body out straight in the air and hold. Roman chair can also be done as a moving stretch/strengthener. Slowly lower your upper body, keeping weight off the low back by pulling upward with abdominal muscles. The body hangs down arched, but core muscles pull upward to keep pressure off the low back. This is an important concept for all the many moves where back extension is needed. Pull up to straight position, hold, and repeat.

Figure 4-22. Roman chair

Medicine Ball Swing. Swing a heavy ball or other object overhead. Do not let your hip tilt forward in front and your low back arch (Figure 4-23, left). Use muscles to hold spine and hip position (right). Belt line is level. Hip is vertical, not tilted from leg to side-hip crest.

To strengthen while training balance, swing the medicine ball while standing on one foot.

Figure 4-23. Left—Medicine ball swing with lower back improperly arched and hip tilted. Right—Compare to neutral spine. Straightening uses core muscles to power the move.

Why Putting Your Hands Under Your Hips for Leg Lifts Does Not Use Abdominal Muscles. Putting the hands under the hips for leg lifts is often taught with the assumption that it "protects" the back by preventing arching from the weight of your legs. However, it is your own abdominal muscles that are supposed to do that. Using your hands to tip the hip is what prevents the abs from working, the opposite of the intention.

To feel for yourself how this works, lie on your back. Arch your back and lift the lower back far from the floor. Lift your ribs up. Now lift both legs a few inches from the floor. The arching will pinch and pressure the lower back. Now start again, this time pressing the small of your lower back against the floor. Push your ribs down. Do not tighten; just move your body. You will feel your abdominal muscles working.

Keep your lower back pressed, and lift both legs again, only a few inches. Pressure in the lower back should be gone, and a new feeling of using abs should begin. Use your own muscles, not your hands, to position your back so that arching does not pressure your lower back.

Partner Core Conditioning

Partner Isometric Abs. Lie on your back with your arms by your ears. Hands are an inch or so above the ground. Lift your arms up against the weight of your partner pressing down on your hands. Pulse your arms up and down, not letting your back arch. Progress until you can lift the weight of your partner. Keep the lift no more than about a foot above the ground.

Figure 4-24. Partner isometric abs, shown properly lying flat throughout the lift. Spine straight and neutral, not pulled into an arch by the resistance of the partner being lifted.

Punching With Bands. Loop your stretchy band around a partner's band in the middle. Each of you holds the ends of your own band. Stand back to back and move apart to put tension on the bands. Hold the bands so that they pass under your arms, so that it does not rub your skin.

Practice all punches without letting the tension of the band pull you backward into an arch. Use muscles to hold straight position against the tension of the bands, without leaning forward.

Figure 4-25. Left—Punching with bands with low back improperly arched, hip tilted, and leaning backward. Right—Straightened to neutral spine, holding upright against resistance.

Throws and Overhead Training With Bands. Loop your stretchy band around a partner's band in the middle. Each of you holds the ends of your own band. Stand back to back and move apart to put tension on the bands. Stand straight against the tension of the band. Practice overhead movements without letting the bands pull your lower back into an arch. Use muscles to hold straight position without arms being pulled behind you, Figure 4-26.

Figure 4-26. Left—Throwing training using bands, shown with the low back improperly allowed to arch under the backward pull of the band. Right—Straightened to neutral.

Let Go of Ineffective Core Exercises

Healthy use of abdominal and core musculature is not tightening. You cannot move or breathe properly with tight muscles. It is not functional to exercise by curling forward for crunches and other forward bends. Back support is not automatic from the core muscles. It comes when abdominal muscles are used to reposition the spine voluntarily to reduce unhealthy overarching in the lower back to prevent back pain. Use your abdominal muscles to keep your spine in healthy position all the time when standing and moving.

The mastery of using abdominal muscles is to prevent letting the low back overarch during all daily actions. This way is different than lying on the floor to do crunches, then standing up with the lower back arched and no understanding. Let go of the old ideas that crunches and other forward bending will help your back, your posture, or work your core in a beneficial way.

An old story tells about clinging to ineffective ideals. Once there lived a village of creatures along the bottom of a great crystal river. Each creature in its own manner clung tightly to the twigs and rocks of the river bottom, for clinging was their way of life, and resisting the current was what each had learned from birth. But one creature said at last, "I shall let go, and let the current take me away from here. Clinging, I shall die."

The other creatures laughed and said, "Fool! You're wrong. The current will throw you tumbled and smashed across the rocks. You will die quicker!"

But the one heeded them not, and taking a breath, let go, and was tumbled and smashed by the current across the rocks. In time, as the creature continued to refuse to cling, the current lifted him free from the bottom and he was bruised and hurt no more.

The creatures downstream, to whom he was a stranger, cried, "See a miracle! A creature like ourselves, yet he flies! He will save us." The one carried in the current said, "I am the same as you. The river delights to lift us all free, if only we dare let go."

But, they cried the more, clinging tightly to the rocks, and told stories of the one who would save them.

"You will break the bow if you keep it always stretched."
—Phaedrus, first century Roman writer

Healthy Flexibility and Stretching

This chapter tells how training for flexibility is more than doing stretches. It shows how to find and fix unhealthy tightness that prevents normal movement. The stretches in this chapter retrain you to be flexible while maintaining stable joint position, to keep joints healthy during daily life, and while increasing martial arts strength, function, and ability.

Functional Flexibility

Flexibility training for martial arts has two goals; healthier function in daily life, and healthier movement in martial arts. The more active you are in real life, the more those two will be the same. Traditionally, stretches were the same movement needed during actual techniques. Later stretches became less like the original motion. It also became common to stretch in ways that don't train range of motion that is healthy for the body and helpful to movement. Functional stretches are stretches that move the body in ways needed for real life health and function. Functional stretches restore the muscle length needed for healthy straight posture, and prevent strain on joints when moving to needed positions for daily life and fighting maneuvers.

Use Stretches to Prevent, Not Add to, Bad Posture

Martial arts moves are more effective when done with straight positioning of the back and neck. Rounding the back and neck in poor position is something to avoid. Sitting, standing and moving with round shoulders and back is already done for much of the day over a desk, work area, steering wheel, and computer. You do not need to stretch by rounding your shoulders, back, and neck more. Many common stretches can be discarded because they are not needed and add to bad positioning habits. You do not need stretches that round your back and shoulders to touch the toes and bring legs toward to the chest. There is no need to add to round shoulders through stretching the back of your shoulders by pulling one arm across the front of the body. Stretching your legs by leaning over and rounding your back is ineffective as a stretch and transfers your body weight to the discs of the lower back. The result of stretching rounded and living rounded is becoming too tight for fighting moves or even to stand up straight. Many achy and injured backs, necks, and shoulders result.

What is Straight Positioning?

To check to see how you stand, stand with your back near a wall, but not touching it. Back up until something touches the wall. Did you touch your behind first? That may meant you tilt forward when standing. Did the upper back touch first? It may be that you lean or arch back when standing. Not standing straight is often a result of tight muscles.

When you touch your heels, hips, and upper back against the wall, is your head still not touching the wall? Holding your head forward of a straight position is called "a forward head." The forward head is a posture that results in much neck, upper back, and shoulder pain.

Figure 5.1. If you cannot stand comfortably straight, you are too tight. Left—Tilting forward. Middle—slouching backward. Right—Forward head and neck. These bad postures are common causes of pain, headache, hip dysfunction, and bad fighting technique.

Are You Too Tight to Stand Straight?

When you stand with your back against the wall, the back of your head, upper back, backside, and heels should touch comfortably. That is upright position, Figure 5-2.

Does your chin jut forward or lift up? If you are too tight to stand comfortably, you are probably standing and moving all the time in unhealthy bent positions that strain the neck, back, hip, and other areas. Do you have to arch your back to touch the back of your head? A small space should remain between the lower back and wall, but not a large space. If the lower back increases in arch, you are too tight to stand straight with neutral spine to prevent lower back pain.

Figure 5-2. You are standing straight when your heels, hip, upper back, and head line up against a flat surface comfortably, without straining, arching your back, or lifting your chin.

Good head position is important in martial arts. A forward head is closer to the opponent, and easier to hit. In case of a head strike, a tilted angle of the neck to the brain and skull is unhealthy and more likely to result in brain injury.

Figure 5-3. Left—A forward head is not healthy for daily life or martial arts. Right—Keep head position in line, with the corner of the jaw over centerline of the shoulder.

When you lie on your back with your legs out straight, are you comfortable without a pillow under your head or knees? If you cannot lie flat, the front of your body is tight. If you are too tight to lie flat without your ribs or chin jutting upward, you are too tight to stand upright without the same thing happening.

Anterior tightness often comes from spending the day bending forward, without standing straight or stretching backward. When you lie on your back, you should be able to lie comfortably, even with both arms by your ears against the floor. If you have to arch your back, your shoulders are too tight to reach overhead without pressuring other areas like your neck and lower back.

When Can Stretches Help?

Tightness hurts many body areas. Tight chest and shoulders make round-shouldered bad posture seem right. Tight hips, calves, and Achilles tendons make "duck-footed" or toe-out posture feel natural. Walking this way wears the ankles, knees, hips, and big toe. Tight feet add to plantar fasciitis or pain on the bottom of the foot and heel. Tight hamstrings are prone to pulls. Tight anterior hip contributes to walking bent forward, and is a hidden cause of groin pulls. Common stretches that bend forward only add to these problems.

Flexibility training for the martial arts needs to address healthy joint positioning to stand and move without strain. Main stretches for health are the front of the shoulder and chest, top of the shoulder, front hip and thigh, extension stretches for the back (extending backward) instead of flexion (bending forward), hamstring, Achilles tendon, hands, feet, and toes. For complete health, remember to stretch face muscles by smiling.

Front of the Shoulder and Chest—Pectoral Stretch

The pectoral stretch is an important stretch to restore healthy resting length to the front of the chest. Then you can stand straight and reduce upper body injury from bad positioning. If it is uncomfortable to stand with your back against a wall, touching the back of your head without straining or lifting your chin, do the pectoral stretch, Figure 5-5.

Tight chest muscles pull the shoulders forward and turn the arm bones inward, Figure 5-4. Arm activity like strikes and throws with tight, abnormal shoulder and arm position can eventually damage the shoulder and surrounding soft tissue including the four muscles that make up the rotator cuff.

To see how joint position changes with tightness, stand up with both arms relaxed at your sides. Without moving your arms, glance down at your hands. Note if your thumbs point toward each other (Figure 5-4).

Rotation inward usually means the muscles of the chest that connect to the arm at the shoulder are tight and short. Trying to hold thumbs facing forward, as they should be (Figure 5-6), may feel tight or unnatural. The answer is not to force thumbs to face forward, but stretch to make it natural and comfortable.

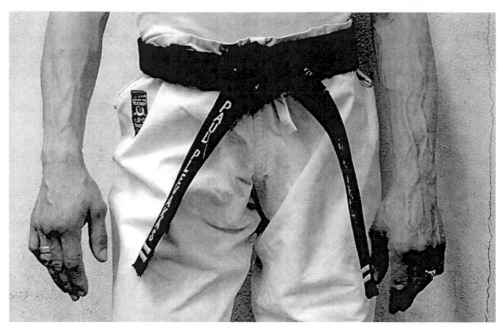

Figure 5-4. Do your thumbs face inward and toward each other when standing relaxed? Tight chest muscles promote round shoulders and inward-facing arms. The abnormal "crabbed" position of the arms can make your shoulders and neck hurt over time.

To stretch the front chest muscles, stand close to a wall, facing it. Lift one bent elbow out to the side. Touch the inside of your elbow to the wall. Turn your body and feet away from the wall, using the wall to brace your elbow far behind you. Feel the stretch in the front chest muscles only. Keep your shoulder down and relaxed. Don't arch your lower back, or lean your head forward. Hold a few seconds, breathe in, and change sides while breathing out.

Figure 5-5. The pectoral stretch prevents round-shouldered tightness that promotes neck, shoulder, and upper back pain. Left—Face the wall. Brace your bent elbow. Right—Turn away, leaving the bent arm far behind you. Feel stretch in front chest muscles, not shoulder.

After holding the pectoral stretch for a few seconds on each arm, relax arms down to your sides. Look down and observe thumb positioning. Thumbs should now be facing forward.

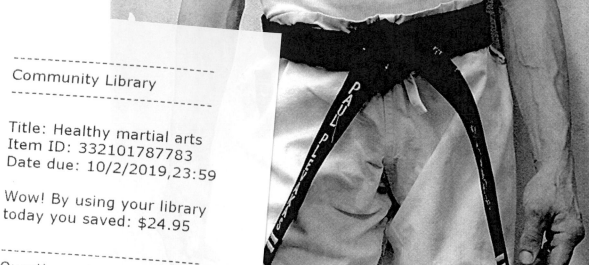

...rs are in healthy position with the arms relaxed at the sides, ...etches make this healthy position comfortable and natural.

Try the wall stand again. Stand with your back against the wall, with heels, hip, upper back, and the back of the head touching. Standing straight should now be more comfortable.

Do this pectoral stretch each morning, before training, and throughout the day. Check yourself often against a wall to see if you can comfortably stand straight. Remember to hold the new good posture. Don't slump back to unhealthy shoulder angles. The stretch does not make you stand straight, it makes it possible for you to stand straight. You do the rest.

Trapezius Stretch and Triceps Stretch

The trapezius stretch is the second stretch to restore healthy resting length to the upper body. Then you can stand straight and reduce upper body injury from bad positioning.

Stand straight. Place one hand behind the opposite hip, as if in an opposite pants pocket. Tilt head toward the hand, stretching the side of the neck and body, as you slide the other hand down toward your knee, Figure 5-7. Breathe in and breathe out while changing sides. Hold each side for a few seconds. Keep breathing. Don't lean forward. Try the wall stand check again. It should be more comfortable and easy.

To add the third stretch of this series, the triceps stretch, face a wall closely and place the back of your bent elbow against the wall high over your head. Press your body toward the wall to stretch the back of your arm. Turn your body until you feel the needed stretch. This stretch is instead of pulling your elbow over your head with the other hand.

Do the pectoral, trapezius, and triceps stretches first thing in the morning, before training, and throughout the day. Check yourself against a wall for straight positioning after doing them. It should change to straight and comfortable if you have done them right. Another check for tightness is see if you can put both hands on your hips and pull your shoulders back. With these stretches to restore resting length, it should be comfortable.

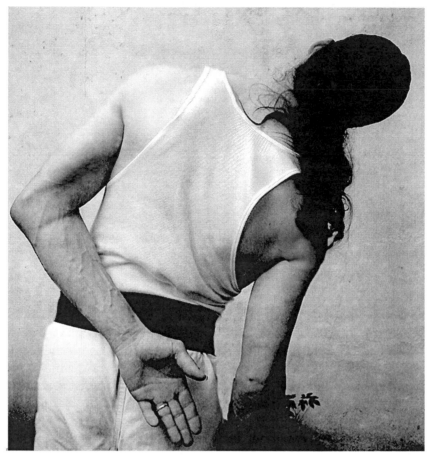

Figure 5-7. The trapezius stretch reverses round-shouldered tightness that promotes neck and upper back pain. Stretch to the side without bending forward.

Do not pull the neck to the side by pulling your head. Pulling compresses the spine. Just tilt your head and body to the side to stretch the entire length. A good way to check positioning when doing the trapezius stretch is to stay with your back against the wall. Keep your heels, hips, upper back and the back of your head against the wall, so you can know that you are not tilting forward and losing the stretch.

Hip and Thigh

The hip needs to generate high force in martial arts. It must be able to straighten and move without tightness pulling it into unhealthy position that reduces power and strains the low back and hip.

It is common in modern life to keep the hip bent most of the day, from sitting, then train by bending and tightening the hip further. The bent position tightens the front of the hip. Back pain, hip pain, faulty and restricted movement often result.

Watch for tightness in front of the hip during front kicks. When a tight kicker raises one leg, the hip tilts under (lower back rounds) and the standing leg bends forward as well, Figure 5-8. The front hip never gets flexibility through kicks. A sudden kick or leg lift can result in groin pull. Sometimes the standing leg may be pulled so far out from under, a fall results.

Figure 5-8. When the front of the hip is tight, the standing leg pulls forward as the kicking leg raises. Kicking power decreases. Note the badly-rounded upper back, and forward head and chin position. Instead, the standing leg should be able to stay straighter (not locked), with the hip neutral not tilted, upper spine straight, with the chin in.

Many common exercises and stretches concentrate on hip flexion, increasing the problem of anterior hip tightness. It is important to retrain the hip away from a bent-forward position. Following are several front hip stretches. They are multi-joint motions, which is the way the body needs to move in life. Several are moving stretches, which more closely match how muscles lengthen under loading and moving conditions.

Lunge and Center Stance. The lunge is an important functional stretch for the hip, thigh, Achilles tendon, and foot. The lunge is different from the center stance. In the center stance (and front stance) the back foot turns outward. In the lunge, the back foot is parallel to the front foot, not turned. Keeping the back foot straight in the lunge gives a better stretch to the back leg and hip.

For both the lunge and center stance, center your weight between both legs. Keep the front knee over the front foot, not leaning forward. When you tuck your hip to neutral, without leaning the upper body forward or backward, you will immediately feel a new strength in the torso and core, and the stretch move to the front of the hip, and thigh of the rear leg.

Figure 5-9. The center stance is a multi-joint stretch. Left—Don't lean back or arch the lower back. Right—Tuck the hip under to level the hip and bring spine to upright neutral. Keep the front knee over the front foot, not forward. To increase stretch on the rear leg, change the stance to a lunge by keeping the rear foot straight, not toe-out.

Dynamic (Moving) Lunge Stretch. Hold a wide lunge stance with your hip tucked under to neutral. Keep your back straight, back foot parallel to the front, with the back heel raised. Bend both knees to lower straight down until the back knee is just above the floor. Rise and lower to get a moving stretch. Ten lunges on each leg warm the body enough to warm-up for more stretching, and use muscles together in functional ways.

Figure 5-10. The moving lunge is an effective stretch for many areas at once. Keep the back foot straight forward, not turned. Tuck the hip under until level for neutral spine. Stretch increases on the hip of the rear leg. Keep both feet in place. Lower and rise many times.

Muay Lunge Stretch. Before every fight and bout in Muay Thai, a traditional lunging stretch, moving forward and back, is done as part of prayer. It can be hard on the knees and does not give as much stretch as the lunge for the back of the leg.

Figure 5-11. Traditional Thai preparation honors the teachers, the camp the boxer fights for, and stretches the hip and thigh through a moving range

Facedown Hip Stretch. The facedown hip stretch quickly restores ability of the hip to extend. It has three parts. To begin, lie face down. Extend one leg comfortably out to the side. Lie flat without turning your body or lifting your hip. Your foot faces out straight, not bent to the floor, Figure 5-12. Hold a few moments while breathing easily. Prop up on elbows to increase the stretch, Figure 5-13. Hold a few moments, then bend the back knee to increase the stretch, Figure 5-14. The quadriceps muscle crosses both the hip and the knee. Bending both the hip and knee increases the stretch. Hold each position comfortably without straining. Keep breathing. Lower and change sides.

Figure 5-12. To start the facedown hip stretch, lie flat with one leg out straight to the side. Keep both hips touching the ground, not turned or lifted. The next two parts of the stretch follow on next page, in Figure 5-13 and Figure 5-14.

Figure 5-13. Hip stretch part 2. Increase stretch by propping on elbows or hands. If pinching is felt in the lower back, tuck the hip to move stretch from the lower back to the front hip.

Figure 5-14. Part 3. Bend the back knee for more stretch to the front of the hip and thigh

Rocket Ship Hip Stretch. Rocket ship is a fun anterior (front) hip stretch that helps prepare for straddle stretches. Lie face down. Bring one bent knee out to the side, and hold. Keep your hip and body flat to the ground, not turned, Figure 5-15. Switch sides and repeat. Then bring both bent knees up and out to each side while lying flat. Feet can come up from the ground until flexibility increases.

Figure 5-15. Rocket ship hip stretch. Lie flat with knees bent out to each side.

The rocket ship stretch replaces the "butterfly" or groin stretch, sitting with feet together (prayer foot) and knees out. In the butterfly stretch, the back is often allowed to round, and the hip does not get a good stretch.

Try the rocket ship stretch face up. Instead of touching the soles of the feet, cross the ankles a small amount so that the lower legs cross side by side like matchsticks. Both lower legs lie on the ground, not the ankles. Let the stretch come from the front of the hip. Increase the stretch by raising both arms to the floor above your head, elbows by your ears without letting the low back arch from the floor.

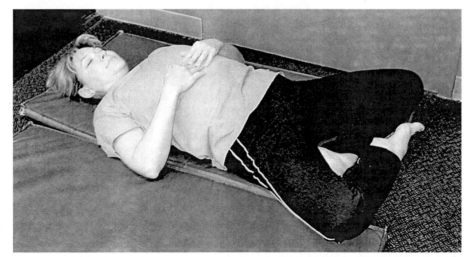

Figure 5-16. The rocket ship hip stretch replaces the sitting stretch. Rocket ship is a good stretch for the hip and leg without the usual spine rounding of the sitting stretch.

Figure 4 Hip Stretch Lying Down. Lie face up, knees bent, feet on floor. Cross one ankle over opposite knee. Move foot on floor in direction of raised foot to greatly increase posterior stretch. Press the crossed knee away with your hands to increase anterior stretch. Lift the foot from the floor, hold, still pressing the knee with your hand. Drop both crossed legs to one side, gently. Keeping legs crossed, bring legs down to the other side. At each side, increase the stretch by pressing the crossed knee away with your hand. Repeat with other ankle crossed.

Figure 5-17. Figure 4 hip lying down. Left—Press knee away with hands. Right—with turn.

Figure 4 Sitting. Sit with feet dangling or on the floor. Cross one ankle over the other knee. Press the crossed knee downward. Lift your chest up, chin in, as you lean slightly forward.

Figure 5-18. Figure 4 hip stretch sitting. Keep your back straight and chin in. Press the bent knee downward and away. Keep ankle straight not turned. Lift your chest to feel the stretch.

Figure 4 Standing. Stand on one leg. Cross the opposite ankle over the standing knee, as if putting on a shoe. Bend the standing leg until hip stretch is felt. Keep your back upright, chin in, and shoulders back. Get a daily stretch by putting on shoes and socks this way. Get a better stretch and more balance exercise by retrieving the shoe and sock from the floor while keeping the ankle crossed in this stretch position.

Iliotibial Band Stretch

The iliotibial band, or IT band is a tough fibrous reinforcement to the side muscles of the thigh. The IT band connects from the side of the hip to the side of the knee. When it is tight, it can rub or snap over the hip or knee causing pain, or pull the leg so that it rotates to a toe-out position when walking. The change in position to toe-out creates unhealthy pressure over time, on the joints of the foot, leg, and back.

Sitting Iliotibial Band Stretch. This is a quick stretch for both legs at once. Sit with knees crossed, feet straight out to each side. Keep both feet forward, away from the body. Keep knees down. Sit up straight to feel the stretch at the hip. Pull shins to help upright sitting.

Figure 5-19. Sitting iliotibial band stretch. Keep feet forward of the body, not near the hips. Stretch will be felt in the hip, not knees. Sit up and lift the chest to feel the stretch in the hip.

Lying Iliotibial Band Stretch. Lie face up with legs far apart. Leave one leg wide out to the side. Cross the other leg over it at the ankle. Remain lying flat on the floor without turning or lifting either hip. Let the stretch come from the side of the body and leg. Hold for a few seconds. Move the top leg far to the other side, and cross the other leg over it to stretch the other side. Keep breathing.

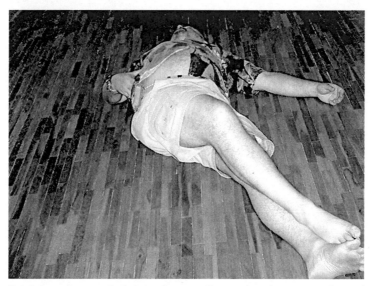

Figure 5-20. Iliotibial band stretch lying down. Cross one leg over the other leg, far to one side. Lie with both hips flat down, don't turn. Get the stretch from the side of the body. Hold for a few seconds on each side.

Quadriceps

Quadriceps Standing Stretch. Hip position is key in this stretch. This stretch is often ineffectively done with the hip tipped down in front and bent at the leg crease, with the back arched. Instead, tuck your hip under to immediately feel a change in the stretch to the front of the thigh. Push your foot away from your body into your hand. Don't pull your foot in to the behind.

It is sometimes taught that pushing the foot away should not be done because it makes the lower back arch. You control whether your back arches or not. Tip the bottom of your hip under to prevent arching, and to get the intended stretch.

To better train the stretch and balance, when starting the stretch, don't bend your leg forward at the hip to reach your foot. Lift your knee up in back and reach back.

Figure 5-21. Left—Arching your back loses the stretch on the thigh. Note the downward tilt to the front of the belt caused by the arched lower back. Right—Instead, level your hips by tucking the bottom of the hip under. Tucking lengthens and straightens the front of the hip and thigh, which is the purpose of the stretch.

Quadriceps Stretch Lying Down. Lie on one side, with both knees bent in front. Extend your top leg behind you, foot in hand. Roll top shoulder back and straighten your arm. Push your foot into your hand, away from your body. Keep the bottom knee bent in front.

Figure 5-22. Stretch the quadriceps and front of the hip lying on your side. Keep the bottom leg bent in front of you. Lower the top knee toward the floor. Rest your head on your arm if you like.

Upper and Lower Back Extension

Upper Body Extension. The upper body (or upper back) extension is a functional stretch that also strengthens. Bending forward loads the discs. Done properly, extension (bending backward) unloads them without compressing them under body weight. Lie face down, hands under chin or at your sides. Slowly lift upper body a few inches, then lower, many times. Keep neck straight, not craned. Lift from the chest and entire back, not neck.

Lower Body and Hip Extension. Lie face down, hands under chin or at your sides. Keep knees straight. Slowly lift legs a few inches, then lower. Or start by lifting one leg at a time, then progress to both.

Figure 5-23. Use muscles to lift the upper (left) and lower body (right) to get a moving stretch that strengthens without loading the discs.

Extension Stretches. To get an extension stretch for your upper body over a bed or bench, lie face up with your upper body hanging off the edge. Keep hips and legs on the bed, and hang your upper body down, from about mid-back level. Use your abdominal muscles to pull up enough while you hang to take compression off your low back.

To stretch the lower body in extension over a bed, lie face up with both legs hanging off the edge. Keep the edge of the bed under your hip. Don't let the lower back arch. Push your low back downward using abdominal muscles to keep the low back from pinching. Get the stretch from the front of the hip. Chapter 3 on Strength tells more about extension.

Hamstrings

It is common to stretch the hamstrings thinking it will somehow prevent back pain. It is also common to stretch the hamstrings in ways that hurt the back. Bending forward from a stand can give a stretch to the hamstrings, but eventually can degenerate the discs of lower back. It is also not the most effective way to stretch the hamstrings. Following are healthier, more effective hamstring stretches, without harm to the discs.

Standing Hamstring Stretch. Prop one foot on a bench or ledge. Keep the standing foot straight forward, not turned out. Drop the hip of the lifted leg down and square with the standing leg. Arch the low back slightly to lengthen the hamstring. Don't let the hip tuck or pull under. Don't round the back. These reduce the stretch on the hamstrings. People often stretch bent over, and wonder why they are still tight even though they stretch. It is because they are not getting the stretch.

Figure 5-24. Note the drawing of the low back vertebrae in each photo. Left—Forward bending generates outward pressure that eventually can push discs outward, degenerating and herniating them. Right—Keep the back upright and the standing foot facing straight ahead, not turned out, for better hamstring stretch.

Foot-on-Wall Hamstring Stretch. The foot-on-wall stretch is similar to the standing hamstring stretch, but gives a better and more functional stretch. Stand about arm's length in front of a wall, both feet parallel, not turned out. Place one foot flat against the wall, about hip height. Starting arm's-length from the wall may seen too close, but will improve the stretch. Keep the standing foot facing straight forward, not turned out. Lift your chest and stand straight. Do not let the standing leg and hip curl under, which reduces the stretch and reinforces unhealthy and ineffective kicking technique. Train stabilization for real life, and when kicking. Practice healthy back posture by standing straight, not rounding.

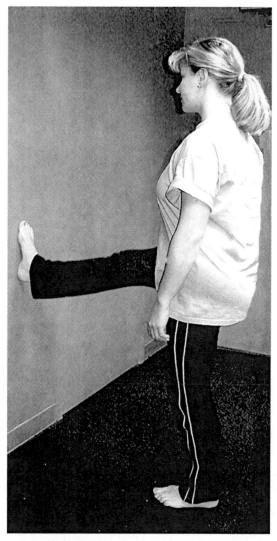

Figure 5-25. The foot-on-wall hamstring stretch is a quick, effective, and functional hamstring stretch if the body and standing foot are kept facing straight forward, not turned

Lying Hamstring Stretch. To stretch hamstrings without the forward bending pressure that loads the discs, lie on the floor and lift one leg pointing to the sky. Keep the other leg straight and flat on the floor, toes up, not outward. It is not the case that the bottom knee and hip should be bent. Bending allows the anterior hip to remain tight, and reduces the stretch. It is also not functional. For walking, running and kicking you need to extend the forward leg without the back leg bending forward also. When stretching, if the leg on the floor lifts upward, the front of the hip is tight. Hip tightness can cause hamstring and groin pulls during front kicks, jumps, and quick stance changes, and the standing leg can be pulled forward when kicking, causing a fall.

To prevent anterior hip tightness, keep your leg flat on the floor when raising the other leg for hamstring stretches, and stretch the anterior hip with tucked-hip lunges, described previously. Keep shoulders and neck relaxed on the floor. Don't round the back and call it a leg stretch. If you are too tight to lie flat with one leg lifted, you are too tight to stand straight and walk, run, or kick.

Figure 5-26. To increase hamstring stretch and prevent rounding the back, lie flat and lift one leg. Note the straight position of the two drawn-in vertebrae and evenly distributed pressure on the disc between them. If the other leg flat cannot lie flat, the front of that hip is too tight. Do lunge stretches to fix hip tightness.

Double Hamstring Stretch. To stretch both legs at the same time, lie on your back with both legs overhead. To get the intended stretch, press the low back and hip on the floor, don't let them round upward. Arch the low back to lengthen the stretch. This kind of arching does not compress body weight on vertebral joints. It positions the hip to lengthen the hamstring. Don't lift the hips or round the back. Bend your ankles and pull your toes back to stretch further.

Downward Dog. A good stretch for hamstrings and several other areas at once is "downward dog," described more in the Achilles and foot stretches later in this chapter.

Figure 5-27. By keeping weight on hands, downward dog stretches many areas at once without compressing discs outward, common in standing and sitting bending forward stretches. Press heels down, feet parallel not turning outward. Lift your hips and push back.

Sitting Hamstring Stretch. Sitting bent forward may work as a stretch, but is not a healthy way to stretch the hamstrings. Rounding reduces the hamstring stretch and pressures the discs. Leaning forward, rounded or straight, greatly increases outward (herniating) pressure on the discs. One way to minimize problems is to bring the leg upward to you, keeping your back straight. Don't concentrate on lifting the leg high. Practice feeling the better stretch that you get with your back upright and straight, without forcing. Turning your back to the leg is another way to reduce pressure on the discs from bending forward.

Figure 5-28. If you sit to stretch, keep your back straight to better stretch your leg. Rounding while sitting presses the discs outward under body weight, damaging them over time.

Splits

The split stretches the hamstring of the front leg, and front hip muscles of the back leg, called hip flexors. Properly practiced, wide stances help kicking range and injury prevention in high kicks, jumps, stances, leg blocks, and makes some leg locking and trapping moves less painful or injurious.

To progress to split, stand in the lowest possible lunge stance, feet parallel with back foot straight, not turned. Turning the foot out or sitting to one side loses the stretch on the back hip. Lift the heel of the back leg. Keep the back knee pointing downward. Keep the upper body upright, not leaning or curling forward. The stretch on the hip is diminished if you bend forward.

Stand and balance in the low split stance. Stay as high above the floor as needed, but keep upper body position straight and back heel lifted.

Figure 5-29. Flexibility and positioning for the split is better practiced by standing in low lunge than sitting on the floor. Remain upright, don't lean forward. Leaning forward loses the stretch in the front hip muscles of the rear leg.

Figure 5-30. Ineffective positioning: Leaning forward (left) and sitting to the side (right) both reduce the hip stretch in the back leg. Time is spent without getting the needed stretch, and practices the bad habit of leaning forward.

Gradually work toward lowering to the floor in an upright position without forcing. Notice if you are trying so hard that you tighten your muscles. Tightening is opposite of the goal of stretching. Learn to lengthen the muscles while moving them and maintaining healthy position. Add more balance components by doing low split stances on narrow surfaces.

Practice splits, alternating which leg is in front, not just the easy side. Do not force the hip joint into ranges it is not time for. Forcing the stretch can jam the upper leg bone into the hip joint, or strain the hamstring. You do not need full splits for effective martial arts. You need only healthy muscle length so that you are not pulled into unhealthy position when you move. Low kicks can be more quick and effective in real fighting situations than high kicks.

Figure 5-31. Keep the upper body upright for split stances, not leaning forward, to get the important benefit of stretch to the front hip muscles of the back leg

Sitting Stretches and Straddles

Sitting is one of the least beneficial ways to stretch the legs. Many aches and injuries result from sitting stretches done with rounded posture. It is more effective to stand with one leg up, or lie on the back with one or both legs up, keeping the back straight. Then more stretch comes from the legs and you avoid rounded position, which gradually breaks down the discs of the low back and neck.

The most important component of healthy sitting stretches is not to round the back trying to touch the toes or floor. Sit straight. To do healthier sitting stretches, put both hands behind you and lean your weight on your hands. Lift your chest up. Do not round the back. If you round the back and hip, the stretch is diminished and your body weight shifts to the discs of the low back. Tilt the front of the hip forward, not backward, to get the intended stretch.

To stretch each leg, do not lean the chest forward. A better way is to look toward one leg, and lean backward over the other leg. Lift the chest up and keep the back straight. You will get the same or better leg stretch without rounding the back. Turn and stretch to the other side.

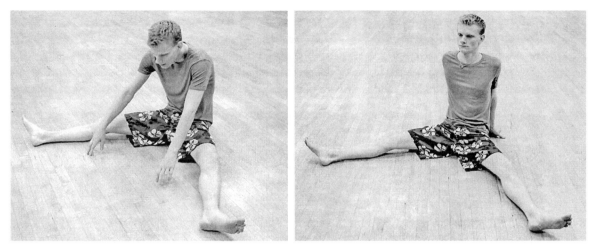

Figure 5-32. Left—Rounding the back makes the stretch ineffective, practices bad posture, and increases pressure on low back discs. Right—Instead, put hands behind you and lean weight on hands. Lift the chest and push the back straight. Learn to rock the top of the hip forward (tilt pelvis) without rounding the back. As flexibility increases, you will be able to rest weight on hands in front without rounding your lower back.

Figure 5-33. Lean back for a better leg stretch instead of leaning forward over each leg. Rock the pelvis forward instead rounding the back.

Do not force or push the stretch. Do not let anyone push your legs into straddle positions. Forcing and pushing can jam the top of the leg (femur) bone into the hip socket, adding to hip joint wear and tear. Let the muscles lengthen, which is the point of the stretch.

Learn how to tilt your hip and pelvis so that your back is straight, not rounded. If your hip is too tight for you to sit without rounding your back, it is better not to sit to stretch. Instead, lie down to stretch while you learn to position your hip.

Figure 5-34. Add a balance component with wide stretches on narrow surfaces

Combination Stretches

Use combination stretches to stretch several areas at once for functional movement and better balance.

Standing Bow Stretch. The standing bow stretch helps back and shoulder extension, hamstring, thigh and hip. Done properly, it trains balance, and how to hold good posture while moving in unaccustomed ways. Curling the body forward loses the stretch. Keep your back and hip extended backward. Press your foot away into your hand. Hold your arm away from your body. Don't round your back or shoulders.

Figure 5-35. Standing bow stretch

Standing Leg Stretch. The standing leg stretch trains balance and straight posture while stretching both legs at once. Do not bend or round forward to grasp the leg. Hold the leg as low as necessary to keep the back, neck, and shoulders upright and straight. Use the stretch to train straight position, not to force your body into unhealthy rounded position.

Figure 5-36. Standing leg stretch

Side Plank Stretch. Use the side plank to train balance, arm and hand strength, and straight posture while stretching the legs. **Don't** bend forward or stick your behind out in back to grasp your foot. Hold straight position.

Figure 5-37. Side plank stretch

Back Bend Preparation Stretch. The back bend is a good stretch to combine flexibility, strength, and to relieve bent-forward upper body posture. Lie face-up with both elbows bent overhead, hands facing the shoulders. Knees bent and feet on the floor. For many, this preparatory position is a big stretch for the wrist, elbow, and shoulder. Progress to pushing upward into a back bend.

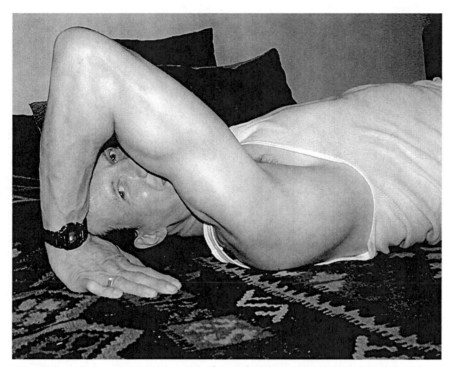

Figure 5-38. Back bend preparation stretch for shoulders, wrists, and hands

Lying Bow Stretch—Face Down Quad, Upper Back, Shoulder, Anterior Hip. Lie face down. Bend both knees and grasp both ankles with hands. Lift thighs from floor. Let shoulders roll back, bringing shoulder blades closer together. Lift and lower several times.

Achilles and Foot

The standard leaning Achilles tendon stretch is the most common stretch. It is not an effective way to stretch the Achilles and foot. More beneficial methods include the lunge, downward dog, Achilles squat, and the foot-on-wall Achilles tendon stretch.

Leaning Achilles Stretch. A common Achilles tendon stretch is to lean forward toward a wall. It is ineffective when done with the hip bent and the backside tilted outward. To improve the stretch, tuck the hip under, as if doing a standing crunch. Keep the back foot straight, not turned out, or the stretch is lost. This stretch, although common, is not a highly effective Achilles stretch. If you are too tight to bend or squat with heels down, your Achilles is too tight. Use the following stretches.

Lunge. A more effective Achilles tendon and foot stretch is the lunge. Stand in a wide center stance, but keep the back foot straight, not turned out. Prevent forward tilt to the hip by tucking, which stretches the front of the hip of the rear leg. Keep the back foot straight, not turned outward. Bend knees to lower to the floor for a moving Achilles and foot stretch. Rise and lower without moving your feet. Repeat many times, then switch legs.

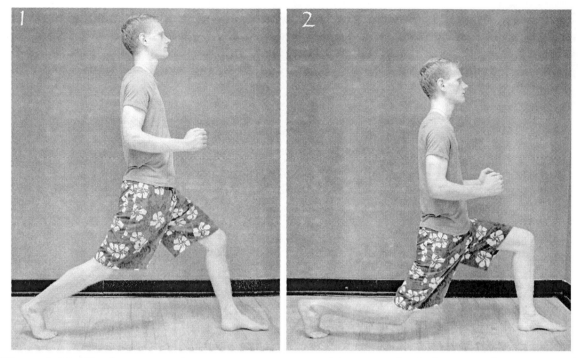

Figure 5-39. The lunge stretches many areas at once. Keep your back foot straight not turned out. Tuck the bottom of the hip under to reduce lower back arch and increase the hip stretch. Lower almost to the floor and rise many times. Prevent sliding the front knee forward as you lower. Keep the front knee over the ankle with body weight centered.

Downward Dog. "Downward dog" is an effective multi-joint stretch. Body weight rests on the hands, so the force of bending forward is not on the discs of the low back. Put your hands and feet on the floor, hands far forward of the feet, like starting a pushup. Keep weight mostly on your hands. Keeping your feet where they are, lift your hips high in the air, pushing backward, letting heels relax to the floor. Don't round or hunch your back. Relax your neck, letting your head hang downward. Keep your feet straight, not turned, weight on rims, not arches. Push your fingers forward with straight, not locked elbows. Push your head and body backward. You probably have seen dogs and cats stretch this way.

Figure 5-40. Downward dog stretches many areas at once and strengthens the upper body. Because body weight is held on the arms, the low back discs are not compressed from forward bending. Start with feet parallel and hands far forward of feet (left). Keep body weight leaning on the hands. Push hands forward to press hips upward and backward. Relax chest and heels downward (right).

Achilles Squat. Use squatting for resting and normal daily tasks to build Achilles tendon stretches into daily life. Keep weight back on your heels, not on toes. Press heels down.

Figure 5-41. Keep heels down and weight back toward the heels to protect the knees while getting a good stretch.

Foot-on-Wall Achilles Stretch. A highly effective Achilles stretch is the Achilles wall stretch. Stand about arm's length in front of a wall, both feet facing straight forward, not turned out. Place one foot flat against the wall around knee height. It will feel as if you are standing too close, but this is the right distance. Press your heel against the wall. Don't round your back or hip, or the stretch is diminished or lost. Lift the chest stand straight to feel the calf and Achilles stretch. Experiment with foot placement for best stretch. Relax and breathe.

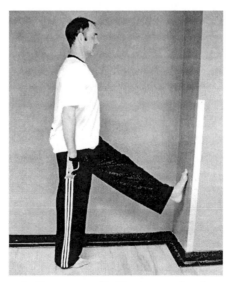

Figure 5-42. Stand arm's length from a wall. Press one heel toward the wall at knee height for a quick, effective Achilles stretch. Keep the standing foot facing straight, not turned. Stand straight and upright, not leaning forward or back. Keep your chin in.

Toe Stretches. Toes must be straight and able to move freely for balance and push-off when moving. If toes don't move freely, or if your shoes push toes together, the shoes are too tight for daily wear. Practice moving toes in all directions often. Stretch toes by pulling them apart side to side with your hands. When standing, don't clench toes or lift toes from the ground.

Built-in Daily Achilles and Foot Stretch. Walking with feet parallel, not turned out, gives a natural stretch across the bottom of the foot and up the Achilles tendon and calf. When the feet turn out, the normal stretch through walking is lost. Turning toe-out (duck-foot) when walking is a common bad habit.

Walk with feet and knees facing straight ahead. When going up stairs, keep heels down when stepping up. Push off the whole foot, including heel, to put the effort through the leg muscles not the knee joint, and get a natural daily stretch for the foot and Achilles. When bending and squatting for any household need, keep heels down. When bending to sit down, keep heels down and don't lean far forward. Keep the upper body upright without sticking your behind out. Do the same when rising from a chair. It makes no sense to tighten your Achilles tendon with poor walking and moving habits all day every day, then hope a few minutes of stretching will prevent injury.

Wall Stretches

Wall stretches improve your sense of straight positioning. Start by standing with your back against a wall. Heels, backside, upper back, and the back of your head should all touch easily. If this is not comfortable or if you have to arch your back or raise your chin, learn the wall stand, the pectoral stretch, and the trapezius stretch shown in the beginning of this chapter. Use them to restore resting length to be able to stand straight. Then use the new, healthy positioning for all you do.

The wall stretches that follow are a few of many stretches that train how to feel straight body positioning. Use this straight positioning to get a better and healthier stretches whenever you stretch and for moving in daily life.

Shoulder Wall Stretch. Stand with your back against the wall. Heels, behind, upper back and the back of your head all touch. A small inward curve remains in the low back, but not a big curve. Reach hands straight overhead so that both hands touch the wall. Don't let the low back increase in arch when you reach overhead. Tuck your hip to reduce the low back curve and get the stretch from the shoulders, not by arching. Touch palms together, prayer style. Straighten your arms. Press both elbows to your ears. Keep shoulders down. Breathe. Feel the straight positioning.

Repeat standing on toes. Keep weight on the big toe and second toe. Don't let body weight teeter on your little toes.

This stretch can also be done on the floor as another way to understand how to get the intended shoulder stretch from the shoulder not by arching the back.

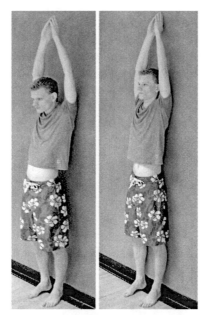

Figure 5-43. Left—When raising arms overhead, don't let the low back increase in arch, or let the head come forward. These unhealthy positions decrease the stretch. Right—Learn to hold straight position for a healthier, functional, and effective stretch.

Upper Body Wall Stretch—Crescent Moon Stretch. Stand against the wall with both hands overhead, as for the shoulder wall stretch above. Gently lean your upper body to one side for a few seconds, then the other side. The hands joined overhead point like a single clock hand to each side. Keep breathing. Keep heels, hips, upper back, and the back of your head all against the wall. Look forward. Don't let the upper body and head come away from the wall as you stretch. Use the wall to learn straight position. Repeat standing on toes. Keep weight on the big toe and second toe. Don't let your body weight teeter on your little toes.

Figure 5-44. Use this wall stretch to learn straight positioning when stretching to the side. Keep your upper body and fingers touching the wall. Don't increase low back arch. Instead, get the stretch from the upper body.

Upper Body and Hip Wall Stretch—Tree in Wind Stretch. Stand against the wall with both hands overhead. Press hands together, elbows to ears. Lift one foot to the inside knee of the standing leg. Press the bent knee toward the wall to stretch the hip. Keep your body facing straight. Turning diminishes the hip stretch. Keep breathing. Bend and hold for a few seconds on each side. Change legs and stretch to both sides standing on the other leg. Don't let your upper body or head come away from the wall. Use the wall to feel straight position. Repeat standing on toes. Don't let your body weight teeter on your little toes. Keep weight on the big toe and second toe.

Figure 5-45. Turn your knee out to the wall. Keep hips, upper body, head, and hands against the wall. Hold a few seconds to each side, change legs and repeat.

Side Body Wall Stretch—Star Stretch. Stand against a wall, feet apart, arms out. Lean far to one side, with heels, hips, upper body, and back of the head touching the wall. A small space remains between the lower back and wall, but not a large space. Reach one arm overhead touching the wall, other arm to your knee. Hold a few seconds, then stretch to the other side. If your lower back hurts from too much arch, press lower back toward wall. Repeat on toes. Don't let body weight shift to side toes. Keep weight over the big toe and second toe.

Figure 5-46. Keep hips, upper body, head, and hands against the wall. Use the wall to train straight body position when stretching, instead of slouching forward.

Wall Kick Stretch. Stand straight against a wall in ready position. Begin a side kick, keeping your kicking leg, hips, upper back, and back of the head touching the wall. Stretch the kicking leg to various heights, keeping straight body position against the wall. Sticking the behind out by bending the hip is an unhealthy and unattractive mistake common to beginners. Use this stretch to learn and practice straightening the hip, instead of keeping it bent forward when kicking. This is an important stretch to reduce hip pain from tight anterior hip, and reduce the tightness that leads to groin pulls during kicks.

Figure 5-47. Use the wall kick stretch to train straight positioning during various style kicks

Hand, Elbow, Shoulder, Wrist, and Upper Body Extension Wall Stretch—Wall Back Bend. Stand about two feet in front of the wall. Reach both arms overhead to touch the wall, fingers facing downward. Don't arch only from the low back or bend the knees much. Get the stretch from the upper body. Lift up in the chest to keep body weight from pressing on the lower back. Keep your chin in, and the weight of your head on your muscles, not hanging backward on your neck. Straighten elbows to increase the stretch. It is fun to "walk" hands down the wall toward, or to, the floor, then back up. Increase the stretch on the front of the hip by doing this stretch with feet together.

Figure 5-48. Done right, the wall back bend can be an effective multi-joint stretch

Use a Partner as a Wall. All the wall stretches can be done as partner stretches. Partners stand back-to-back, serving as each other's wall, to add cooperation and balance to the stretches.

Figure 5-49. The wall star stretch can be done as a back-to-back partner stretch

Partner Stretches

The following four stretches are quick, fun ways to increase flexibility in key areas. They combine balance, integrated body skills, and partner cooperation. Partner stretches are often abused. Do not force or push. Do not practice them in bad posture. Be clear on the purpose to learn and restore healthy body positioning, not damage the joints.

Partner Pectoral Stretch. Stand back-to-back, arms outstretched and touching, hands comfortably linked. Thumbs face up. One partner gently pulls, while the other allows the chest muscles to stretch (Figure 5-50, left), then switch (right).

Figure 5-50. Partner pectoral stretch

Figure 5-51. The partner pectoral stretch can be done with both partners getting a stretch in one arm at the same time. Stand side by side, one facing front, one facing back. Stand straight, arms comfortably bent at the elbow, hands linked. Each partner turns their back gently to the other and lets the arm be pulled back. Don't yank the shoulder at the joint, arch the back, or bend the neck forward. Allow the front chest muscles to lengthen.

Partner Whole Body Stretch. The first partner stretches in stable downward dog. Hands far in front of feet, weight on arms, pushing back, and heels down. Second partner stretches backward, placing his back high or low to change the stretch. Then in a smooth manner, each partner stands and bends the other way. The backward stretching partner becomes the downward dog. At each, make sure entire spine gets mild motion, not pinched at one place.

Figure 5-52. Partner whole body stretch

Partner Hamstring Stretch. The partner who is stretching (Figure 5-53, right) pushes weight backward to the heel of the standing leg and leans into the partner who is helping (left). Lifting the leg shifts the lever point off the low back discs. Lift up in the chest and keep your back straight. Press your abdomen (not upper body) toward the thigh. The helping partner does not force or push the leg upward, just supports the lean.

Figure 5-53. Partner hamstring stretch

What Stretches Harm?

Not all foods are beneficial. Neither are several common stretches. This section tells how to spot and avoid stretches that practice poor positioning, and deform or injure joints over time. This section gives stretches to do instead that are more effective to train flexibility without injury.

Hamstring Stretches That You Don't Need. Bending over from a stand may stretch the legs but slowly degenerates the discs of the low back, and pushes them outward. You wouldn't pick up a package that way. Don't injure your discs by stretching that way. Stretching the hamstrings by bending over opens the vertebra in the back. Over years, bad bending can squeeze discs outward, like squeezing a toothpaste tube, which is one way discs degenerate and herniate. Outward pressure on discs can occur when bending over, whether with a straight (flat) back or rounded. Bent-forward stretches practice a bent-over rounded posture. Poor, bent over posture is a common cause of neck and upper back pain, and poor form in martial arts. Overstretching the back is common in much of daily life from bad sitting position for deskwork, driving, and watching television. More forward rounding from stretches and exercises is not needed. Instead, use the back stretches in the flexibility chapter to rethink and relearn how to stretch.

Figure 5-54. Note the drawn-in vertebrae and disc. Forward bending pinches the disc in front, and pushes outward in back. Over time, hanging your weight forward with excessive bending degenerates discs, pushes them outward until they hurt, and practices rounded posture.

Figure 5-55. Forward rounded posture contributes to upper back and neck pain, degenerating discs, and slouching habits. Notice how much of your day you already spend bending forward for sitting, driving, and working. Notice how many stretches contribute to more rounding.

Avoid assisted stretches where anyone presses your back into rounded position, Figure 5-56. Rounding the back under load forces the vertebrae to open in back. The discs between each vertebra are pushed backward like squeezing a toothpaste tube or water balloon. The most pressure occurs on the vertebrae of the neck and low back. Over many years of abuse, these are the discs that may finally break down (degenerate) and push outward (herniate).

Figure 5-56. Being pushed to stretch farther is hard on the discs

Neck. Shoulder stands and "the plow" involve lying on the upper back, with legs overhead, neck bent forward, and body weight on the neck. The forced, bent forward angle of the neck vertebrae can eventually degenerate and herniate the discs in the neck, and promote bone spur. The pressure of body weight pushing the neck forward practices the poor posture of forward head and round shoulders. Pushing the neck forward stretches the ligaments. Ligaments are not supposed to stretch much. When ligaments become lengthened through stretching, they can no longer do their job of holding bones in healthy position. Poor rounded posture results.

When you stretch your neck by tilting the head to the shoulder, do not pull your neck to the side by pulling your head with the hand. That compresses the spine. Tilt your head to the side, keeping the neck and upper body straight, not leaning forward.

When you stretch your arms overhead, don't bend your neck forward. When you exercise the biceps with dumbbell curls, don't bend the neck forward to "help" the lift. When you do pushups, don't let the neck hang down, bent forward. In short, notice all the exercises, stretches, and daily life (like working at computers and driving) where the common bad habit of bending the neck forward can be identified and retrained to keep straight healthy posture using neck muscles.

When looking up for all movement, whether standing, sitting, or lying face down, keep your chin in. Don't crane your neck. The neck vertebrae are not hinge joints. Use your chest muscles to lift your upper body. Keep shoulders back. Don't just compress your neck joints backward.

Shoulder. Shoulder stretches done by bending over forward with arms lifted in back with clasped hands can eventually damage the anterior shoulder and the low back. The unsupported bending forward promotes disc degeneration and herniation, and practices round-shouldered posture. The bent-over stretch rotates the shoulder so that the joint stretches, but not the muscles, and puts the force of the stretch on the front of the shoulder capsule. Benefit is low and the joint can become compressed and destabilized by overstretching. Don't let anyone pull your arms behind you with your thumbs facing down and your shoulder rotated forward. That presses the arm bone against the front of the shoulder capsule with enough force to damage the shoulder cartilage. There is no need to harm your joints to stretch your muscles. A healthy way to stretch the shoulder is to stretch the muscles using the pectoral stretch described at the beginning of this chapter. Keep thumbs facing upward when stretching arms behind you, and hands above the level of the elbow, to make sure the stretch is in the front muscles of the chest, not the joint.

Knee. Sitting on folded knees and lying back to the floor to stretch the thigh can create several problems. Folding the knee completely under the load of body weight exerts high pressure on the kneecap. The physical size of the thighs pressing at the knee creates a nutcracker effect where the knee joint is slightly pried apart. This effect is smaller in thinner people and larger in those with bigger or more muscular thighs. A third problem occurs because the knee is not shaped to twist. If you can't turn both legs in from the hip, the knee will have to twist. Instead, to stretch the front of the thigh, use the standing or lying quadriceps stretches shown earlier, using the hip tuck to get a better stretch.

Hip. Avoid vigorously oscillating knees (butterfly knees) when sitting with bent knees and soles of feet touching. Don't let anyone stand on or push your knees apart. It can create grinding pressure on your hip socket.

Ankle. When sitting cross-legged, stretch from the hip rather than turning and bending the ankle. Overstretching ligaments on the side of the ankle leaves the ankle prone to sprains.

Change Stretches to Make Them Healthy

Stretch muscles not joints. Don't force joints into such ligament laxity that they no longer seat properly. Like car parts that don't seat, the rubbing results in early wear and tear. Strengthen, rather than just stretch. Unstable joints slowly wear and tear. In a sudden situation, weak, loose joints are predisposed to pulls or dislocation. Keep joints strong with exercise.

Many people strain and force to stretch, forgetting that the purpose of a stretch is to lengthen the muscle and train it how to move in relaxed ways. Check your stretching to make sure you are not grunting, straining, holding your breath, forcing, and tightening. Instead, smile and practice healthy movement.

Chinese proverb teaches, "The best time to plant a tree was twenty years ago. The second best time is now." Now is the time to start stretching in healthier, functional ways.

Flexibility Enhancing Techniques

Stretch Often. Several methods help stretching. It is not true that being muscular reduces flexibility. Not stretching reduces flexibility. Stretch regularly. Like gains from other exercise, flexibility is easily lost.

Stretch the Right Things. Many people round their shoulders and back for much of the day. The back and shoulders get rounded and overstretched. More forward rounding is not a helpful stretch. The front of the chest and hip get tight from bending forward so much all day. Restore healthy length to the front of the upper body by the two stretches in the beginning of this chapter, the pectoral and trapezius stretches. Move throughout your daily life in healthy straight posture. Preventing bent-over posture with straight positioning gives healthy, built-in chest and hip stretch all day. You will prevent your body from getting tight in the first place.

Warming. Be warm enough to sweat before stretching. "Warming-up" literally means raising body temperature. Elasticity increases with temperature. Active warming is easily and quickly accomplished with exercise. Ten or more pushups and lunges warm the body enough to break a light sweat. Lunges have the additional advantage of functional warming and integrated use of the legs, enhancing muscle fiber firing in sequence needed for activity. There is no need to bicycle or jog ten minutes. Don't be afraid of exercise without air conditioning. Within limits, a warmer environment helps. Passive warming in a hot tub or shower, or locally applied heat also helps.

Stretch What You Think You're Stretching. The main way to increase flexibility is to stretch what you think you are stretching. It is common for someone to lean over, thinking they are stretching their hamstrings. They are often rounding the back instead of getting the stretch from the leg. In standing hamstring stretches with one leg up, if the standing foot is turned, out the angle of stretch is not on the hamstring. It is common to lunge forward thinking you are stretching the Achilles tendon, but if the back foot turns out and the hip is bent, there is little or no stretch on the Achilles. It is common to hold a quadriceps stretch with the back arched so that there is little or no stretch on the quadriceps. Doing a hip stretch with the hip bent forward rather than extended backward does not stretch the hip. People wonder why they are not getting flexible or why their back hurts, even though they stretch often.

Do the Purpose of the Stretch, Not Just a Stretch. Make sure to understand what you are stretching, not memorize rules about a position. Once you are clear on the concept of what actions create a stretch, you can easily position yourself without bogging down on details that don't matter. Then ordinary stretching will give greater gains than before. Once you can use intelligent positioning, try three easy techniques, PNF, active assist, and dynamic stretching.

Proprioceptive Neuromuscular Facilitation—PNF. A quick and effective technique to improve immediate flexibility is called push-pull, contract-relax, muscle-energy technique, or proprioceptive neuromuscular facilitation (PNF). While holding any given stretch at maximum comfortable stretch, push (contract) against resistance in the direction opposite the stretch for four or five seconds without moving or reducing the stretch, to fatigue the muscle. Then pull (relax) into the stretch. Use this technique slowly and safely for any desired stretch.

To use this technique for hamstring flexibility, lie face-up with one leg lifted. Keep shoulders, head, and the other leg on the floor. Hold the back of your lifted leg at maximum comfortable stretch. Push the leg downward against the resistance of your hands. Hold while pushing downward for about five counts to fatigue the hamstrings. Stop pushing and relax the leg. Pull the leg up gently toward your chest. It should immediately gain a greater stretch. Repeat, pushing down against hands at the new stretch length, then gently pull in to the next greater stretch. Keep breathing. Repeat for three stretches on each leg. This same stretch can be done standing with one leg against the wall or bench. If a partner is assisting by being the resistance to the leg, do not let them press your leg forward so that the hip joint presses into the socket. The partner gently pulls the leg away from the socket when assisting the stretch.

To stretch triceps using PNF, lift one arm overhead, elbow bent by your ear, allowing the hand to hang straight back. Don't arch your back to raise the arm. Keep your torso and head straight, not bent forward or back. Without moving the raised elbow forward, press the raised elbow in front against the other hand (or a wall) for five counts to fatigue the triceps. Release the press and pull back. An immediate and easily gained farther stretch should result. Repeat for three stretches on each arm. This can be done against a wall without a partner, using the wall to brace the elbow while pushing against the wall.

Active Assist. In "active assist," the opposite muscle assists in pulling the stretch. For example, the quadriceps (thigh muscles) assists the hamstring stretch. To stretch the hamstrings with active assist, lie on the back with one leg lifted. Shoulders, head, and the other leg stay flat on the floor. Instead of holding the lifted leg with hands, use the quadriceps muscle of the lifted leg to pull the leg toward the body. Maintain the held position in the air for four to five seconds, then relax and pull the leg further in toward the body using hands. Repeat for three stretches on each leg. Then try this standing, lifting the leg up with your own muscles, not hands.

To stretch triceps using active assist, lift one arm overhead, elbow bent by the ear, allowing the hand to hang straight back. Arching your low back to raise your arm reduces the stretch. Keep your body and neck straight without bending forward or back.

Use the muscles of the back and shoulder to pull your raised arm further back, instead of pushing with the other hand. Maintain the held position in the air for four to five seconds, then relax and push the arm further back using the other hand. Repeat for three stretches on each arm.

Dynamic Stretching. Functional movement is training in the manner useful to real life. Many stretches are static and non-moving. However, continuously and rapidly changing muscle lengths are needed when moving in martial arts. It is important to practice stretches as needed for movement. It is a theory that bringing the limbs through a moving stretch to maximum length first thing in the morning can set their stretching length for the day. Move through all the ranges of motion of the shoulder, hip, and leg needed for punches, strikes and kicks.

To dynamically stretch the front of the hip, quadriceps, calf, Achilles tendon, and bottom of the foot, use the moving lunge. Stand with your front foot far forward of the back foot, back foot straight, not turned out, dipping up and down.

To set the leg range for kicking, in a controlled manner swing the leg through the motion and range needed for each kick. Maintain straight healthy posture of the back and neck. Swing up to the front and to the back. Bending the back trains ineffective positioning. Keep the back and neck straight, and use the leg muscles.

Figure 5-57. Dynamic stretch of the hamstring demonstrated in good and poor form. Left—Rounding the back forward and letting the standing hip pull under makes the stretch ineffective. Rounding also pressures the discs and practices and reinforces slouching. Right—Hold body position straight while swinging the leg, with neck and chin in.

Figure 5-58. Dynamic stretch of the hip to specific targets, practicing movement needed for kicks and knee strikes

Use Stretching in Helpful Ways

Some studies have concluded that stretching does not reduce risk of injury. Other studies have shown that stretching reduces muscle force that can be generated soon after the stretch. Based on these studies, some athletes will not stretch before movements that need strength, or sometimes they will not stretch at all. The answer seems to lie in how stretching is commonly done. Stretching is often done in ineffective ways that does not get the intended stretch. You may stretch, but then move in tight ways. Or stretch in tight, strained ways. Instead, use stretching as a way to restore healthy positioning, not as a "thing" to do for a number of seconds, then forget about. After stretching the shoulder, for example, don't punch with shoulders held tightly hunched. After stretching the front of the chest and hip, don't sit, stand, and practice martial arts with rounded back and shoulders. Keeping the back rounded and stretched weakens it. "You will break the bow if you keep it always stretched." Practice how to lengthen muscles to healthy position, then use the position to advantage.

"Jiu yoku go o sei suru; Flexibility masters hardness."
—Japanese saying

Mental Flexibility

A Japanese story tells of the mental flexibility needed to change thinking, and ultimately, to change actions. A belligerent bushi (samurai) challenged a Zen master to explain the concept of heaven and hell. The monk replied, "No, you are not ready." His honor attacked, the samurai flew in a rage. He pulled his sword. He yelled, "I could kill you for your impertinence." "That," said the monk, "is hell." Startled at the truth, the samurai saw that fury controlled him. He calmed himself. He returned his sword. He bowed. He thanked the monk. "That," said the monk, "is heaven."

"Iron rusts from disuse,
stagnant water loses its purity and in cold weather becomes frozen:
even so does inaction sap the vigour of the mind."
—Leonardo da Vinci

Cardiovascular Conditioning

Good cardiovascular health can help you train harder and get through the physical stress of difficult situations and the period following them. It increases tolerance to exercise in the heat and cold. Improving cardiovascular conditioning can give you the ability to move faster, for longer, similar to the abilities of a younger person. This chapter covers what aerobic and non-aerobic exercise and cardiovascular conditioning mean and how to train your body for better cardiovascular ability for daily health and the martial arts.

What is Good Conditioning?

Until recently, martial arts cardiovascular conditioning used movement of martial arts. Warriors sparred in extended sessions, wearing weighted jackets, maneuvering over stones and logs. They trained while ducking thrown objects and weapons. They trained outdoors in the heat and in the snow. They trained indoors without air conditioning or heat. They trained carrying a training partner and dragging rocks.

Modern conditioning often involves exercising in air conditioning, leaning over expensive machines that cushion all shock and place feet in level position. These remove helpful training qualities. When the body is not exposed to working in hot temperatures, cardiovascular ability does not build enough to supply blood to muscles for work and skin to cool at the same time. When ankles and feet are not trained to hold straight and stable position, they become prone to sprains and turns during turning movement and jumps. When shock absorption is not trained by teaching the legs to decelerate softly with each foot fall and jump, landings become heavy and transmit shock to the hips and spine. The result is loss of useful conditioning for how you live and move. Return to functional use of the body through natural motions in real conditions.

What is Aerobic?

The word "aerobic" does not only mean a type of exercise. It is your body's chemical process of energy production to be alive. Aerobic metabolism goes on during sleep, sitting, standing, moving, and all daily life, as well as during aerobic exercise.

In humans, three body systems make energy. One is aerobic. The other two are not aerobic, so are called anaerobic. All three systems make the same one molecule your body needs to live and move. This molecule is adenosine triphosphate (ATP). ATP isn't stored much in the body. It must be generated all the time. You need less during sleep and more for exercise, but you always need it. The aerobic ATP-making system uses oxygen to combust food into ATP and by-products. The aerobic system makes continuous ATP but is slow because it takes time to process oxygen. Two non-aerobic (anaerobic) systems use the small amount of stored ATP and make another small amount quickly without needing oxygen.

When you start a move or increase intensity, you need quick ATP. The two anaerobic systems work quickly, but run out quickly. You are left without ready fuel. Without oxygen to carry off byproducts, lactic acid and other products build. Your limbs hurt and you gasp for air. Lactic acid is not bad, and is an important fuel, but, it makes you slow down so the slower aerobic system can catch up and get ATP back to your working muscles. The better trained you are, the harder and longer your aerobic and anaerobic systems can work to make and supply fuel before you are too tired to continue. No special pills teach your body to use more oxygen—just simple, free training.

How Does Your Body Use Oxygen and Fuel to Exercise?

When you exercise, your body needs more oxygen to make ATP. Your cells extract more of the oxygen your blood carries from the air you breathe. This does not mean that breathing more oxygen will help. At rest you use only a small part of the oxygen in the air that you breathe. You breathe the rest back out unused.

Average exercise is about ten times more work for your body as just sitting still. That means the exercise increases the oxygen you use by about ten times. You still use only part of the oxygen in the air and breathe out the rest unused. Heavy exercise can increase how much oxygen you need by about twenty times, depending how much aerobic capacity you have. No matter how much oxygen is available, if your body is not in shape to extract and use it, you cannot do the work.

Aerobically fit people can extract more oxygen from air when exercising, so can do more exercise. The better aerobic shape you are in, the more work your body can do without reaching your maximum oxygen carrying capability. World-class athletes have been recorded to reach over 30 times resting rate. A horse, by comparison, has more than twice the best recorded values for humans, even after correcting for size.

Breathing in more oxygen won't increase your ability to extract more oxygen. Eating more food than normal will not increase the rate your body can turn it to energy. Regular aerobic exercise will change your body to increase ability to take oxygen from the air you breathe.

What Changes From Cardiovascular Training?

Many changes happen in the body when you increase cardiovascular fitness. You become able to breathe more air volume in and out. You can move more air faster. Blood volume increases to carry more oxygen. The network of blood vessels expands throughout your lungs and delivery system to your muscles, and the number of oxygen-carrying cells in your blood increases. Fatty deposits diminish in vessels allowing better flow with less blood pressure increase needed. The amount of all the different components and chemicals in the cells that process oxygen and generate ATP increases. Increased blood volume is important when exercising in the heat. You need enough fluid to supply working muscles and to cool the skin. All the many changes that come with better cardiovascular ability are similar to having the physical condition of a younger person.

Aerobic and Non-Aerobic Exercise

High aerobic capacity allows continuous effort in forms, drills, extended sparring, running, skipping rope, and general continuous martial arts activities. This is cardiovascular endurance. Anaerobic or non-aerobic capacity allows fast hard exertions, like flying strikes and throws, and flurries of moves. The highest intensity, brief efforts are mostly anaerobic. Longer, low intensity long efforts are mostly aerobic. All the rest in between are combinations of aerobic and anaerobic. You use both aerobic and non-aerobic reactions in varying amounts for all the times you move at varying speeds and duration.

A slow, easy movement uses almost all aerobic processes, but does not train your heart or circulatory system. Although it is aerobic metabolism, it is not aerobic exercise. Aerobic metabolism includes the aerobic processes that go on all the time to keep you alive. As you work harder, you go higher in your body's ability to supply fuel aerobically. When you start exercise, you add some anaerobic component to make enough ATP. If the exercise continues long enough, you can switch back to more aerobic component. When activities are faster and harder, the body stays with more anaerobic processes. Anaerobic activity uses a few more calories per minute than aerobic exercise. All three systems contribute in different proportions for different length and intensity movement. Train the aerobic and both anaerobic systems for better martial arts.

Training the Three Cardiovascular Systems

The first of the two anaerobic system, called the ATP-PC system, supplies ATP from stored fuel that lasts only seconds. Improve this system through intense runs, lifts, throws, flurries of strikes, kicks, jumps, and other movements hard enough to create fatigue in seconds. Continually work to increase amount of activity done in the same short period of a few seconds.

Train the second anaerobic system, called the gylcolytic system, through hard efforts lasting a few minutes. Finish the last three minutes of long training efforts with the fastest possible pace. Sprint the end of every run. Train your body to go faster, not slower at the end of movements and extended efforts. Alternate fast efforts with slower recovery activity, for example sprint runs with walks, speed punching with slower strikes, and sprint kicks with slower form drills. Jump rope at high speed for 15 seconds, and slower jumping for 15. Increase to jumping 30 seconds, with 15 seconds easy jumping or walking, and so on, increasing time and speed of exertion. Challenge speed by training the same strikes or punches increasingly quickly. Make all-out efforts.

Train the aerobic system through long efforts. Run, spar, swim, bike, practice moves, and jump rope for increasingly long and intense periods. The aerobic system doesn't only increase ability through long aerobic efforts. You need to increase the intensity of longer efforts too. Train to do more in the same time.

Train the aerobic and anaerobic systems together. Divide a bout of time into continuous one minute rounds of activity. Examples: one minute jumping rope, followed by one minute of pushups, back to one minute of rope, then one minute of rapid heavy bag or strikes against a padded wall, then one minute jumping, one minute of rapid heavy bag kicks, one minute of specific striking techniques of your martial art, and so on. Then rest and return to the next bout of one-minute training activities.

Partners can train by doing one minute of intense strike-block combinations from their art, with one-minute periods of pushups, jumping high in the air, squats, lunges, and partner strength combinations shown in Chapter 3 on strength training.

Vary resting time between bouts to train ability to recover and ability to work fatigued. Keep moving following intense exercise, as light exercise uses and removes the lactic acid made by exercise faster than through complete rest.

The aerobic and anaerobic systems help each other recover. Train to improve ability to recover quickly from both short hard effort and longer lower intensity efforts. Vary exertion levels for variety of ability and use. Vary the type of workout. Cross train with varied activities. Intersperse long efforts with speed bursts. Practice moving through forms, katas, and running in zigzags, with rapid directional change, ducks, swoops, and jumps for balance, stability, proficiency, and joint stabilization.

Add different workouts and skill combinations from week to week and month to month. Use healthy, thought-out, challenging, and interesting cardiovascular training to improve many aspects of your life and martial arts at once.

Healthy Joint Positioning and Stability During Cardiovascular Training

- Keep good joint positioning with body weight held up on the muscles, not sagging downward on the joints.

- Don't jump and strike with your back overarched and your hip stuck out in back.

- Keep your hip tucked to prevent a large arch in the lower back. Don't tuck your hip so much that you hunch and round forward. Tuck enough to straighten and shift the weight of your upper body onto your core muscles and off your lower spine. Tucking the hip should not make your knees bend. The tuck comes from your hip.

- Keep your chin in.

- Keep kneecaps facing in the same direction as the feet. Don't let knees or arches sway inward under body weight. Use leg muscles to hold healthy leg positioning.

- When landing from jumps, land on toe, and roll to heel while bending knees.

Figure 6-1. Don't let knees sway inward when landing from any jump or step. Inward pressure strains knee cartilage.

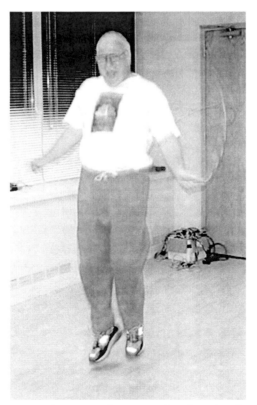

Figure 6-2. Prevent joint trauma by using leg muscles for shock absorption and healthy leg and foot positioning. Land lightly, using thigh and trunk muscles to decelerate. Keep knees and feet facing forward.

Spiritual Heart

"There is no exercise better for the heart than reaching down and lifting people up."
—John Andrew Holmes

"Before the beginning of great brilliance,
there must be chaos.
Before a brilliant person begins something great,
they must look foolish to the crowd."
—I Ching

Balance and Agility

Stances are called kihon in Japanese. Forms are kata in Japanese and Okinawan styles, kuen in Chinese, poomse in Korean, and kon muay in Thai. Fighting and sparring is kumite in Japanese, san da in Chinese, and kyuroogi in Korean. In any language, all require different amounts, kinds, and speed of balance. Good balance is crucial for ease of movement in daily life and martial arts, and preventing sprains and falls. Balance is easily and highly trainable. Many fun activities train balance since balance is used in many ways for real life and in the martial arts. This chapter tells how to develop balance and agility for health and better martial arts ability.

Balance is Use or Lose

Balance is a "use or lose" skill. You will not have good balance unless you use it in your daily life. Many fitness-training programs do not train balance. Injury and disuse diminish balance. Don't be discouraged when first practicing balance. It will improve with practice.

Double Leg Balance Training

- Stand to exercise. Standing is functional exercise, and healthier for the back than sitting to lift weights or stretch.

- Practice getting up from the floor in a smooth manner without hands and back down without hands. Repeat ten times. Repeat ten times holding a package.

- Stand on tiptoe. Maintain good foot posture by keeping body weight over the big toe and second toe, not teetering on the outside of the foot. Ankles straight. Raise and lower ten times.

- Walk over uneven ground. Carefully work up to moving quickly over uneven ground to be able to prevent ankle injury and falls.

- Walk following any line, straight, curved, or uneven. Then walk the line backward, then sideways. Cross feet, first one in front then the other behind, in a style sometimes called "grapevine walking." Sports players practice running like this quickly.

Figure 7-1. After practicing balance on lines on the ground, try raised surfaces. Learn to stand, then walk, then jump and move quickly, forward, backward, and sideways over lines of all configurations.

- Kneel on a large exercise ball. Stand on rolling surfaces.

- Do squats and lunges on wobbly cushions and surfaces.

- Walk on fence rails.

- Use a skateboard. Go skating.

- Put a board over a rock to make a balance board and balance on it.

- Jump in and out of tires and other objects. Walk on the rims. Work up to running in and out of tires.

Figure 7-2. You don't need expensive balance equipment. Use available objects of all shapes to practice balance.

Single Leg Balance

Single leg balance training trains balance at the same time as strengthening the shin muscles in functional ways.

- Put on and take off pants, socks, and shoes standing up, for balance and flexibility.

- Stand on one foot for increasing periods of time. Stand on one foot while on the phone or washing dishes. Stand straight. Don't let body weight sag inward on the knee and downward on the arch of the foot. Maintain straight neutral foot and knee position by using muscles and balance. Increase time of balance on each leg.

- Stand on one leg and point to things with the other. Turn lights on and off with the raised foot. Open and close drawers with your foot. Maintain healthy standing foot position without sagging inward on the knee or arch, flattening the foot.

- Throw and catch things standing on one foot. Lift weight standing on one foot.

- Raise and lower on the toes of only one foot. Maintain healthy foot position with weight centered over the big and second toe. To increase skills, practice balancing with eyes closed.

- Start in the ready position of your martial art. Chamber the leg for a front kick and hold the chambered position. Extend the kick slowly. Hold the leg extended, rechamber and hold. Repeat ten times. Repeat for ten slow side kicks, then ten slow back kicks. Do all your practice on both legs, not just the "easy" side. Remember to do the purpose of the exercise, which is to train healthy function. Don't just do a meaningless series of repetitions in tight or unhealthy position.

Figure 7-3. Practice repeated kicks on one leg, holding healthy straight body positioning

- Stretch legs standing up. Stand and lift one leg up to the front. Maintain upper back straight, not rounding forward. Shoulders back. Keep standing leg straight, but not locked. Hold for at least three normal breaths. Move the same leg out to the side.

Maintain upper back, torso, and standing leg straight. Hold the leg with your hand if it helps. Hold for at least three normal breaths. Without changing straight upper body position, or touching down to the floor, move the same leg behind you for a standing quadriceps stretch. Tuck the hip. Still holding your foot in hand, tip your body forward to stand balancing with your body and free arm pointing forward. Chapter 5 on flexibility teaches more balancing flexibility stretches.

Figure 7-4. Stretch standing up. Keep upper body straight. Avoid letting weight roll inward on the ankle. Instead, hold healthier straight position, with weight on the sole, not arch.

Moving Balance
Ancient Balance Traditions of Muay Talay and Monk's Pillars. To increase skill and balance challenge, fighting is sometimes conducted on raised surfaces. In Muay Talay (water boxing), fighting is done on a bamboo rail suspended over water. The mei-hwa-chuang are the plum flower fighting stumps, also called monk's pillars. These are a series of posts in the ground in specific numbers and patterns for different style practice and fighting.

Hop-gar, White Crane, and some lion dances use the plum pillars. There are stories of sharpened stakes put in the ground between the stumps to make balance training more compelling. In kung fu, posts were long used for balance training and combat testing. Find or make your own safe training lumps, stones, walls, and posts to practice balance. Step up, then learn to hop up onto posts, stumps, and other raised small surfaces.

Figure 7-5. Find balance opportunities wherever you go. Jump and balance on raised posts and rocks for ready-made Monk's Pillar training. Straight position trains strength and focus.

Simple Moving Balance Ideas

• Hop on a line. Hop the line backward. Slalom hop the line, then slalom hop the line backward. To slalom hop means to move forward while hopping side-to-side over the line without touching it.

• Hop from one line, space, marking, or crack in the sidewalk or ground to the next. When landing from any hop or jump, use shock absorption by bending knees and using muscles to slow and pad landing.

- Do pushups with your hands on a balance ball or other wobbly object. Keep your hip tucked under, not letting the back arch or slump toward the floor. Do pushups with both hands on different balance balls.

- Do headstands, handstands and other inverted balancing poses.

- When rolling up to inverted balance poses, do not bend the neck forward, as done for shoulder stands, or "plow" stretches. Bending the neck forward sharply under body weight eventually breaks down the discs and promotes bad neck posture. Keep the neck straight and weight on the muscles not joints of the neck.

Figure 7-6. Inverted balancing poses help balance. Instead of poses that bend the neck forward, damaging the discs, keep the neck straight with weight on the muscles, not the neck joints.

- Do handstands against the wall until you can hold yourself up. Then practice walking on your hands. Recover to your feet softly, either forward or backward, not letting knees sway inward on landing.

- Practice safely until you can walk on your hands on raised surfaces.

Figure 7-7. Walk on your hands to practice strength and balance together. Start on the floor against a wall, shifting hand to hand, and gradually increase balance.

Balance Training After Injury

After illness or surgery, balance ability quickly diminishes. Get on your feet as soon and often as possible. Check to make sure you are not overcompensating by overly widening your stance, waddling side to side, or leaning forward when walking. Stand up straight. Retrain normal gait. The injured area and the rest of your body need that.

After an ankle or knee injury, balance will be poor in the injured leg. Use of brace reduces the need for the leg to make its own adjustments, further diminishing balance. As soon as possible after your injury, begin gentle single leg balance training without the brace or support device. Use your own muscles to hold healthy joint positioning of your knee and ankle. Use bracing as a temporary aid for contingencies like a tournament that come up before balance is restored.

Spiritual Balance

"Given enough time, any man may master the physical.
With enough knowledge, any man may become wise.
It is the true warrior who can master both, and surpass the result."
—Tien T'ai

"He who hesitates, meditates in a horizontal position"
—Ed Parker

Speed

You need speed for quick blocks and strikes. You need to react quickly, move quickly, and "not be there" quickly. Speed must be trained. You won't be fast unless you practice fast. This chapter shows how to develop speed.

Muscle Fiber Types

How fast can your arm move to redirect a punch? It has to be faster than your opponent can punch. When your muscles move your bones, they do that by contracting and shortening the long cells called muscles fibers that make up the muscle.

Muscles have different kinds of fibers. Some fibers contract quickly but get tired quickly. Others are slower but can last longer. The faster and slower fibers are called fast and slow twitch. You use both fast and slow twitch fibers for all movement. Each helps in the way it works best. Slow twitch fibers use more oxygen. They are called oxidative, or Type I fibers. You need these for long steady efforts. Two kinds of fast twitch fibers (IIa and IIb) work more during bursts of strength and speed.

You have probably already seen fast and slow twitch muscle fibers. The slow fibers that use oxygen have dark blood pigment and are called dark meat. You find dark meat in parts of the body, like legs, that do long, continuous efforts like standing and moving around. The fast twitch fibers don't have this oxygen-using pigment, and make up the lighter white meat.

Everyone has both kinds of fibers. Some people have a bit more of slow twitch fibers than fast twitch, giving them a natural tendency to be better at endurance than speed and strength. Other people have more fast twitch fibers, helping them prefer quick strong moves. All the muscle fibers respond to training. That means you can improve both speed and endurance with training. People with more natural ability for speed but less endurance, can improve endurance ability by training with more endurance work. Martial artists with more slow fibers need to train more speed. People who are already fast can get faster with speed training. It's not fiber type, but training that determines final ability.

Train Fast to Be Fast

You will not be fast unless you train fast. Each martial arts skill uses speed differently. You must train speed with each different skill. Practice speed while moving a light weight like your own arm to punch fast. Practice speed while moving a heavy weight, like throwing an opponent, to be able to move heavy things quickly.

The practice of slow weight lifting, sometimes called "super slow" does not train the speed needed for martial arts moves. Slow training increases the total time spent lifting, so increases strength. It will not develop speed for moving heavy objects. You can become as strong or stronger, and faster too, by lifting weights quickly, using more lifts so that total muscle work is the same. Injury potential rises with speed of movement, another reason to properly train speed.

"Why should I practice running slow? I already know how to run slow. I want to learn to run fast. Everyone said, 'Emil, you are a fool!' But when I first won the European Championship, they said, 'Emil, you are a genius!'"
—Emil Zatopek, legendarily fast runner, achieving "the impossible" at the 1952 Helsinki Olympic Games. He set Olympic records in the 5,000 meters, the 10,000 meters, and the Marathon.

Ratios of Strength to Speed

Throws, kicks, sweeps, holds, and strikes that contact the opponent need strength combined with speed. These moves have a higher strength to speed ratio. Locks, parries, and slips use more speed-dominated ability. Fighting situations require both in constantly changing proportions. Train to develop both.

"Standing before me my enemy strikes, but I am already safely behind him."
—Morihei Ueshiba, founder of Aikido

Individual Speed Drills

Several drills train speed for the many ways it is needed in life and martial arts, for moving light and heavy weight quickly. Start with these and tailor your own from them.

Light Weight Speed Drills—Speed Dominated Power. Moving a light weight quickly.
- Punch at a candle flame to extinguish it.

- Punch as fast as possible. Then repeat twice in rapid succession. Then three times, then four. Bring the elbow back to your side between each side, rapidly. Launch your fist forward and back, straight like a piston or like sawing wood. Repeat on the other arm. Practice both arms, not just the faster arm.

- To practice full arm movement quickly, put a paper under your bent elbow by your side in a punching ready position. Strike and return to ready position without letting the paper fall. Repeat 20 times.

- Reach and grab a moving kime (target) bag as fast as possible. Repeat 20 times.

- Front kick as fast as possible. Then repeat twice in rapid succession. Then three times, then four. Train to fire your kicks steadily and strongly each time. Work to do the same number of properly done kicks in less time. Then repeat with side kicks, back kicks, spinning kicks, and others. Repeat on the other leg. Practice both legs, not just the faster, easier leg.

- Run short distances at maximum speed. Rest 10 seconds. Repeat 10 times. Start at 15 yards, then 25, then 50 yards. Time yourself and work to run faster for each set distance. Work to increase speed.

- Run short timed bursts at maximum speed. See how far you can run in 5 seconds. Rest 30 seconds. Repeat 10 times. Work to increase distance covered in each 5-second bout. Then try 10-second bouts, then 25, then 30-second bouts at top speed.

- Throw a ball in the air. Punch one time then catch the ball. Throw to the same height and punch twice before catching. With each throw increase the number of punches. Use a ceiling to limit how high you can throw the ball.

- Throw a ball in the air. Kick one time then catch the ball. Throw to the same height and kick twice before catching. With each throw increase the number of kicks. Work to increase number of kicks in the same amount of time.

- Movies sometimes show someone snatching a fly from the air, then releasing unharmed. Instead of interfering with other living things, throw bits of paper in the air. Snatch them from the air as they flutter. Throw increasing numbers in the air, trying to catch them all with one and both hands.

- Stretch your feet and toes. Pull toes apart so that they are not stuck together and can move freely. Stretching your feet, by itself, will not make you faster, but stiff toes and feet can slow you. Stretching can allow you to use the speed you already have.

- Relax your body. Check your shoulders for hunching. You can't move quickly when tight.

- Relax your mind. You can't make quick decisions of where to move if you are burdened with worry or conflicting ideas. It is an old saying, "To travel quickly, travel lightly. Take off envy, jealousy, unforgiveness, selfishness, and fear."

Heavy Weight Speed Drills—Strength Dominated Power. Strength component speed drills practice moving a heavy weight quickly, both body weight and external weight.

Do not do drills that will injure yourself or others. Always train to go faster. Use control and train positioning joints safely. As you increase the strength component of speed, you move into the realm of power. Training for power is covered more in Chapter 3 on strength.

- Do one pushup at high speed, rest, repeat, until reaching 10 high-speed pushups without stopping. Do not let the low back arch or hike upward. Practice lifting a weight, with increasing speed, paying close attention to safety and joint positioning.

- Do standing lunges quickly. Stand with one foot in front and one far back. Keep feet parallel, not turned out. Bend both knees to lower to just above the floor and raise, keeping feet in place. Healthy lunge positioning is detailed in Chapter 3 on strength. Do standing lunges first singly, then in speed bursts of five and ten down and up.

- Quickly sit or kneel on the floor, and rise to a stand. Try this, carefully, wearing a backpack with increasing weight. Maintain speed. Don't let the increasing weight slow you. Repeat many times.

- Practice throwing a heavy ball or other heavy object at a small target.

- Tie a stretchy band behind you, or use a cable weight. Punch forward, using the band or cable as resistance holding your arm back. Maintain punching speed against the increased resistance. Do increasing numbers of quick punches. First five, then ten, then twenty strikes at a time on each arm.

- Use the same band or cable tied to your foot to train rapid kicks. Alternate shorter rests of five seconds and longer rests of up to 30 seconds between bouts. Holding a cable or band behind you increases the resistance to forward motion. Holding hand weights increases downward force and does not resist against forward motion.

- Devise speed games that train varying proportions of speed and strength. Run dragging a tire on a rope. Pull a child on the tire. Push a car. Run pulling a rickshaw. Push a weight up a hill.

Partner Speed Drills

- Have a friend hold a piece of paper near your hand and drop it without warning. Practice catching.

- To increase speed in response to visual cues, have a partner point a flash light beam at the ground, moving it quickly from point to point. Jump quickly to each new point. Practice this drill jumping with both feet, then hopping with one foot. Do a few dozen points for each kind of jump on each leg. Then do the same drill kicking at each point.

- Kneel on the floor. Have a partner point a flash light beam at the ground, moving it quickly from point to point. Use your hand for punches and strikes at the beam on the floor. Do a few dozen points on each hand. Then try both hands punching together. Then practice striking each point by blocking with one arm and striking with the other simultaneously.

- To increase quick response to auditory cues, one partner makes sound by tapping a stick or other object. At the sound, you strike a target.

- For practice with auditory cues that involve discrimination, use a target with various points, for example a silhouette. The partner quickly names points: "hand, neck, elbow..." You must strike the named target. The same can be done with a target of colored dots or a target of shapes.

- Face a partner. Punch each other (tap lightly). The one who contacts first gains a point. Repeat the drill with one partner punching, the other blocking. The blocking partner must respond quickly to block the punch.

- Have a friend poke at your feet quickly with a non-sharp stick, or squirt you with a water pistol. Jump and duck to avoid hits.

- Throw a ball to a partner. They punch once then catch the ball. They throw the ball back to you. You punch twice before catching. Throw the ball back to the partner who punches three times before catching. Increase the number with each pass. Repeat the same drill with kicks.

- Stand facing a target. Your partner stands next to the target facing you, holding a piece of chalk. You advance quickly in a single move to strike the target. Withdraw your arm quickly before the partner can mark your arm with the chalk to train quick strikes and avoidance of return grabs. Do 20 strikes and exchange places.

- Stand facing a target. Your partner stands next to the target facing you, holding a piece of chalk. You advance quickly in a single move to strike the target. Retreat quickly before the partner can mark the knee of your pants with the chalk. Do 20 strikes and note the number of chalk marks on your pants. This trains quick footwork.

"Tell the truth and run."
—Yugoslavian Proverb

Spiritual Speed

During a soccer match between two Brazilian teams, the first goal was scored within three seconds after kickoff.

The goalie was still on one knee with head bowed in prayer.

There is a time for prayer. There is also a time for speedy action.

"Most people would rather die than think:
Many do. "
—Bertrand Russell

Healthy Mind

Your brain is like your muscles. Use, or lose your skills. Your mind needs stimulation and conditioning. To be a martial artist you need to train your brain to develop coping, evaluating, and decision-making. This chapter gives fun exercises for the mind.

Brain Training

Practice puzzles. Learn chess. Teach children chess and mind stimulating games for home and travel, where you interact with them instead of television. Practice stimulating activity for memory, reasoning, speed of processing.

Figure 9-1. Children thrive on learning and thinking

In Zen, mental riddles called Koan are practiced. They have no answer, so that the brain continues to work at finding the answer. In this work, it becomes quiet in focus.

Practice the foreign language of your martial art. Learn the foreign language of a friend or of your family.

In martial arts it is traditional to practice an art form like bonsai, haiku, shodo (calligraphy), sumi-e (brush painting) or ikebana (flower arranging). Find a form to dedicate your mind: music, dance, drawing, painting, gardening, carving, and other work that combines the mind and the hands.

Examples of thinking for better exercise and injury prevention are given throughout the book. "Mens sana in corpore sano; A healthy mind in a healthy body."

Figure 9-2. Shodo, the way of the brush

Awareness

Practice remembering the people you pass in a crowd. When a group passes, see if you can name how many there were, what they were wearing, and what they were carrying. Can you tell the make and model, or color of the cars that pass? License numbers? Could you tell someone what time it was when they passed?

It is normal, even healthy, to filter extraneous information. It is not a bad thing if you can't recall all observed events, but it is good to develop powers of observation for safety in the streets. Try practicing this martial arts awareness game: if you see a friend or someone you know before they see you, you get one point. If they see you first before you see them, you lose 100 points.

"When one of us says, 'Look there is nothing out there,' what we are really saying is, 'I cannot see.'"
—Terry Tempest Williams

Here is a story of the awareness of the answers that are always there. A young man answered an ad in the newspaper for a job as telegraph operator. He went to the telegraph office for an interview. Many applicants arrived. They were all told to fill out a form and wait to be called. He filled out the form and sat down to wait. Customers came and went. A telegraph machine clacked in the background.

The young man stood up, crossed the room to the door of the office, and walked in. The other applicants wondered why. They decided that, since no one had been summoned to interview, the man should be reprimanded for not following instructions.

A few minutes later the young man came from the office with the interviewer, who announced, "Thank you all for coming. The job has been filled."

The applicants said, "We have been waiting longer than he, and we never got a chance to be interviewed. We listened!" The employer said, "Listen." They head the tapping of the machines. All the time they were sitting, the telegraph had been ticking out the message: "If you understand this, come in. The job is yours." All of them were summoned, but he heard and understood.

Remember that martial arts class is always in session in the real world. Be there mentally.

Be Clear on the Concept
Are you doing what you think you are doing? When you exercise for health or to better your life, are you exercising in unhealthy ways? Are you doing exercise with your back in rounded poor posture? Do you sit in poor posture waiting for class to start? When reading this book on improving health? Students who go to martial arts for the discipline but use poor posture, chew gum, complain when its hard, insult their teachers, and go out drinking and smoking after class are missing the concept of the martial arts. Stay positive, in healthy joint positions, and focused when working on an art that is supposed to embody positive thinking, posture, and discipline.

Mental Clarity in Real Life
A common interpretation of meditation is that quieting the mind is like letting the waters of a pond to become still. Swirling pollutions separate from the water and fall, leaving the water clear, pure, and still.

The problem with leaving the practice half finished like this is that, for many people, like throwing even a small pebble in the water, the smallest disturbance to the person swirls up all the uncleanliness, clouding their mind and sometimes pouring out of their mouth. They are only able to function when all is calm and still. They can't handle being stirred because the junk is still all there. Anyone can meditate in the quiet dark, staring at a candle. Can you stay focused in real life when the phone is ringing and the babies (of all kinds) are screaming?

Long ago, only the rich, and the subsidized monks had the luxury of time to practice meditating as a separate practice from life. Everyone else, including the warriors and the original monks of the Shaolin practiced meditations during all their other practices, when practicing archery, when breaking boards, when gardening and cooking.

Instead of only practicing mediation when sitting quietly, remember to keep the mental skill of clarity, focus, and turning away negative thoughts when doing housework, exercise, and during interactions with others. If you can't do this, it is only that you need practice.

"Anyone can hold the helm when the sea is calm."
—Publius Sirus

Focus

What can you do when thoughts nag at you at night and you can't sleep? Thoughts tumble around of sadness and resentment of things that could have or should have been, or not been. Night is time for sleep and health. Your adversary would be happy to know he has power over you, even in your own bed. You must reclaim your focus. Say to yourself, "This is my time. I will sleep. I will think of this another time, but now it is time for sleep."

Decision Making

There was a wild horse tied up and left by its owner in a narrow alleyway. All who came upon it pondered and debated how to pass without being kicked. One tried running past and was tumbled to the ground, but still not able to get beyond. Another tried jumping over the horse's legs as it kicked, with the same result. Another attempted to pass through the horse's legs but got trampled.

A crowd assembled and debated how to pass the horse, with many theories.

Finally, Master Kung passed by. The crowd said, "Here is Master Kung. He'll know how to deal with this!"

Master Kung looked at the wild horse, smiled, and walked to the next alley to continue on his way.

If you think you must only muscle your way through something, remember rational thought. "Life is simpler when you plow around the stump."

Wabi Sabi

Wabi sabi is a Japanese concept of aesthetics, stressing unpretentiousness, plainness, earthiness, and satisfaction with imperfection. It is a comprehensive worldview and aesthetic system. It does not mean to be sloppy or lazy, or to fail then say it's all you could do. Wabi-sabi is a beauty of things imperfect, impermanent, and incomplete. It is finding the beauty of modest, unconventional, and humble things. In understanding wabi sabi, you will unclutter your mind to be unpretentious, content, earthy, and simple.

"I like living. I have sometimes been wildly, despairingly, acutely
miserable, racked with sorrow,
but through it all I still know quite certainly
that just to be alive is a grand thing."
—Agatha Christie

Healthy Spirit

Healthy spirit involves many things. The aim of the martial arts is to train them all. Along
with kicks and strikes, self-discipline, gentle behavior, sportsmanship, respect, and peaceful
mind are developed. This chapter gives stories, quotations, and ideas to use as mental tools to
develop many aspects of healthy spirit.

Budo

The concept of "the do" (the tao) means "the way." Budo means "the way of the combat."
This does not mean going around hurting things. It includes all the aspects of mental and
physical discipline and technique that work together to make you able to win. Winning
means to be a good and happy person in life, and becoming powerful inside so that things do
not upset your thinking and path. Budo guides you through your years of practicing peaceful
behavior with healthy mind, spirit, and ethics. Budo emphasizes developing physical, mental,
and spiritual control and depth. This is not just three times a week doing pushups and
sparring in the training hall, but in the supermarket when the person in front of you takes
too long. Can you smile with real joy, as if at a child who tumbles over trying to walk? This
is the true winner. When will it be you?

Effort

Effort does not just mean succeeding. It means doing. You may try a move and fall over
every time. That does not mean you are failing. You are the person building a tall tower. You
are not finished yet. It is exciting watching the construction. A baby who falls over when
learning to walk is not a failure and neither are you. We are not finished yet. That is good, it
means we are still alive.

"The real glory is being knocked to your knees and then coming back.
That's real glory. That's the essence of it."
—Vince Lombardi

Respect
In Thai martial arts, respecting teachers and elders is foremost. Every fight begins with rituals of honoring parents, and the Ram Muay, a spirit dance to show respect and thanks, and ask blessings from the teachers, the Kruu Muay Thai. Live your daily life with thanks for what you have learned. Thankfulness and respect are empowering to your own spirit.

"You can easily judge the character of someone by how they treat those who can do nothing for them or to them."
—Variously attributed to several people including Malcolm Forbes

Discipline
Students ask what is the secret to discipline; how can they get discipline? How can you not have discipline? How else will you get things done? How else will you achieve what you want? It's just common sense that you have to do what needs doing until you succeed.

"When a person trains once, nothing happens. When a person forces himself to do a thing a hundred or a thousand times, then he certainly has developed in more ways than physical. Is it raining? That doesn't matter. Am I tired? That doesn't matter, either. Then willpower will be no problem."
—Emil Zatopek, epic Olympic runner, legendary for achievement and discipline

Adversity

A student was sad that life was hard. He did not know how he was going to make it and wanted to give up. The cook saw him and took him to the kitchen. There the cook showed him three pots boiling on the coals. In one, the cook placed carrots, in the other she placed eggs, and in the last she placed ground coffee beans. She let them sit and boil, without saying a word.

The student impatiently wondered what this had to do with anything. He had problems, and wanted someone to help him. After some time, the cook pulled the carrots out. She pulled the eggs out. Then she ladled the coffee out. Turning to the student she asked, "What do you see?" With scorn, the student replied, "Carrots, eggs, and coffee."

The cook brought him closer and asked him to feel the carrots. He did and said they were soft. The cook asked him to take an egg and break it. After pulling off the shell, he observed the hard-boiled egg. The cook asked him to sip the coffee. His face wrinkled from the strength of the coffee. Humbly, he asked, "What does it mean, Master?" She explained, "Each of them faced the same adversity, the same temperature of boiling water. Each reacted differently, according to their substance."

"The carrot began strong. After going through boiling water, it became soft and weak. The egg started out soft inside. After going through the boiling water, it became brittle outside and hardened inside. The coffee beans became stronger and richer."

"Which are you?" the cook asked? When adversity occurs, how do you respond? Are you the carrot that seems hard, but with the smallest amount of pain, you wilt and become soft with no strength? Are you the egg, which starts off with a malleable heart and fluid spirit? But after a death, a breakup, a layoff, you became brittle, hardened and stiff. Your shell looks the same, but you are hardened with a stiff spirit and heart, internally. Or are you like the coffee bean? When the water gets hottest, it releases better taste and richness. When things are worst, you reach inside to put out greatness. How do you handle adversity?

Are you a carrot, an egg, or a coffee bean?

The story does not end there. What about the water in the pots? It is popular to retell the story of the butterfly that flaps his wings here, causing events that eventually lead to the volcano erupting at the other side of the world. It is important to know that your actions have consequences to others. It is important to not do things that hurt others. For yourself, you must not be fragile and so easily affected. Water boils and freezes. It pours, evaporates, falls again. It remains the same water. Unharmed. You can't grab water. When adversity grabs at you, become better like the coffee bean, but remain as serene and unaffected as water.

Intoku

What good is being good if no one knows about it? It is an art. Just as the number one can never be reduced to zero, a kind act or good deed or accomplishment is never completely erased. Neither is an unkind deed. Do not do unkind things. Do good, even if no one knows. Intoku is good done in secret.

"The work an unknown good man has done is like a vein of water flowing hidden underground, secretly making the ground green."
—Thomas Carlyle, Scottish writer born 1795

Perseverance

No matter what defeat or sadness you feel, keep putting one foot in front of the other toward your goals. It may be called "faking it," but just keep moving. Things will clear up. By then, you've put many feet in front of the other and gotten farther to where you want.

"Nothing in the world will take the place of persistence. Talent will not; nothing is more common than the unsuccessful person with talent. Genius will not; unrewarded genius is almost a proverb. Education will not; the world is full of educated derelicts. Persistence and determination alone are omnipotent. The slogan "press on" has solved and always will solve the problems of the human race."
—Calvin Coolidge, 30th President of the United States from 1923-1929

"Fall seven times, stand up eight."
—Japanese proverb

Mastering Emotions

If someone came up to you and said, "I command you to jump up and down and shout," would you do that? If someone came up to you and said, "I command that you do not sleep tonight," would you obey? Does this sound ridiculous? Can you remember a time when something negative happened. Did you stomp around? Did you shout, "How could they do that? How could they say that?" Did you stay awake, going over it in your mind, unable to sleep? Would your adversary be happy to know they control you completely?

What if someone walked up to you and said, "I am going to install this metal device onto your body, and whenever I touch it, you will jump and shout, and not sleep; you will do what I want." Does this sound ridiculous? It is. But it is still real. This device is called a button. Whenever a person presses your buttons, are you controlled? When people do things, does it control how you feel and what you do?

If a small child came up to you and said, "You're a poopy-head!" would you be hurt? Would you call your friends, outraged? Would you ask everyone, "Do you think it's true?" Probably not. Why not? The child has no power over you. His making a statement does not render it true. Transfer this thinking to others who call you names or claim to judge you. Smile indulgently at them. Instead of them having power over you, they are reduced to an unaware and mildly cute small child.

"To win one hundred victories in one hundred battles is not the highest skill. To subdue the enemy without fighting is the highest skill."
—Sun Tsu, The Art of War

Repeated Problems

When you find yourself in an unfavorable situation, see if you went toward it because it felt familiar. In a room of 100 people, it often happens that the two depressed people find each other. Make sure that you are not going toward unfavorable things. An amoeba will ooze away from a pin stuck in it. Will you move away from something painful?

Sometimes bad things just happen. That is how it works. But other times, why do bad things happen over and over? A lesson will be presented until it is learned.

When Other People Repeat Problems

Are you surprised and upset every time stupid people act stupidly again, and when undisciplined people do undisciplined things? It's nice to think well of people and hold them to the excellence that they can do. But the sun rises every day. Don't let it catch you by surprise.

Habits

"We are what we repeatedly do."
—Aristotle

Addictions

Having a problem is not the problem. It is the attachment to the problem.

Impermanence

All life is impermanence. Sadness about loss can be reduced when remembering that everything in life is temporary, transient, changeable, impermanent. It is supposed to be that way

Working Against Yourself

"Man stands in his own shadow and wonders why it is dark. "
—Zen saying

Negativity

Make the energy to do positive acts and think positive things. Instead of spending time talking against yourself– "I can't do that, I'll never be able to do that, I'll never succeed," —take the energy and just keep moving toward a goal.

"Argue for your limitations and they are yours."
—Richard Bach

It's also true that you don't want to accept everything without thinking. Keep an open mind, but not so open that your brains fall out.

Fear of Failure

Avoid fear or failure by releasing attachment to the outcome. To avoid the dread of trying something or counting on something and fearing it will not happen the way you want, release your attachment to what will happen.

"Don't listen to anyone who tells you that you can't do this or that. That's nonsense. Make up your mind, you'll never use crutches or a stick, then have a go at everything. Go to school, join in all the games you can. Go anywhere you want to. But never, never let them persuade you that things are too difficult or impossible."
—Sir Douglas Bader (1910-1982), British fighter pilot who lost both legs in a flying accident, but still fought in World War II. He was knighted for his work with the disabled. The quotation is from his talk to a 14-year-old boy who had lost a leg after a car accident.

"In great attempts, it is glorious even to fail."
—Cassius Longinus, Greek philosopher ca. 210–273 A.D.

Fear of Life

Nelson Mandela talked about breaking away from fear: "Our deepest fear is not that we are inadequate. Our deepest fear is that we are powerful beyond measure. It is our light, not our darkness, that most frightens us. We ask ourselves, who am I to be brilliant, gorgeous, talented and fabulous? Actually, who are you not to be? Your playing small doesn't serve the world. There's nothing enlightened about shrinking so that other people won't feel insecure about you. We were born to manifest the glory that is within us. It's not just in some of us; it's in everyone. As we let our light shine, we unconsciously give other people permission to do the same. As we are liberated from our own fear, our presence automatically liberates others."
—Nelson Mandela, Inaugural speech, 1994

Expecting Life to Be Fair

Life is not set up to be fair. Expecting it to be fair is an overdeveloped sense of entitlement. A saying illustrates this: "Expecting the world to treat you fairly because you are a good person is like expecting the bull not to attack you because you are a vegetarian."

Losing a Fight

Lose well. It is called sportsmanship. We learned it as kids. Show that you learned it. Make no excuses. Blame no others. It is a normal part of life. Aside from tie scores, you will score more or fewer points than your opponent. When it is fewer, smile, shake their hand. Find a sincere comment to praise them. If your children are watching you compete, teach them to do the same. When you are watching your children compete, you do the same.

"He that is good at making excuses is seldom good at anything else."
—Benjamin Franklin

Losing is not always losing. Work together in a team effort to help a teammate to success. Let others win. That is sometimes how you win most.

"When someone does something good, applaud. You will make two people happy."
—Samuel Goldwyn

When an Olympic runner comes in second, is that losing? Do they throw their silver medal on the ground and stomp away? What we like to see is their victorious smile. They competed. They lived. When they stumble, they get back up and raise arms high overhead with a smile, and we cheer. Remember, "No ego, no cry." When you lose, whether a job or a meet, say, "It was great. I had the time of my life." Then who is the winner?

"Victory and defeat are not polar opposites."
—Former US Senator Bob Dole

Keep Going

Sometimes you are so overwhelmed by disappointment and loss and pain that you do not know what to do. The answer is only to not make things worse. They have hurt you. Don't add to that. You must eat. You must sleep. Grieve all you want, but take care of yourself. If you can't look at food, put the nutrients you need in a blender, hold your nose if you must, but drink it down and keep your body going. Keep one foot moving in front of the next. Comb your hair. Do your training. The hard time will pass.

Understanding

An important gift to give someone is understanding. When someone doesn't feel understood by you, they feel isolated from you. You do not have to agree with them to understand them. When someone feels understood, they no longer feel they have to insist on their point. It is a gift for both of you.

Sense of Humor

There is a Buddhist saying that laughter is the language of the Gods. Keep your sense of humor. Joe Louis, boxing heavyweight champion, explained why he did not hit a motorist after the motorist abused him following an accident, "Why should I? When somebody insulted Caruso, did he sing an aria for them?"

Need

Wanting to win is fine. Needing to win is not healthy. Don't let yourself be so needy or insecure that you need to win. Don't ruin your finances so that you need the prize money and have no margin from savings and other work. Don't compromise yourself because you need a million dollars. Or one dollar.

Do things from love, and fun, and wanting to, and for the spirit of learning. You and your family are better off with your healthy spirit, than with a desperate person who hinges worth on one event, or from event to event.

Seeking Status

Who is important? Are you important only if you have a certain job title or income or fight record? Or live in a certain place? It is not the way of the martial arts to consider yourself better than someone of lower rank, or treat them without respect. It does not matter what job or income you have, it matters how you conduct yourself in life.

A long time ago, there was a bakery where all the bread for the village was baked. The bakers worked though the nights to make fresh hot bread for the village every morning. The little boy of the family greased the pans. That was his job—the lowest job in the bakery. He thought he was not important. He didn't do any of the important things that everyone else did. He thought his life and job did not matter to anyone.

One night he didn't oil the pans. All the bread was ruined. No one had bread that day.

Do every job you have, no matter how small, with happiness. It does not have to be a job that is known about, or with status. We are all important.

"You can stand tall without standing on someone.
You can be a victor without having victims."
—Harriet Woods, American politician

There is a story that at the end of the final exam of the finest MBA program in the country, was one question, "What is the name of the person who cleans the floors of this building?" Anyone not able to answer this did not get a degree that semester. Do you say hello to the people who work so hard to make a beautiful place for you to learn and work? Do you care who they are? They are a special human being like you are. Learn their name. Say hello. See the difference it makes to them and to your world outlook.

Warrior Heart

It is normal to become angry. The skill is what you do with it. It is a practice in the martial arts to learn what is sometimes called "warrior heart." It is not hiding or denying anger, just not making it a negative force. The Thais call it "jai yen" —cool heart. They reduce visible irritation and tone of voice. Jai yen is central to Thai social and business interaction. It means not becoming shaken or agitated by something or somebody. It illustrates the mind/body set of the experienced warrior. Jai yen is part of Muay Thai boxing training. In Japan it is "fudoshin" —unchanging heart. A person with fudoshin is more stable when things happen. It doesn't mean you don't feel and understand and care what is going on. That would indicate other problems. You can be angry. Anger can be a force that gets positive things done. But don't sadden yourself and injure your body with the unhealthy chemicals generated that can hurt your health and heart.

"He who smiles rather than rages is always the stronger."
—Japanese proverb

A story of a boy with an angry heart tells how his father gave him a bag of nails and told him that every time he lost his temper, he must hammer a nail into the fence. The first day the boy had driven 37 nails into the fence. Over the next weeks, as he learned to control his anger, the number of hammered nails dwindled. He discovered it was easier to hold his temper than to drive the nails into the fence. The day came when the boy didn't lose his temper. He told his father. The father told him to pull out one nail each day he was could hold his temper. Days passed until the boy told his father that all the nails were gone. The father led him to the fence. He said, "You've done well son, but look at the holes in the fence. The fence will never be the same. When you say things in anger, they leave a scar like this one. You can put a knife in a man and draw it out. It won't matter how many times you say, "I'm sorry." The wound is still there. A verbal wound is as a physical one." Although the things that others say to you does not anger you, remember that to others a small hurt can hurt all their life. You have far more power when you say helpful things to people and have it help their life forever.

Disapproval

There is an interesting phenomenon that is sometimes true. Stop and check yourself when you find yourself strongly disliking something in someone else. Sometimes it is because it is a characteristic that you dislike in yourself.

Scorn

If you want to do one thing to rid yourself of poison, rid yourself of scorn. Scorn in speech or action is poisonous to the human spirit. Must one person put another down and show contempt before television audiences find a show funny or interesting? Is that the only way they can relate?

"To think bad thoughts is really the easiest thing in the world. If you leave your mind to itself it will spiral down into ever increasing unhappiness. To think good thoughts, however, requires effort. This is one of the things that discipline—training is about."
—James Clavell, *Shogun*

There isn't anyone in the world who doesn't know something wonderful you haven't yet heard. Working positively to listen to them can be more interesting, and ultimately more powerful than scorning them. When someone trains in a different style than yours, instead of rejecting them as wrong, learn something. Anything. If nothing else, if they are insufferable, insisting only their style has merit, learn how great it is to lighten up.

"The noble man emphasizes the good in others, and does not accentuate the bad. The inferior does the reverse."
— Confucius, Chinese philosopher 551-479 B.C.

Who Are You Living For?

To become peaceful, honor your teachers and parents. To become in conflict, live only for them.

"If you race merely for the tributes from others, you will be at the mercy of their expectations."
—Scott Tinley, runner

Being Happy

To be happy, practice being happy. It is like any other skill. Don't look to arbitrary and changeable external circumstances to make you happy. People often ask, "When will I be happy? When will this sadness leave?" The answer is like laundry: it will happen when you do it. It doesn't happen by itself. Yes, time can heal, but not if you practice being unhappy for long periods by waiting for happiness to come by itself. Find something. Take back the power of your own happiness.

"No matter who says what to you, smile and do your own work."
—Agnes Gonxha Bojaxhi (Mother Theresa)

To cheer yourself, cheer someone else. Learn to be happy with all around you. Practicing it will help it become a habit. Keep a mirror at your desk where you can see yourself when you are on the phone. Watch yourself interact with people. Practice being happy enough when talking to smile. When you smile, they will hear it.

"He who allows his day to pass without practicing generosity and enjoying the pleasures of life is like a blacksmith's bellows. He breathes, but he does not live."
—Sanskrit proverb

Joy

Do you practice the martial arts with joy? Do you practice life that way? Do not practice with a scowl, thinking you are more fierce that way. Being masterful does not mean being grim, serious, angry. The one who can practice and have it be his joy is someone to look up to.

"People are able to wonder at the height of mountains, and the huge waves of the sea, the vast compass of the ocean, at the circular motion of the stars, and then pass by themselves without wondering at all."
—St. Augustine

Being Simple

In order to meditate and practice simple things, many people buy special clothes, chairs, candles, scarves, incense, bowls, chimes, oils, rocks, music, clocks, tapes, mats, jewelry, things, and more things. There is no need for expensive props, or any props, to learn how to be simple.

Self–Mastery

"Any person capable of angering you becomes your master."
— Epictetus, Roman philosopher 55-135 A.D.

Helping Others

What is heaven? Sometimes it is in surprising places. An old story tells of a group of people who found themselves at a banquet. Wonderful food filled the table. Their arms and legs were all in splints. They could not bring the food to their mouth, or bend to the table to eat. They realized they were in hell. Weeks passed. They were starving with food right in front of them. Then, one person took the food in his splinted arm and fed it to the person next to him. Everyone did this. They realized they were in heaven.

Looking for Happiness

Long ago in a small village, there was place known as the House of 1000 Mirrors. A small dog learned of this place and decided to visit. When he arrived, he looked through the doorway and smiled in happy expectation. One thousand dogs smiled at him. He said, "This is great." One thousand dogs said, "This is great."

Another little dog traveled far to visit the House of 1000 Mirrors. He climbed the stairs and hung his head low as he looked into the door. One thousand unfriendly looking dogs lowered their head at him. His mouth fell open in fear. One thousand dogs opened their mouths back at him. He thought, "This is a terrible place, everyone is so unfriendly."

What kind of reflections do you see in the people you meet?

Looking for What is Here

Some people pay large sums of money to go away to a resort, retreat, zendo, or ashram to go without telephones, go on a fast, be silent, and sleep on a hard bed, or no bed. Find peace and discipline yourself at home. There is no other place it matters more. Get rid of junk and clutter. Make a healthy meal with family or alone, without television or phone. Say thankful things. Taste your food. Turn down seconds. Breathe. Smile. That is enlightenment.

Giving Thanks

There are groups of mountain monks in Japan, who, after going to the bathroom, give thanks because everything worked. Learn to give thanks for all the little things and big things. When possessions break, give thanks for having possessions, which is more than most of the world has. When your faucet leaks, give thanks that you have running water. Most of the world walks far to carry home heavy water on their back. When you wake up, say "thank you" for that, instead of being unhappy about having chores to do. Don't curse your car or bicycle when it doesn't work; that's unhealthy. Thank it every time it works.

To cheer yourself, cheer up someone else. Do something for someone else. Tell someone "thank you" who has helped you.

In many areas of Asia, almost every store, home, and public building has small personal shrines with offerings of food, drink, flowers, candles, and incense for the spirits. Bottles of water, soda and juice are open, often thoughtfully supplied with a straw, thanking the spirits every day. It is common to see trees with colorful sashes tied. The sashes are gifts to thank the tree and the powers that live in and around the tree for all the good they have done for us in all the many ways.

In Buddhist countries of Southeast Asia, it is customary for men to become monks. They may remain monks for weeks, months, or as long as they want. Becoming a monk honors their parents, their people, and their country. Many Thai families say they prefer their daughters to only marry a man who has been a monk because he has learned patience, simpleness, compassion, respect, and thankfulness.

Most Muay Thai fighters, military personnel, and government officials have been monks, including the King. Thousands of monks walk with bowls early every morning, often barefoot, even in city streets. The people line up to give food and offerings and thanks. It is believed that the monks help the people by letting the people become more meritorious by giving food and thanks. By generosity and thanks to others you can overcome personal fear and selfishness.

Inner Light

Like a stained glass window in the darkness of winter, the way you can see its beauty is the light that shines from within. Don't wait for others to light your way. Light your own light inside. Shine on.

The Lotus
How to Free Yourself of Baggage

The lotus is the most representative image of Buddhism and Budo. In the villages, life is hard. Dust and squalor of daily life are all around. In every rain gully and muddy pool of water, there is probably a buffalo pooping in it, a baby being bathed and pooping in it, and all the dirt and traffic of life going through it.

Through the filth and organic matter, the lotus takes root. It grows and passes through the muck, then blooms in exquisite beauty, untouched by what it passed through.

The symbol of the lotus flower is two hands pressed palm together. This is why we greet each other this way. It is a greeting of the lotus and a fervent wish that no matter what we had to pass through to get here today, that we bloom in beauty, untouched.

The lotus root grows even if hurt or cut or damaged. No matter how you cut them, they grow anyway. This does not mean that anyone can cause hurt without consequence. The person who does the hurting is still stupid. But the lotus can be cut and it does not affect the lotus. It grows as it wants to without any change to its own plan. As can you.

Bloom in beauty.

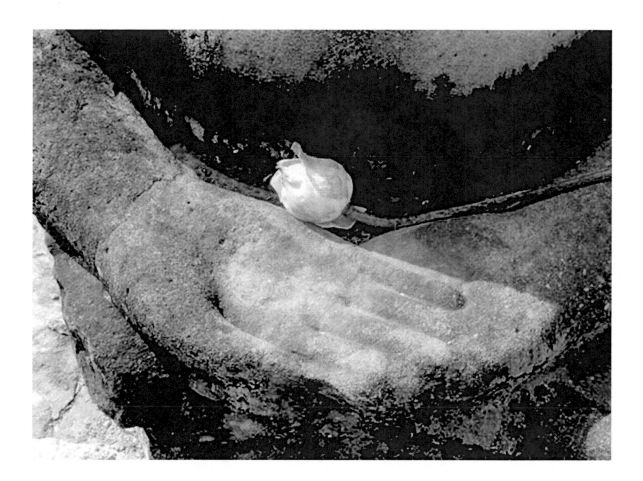

"Whenever I feel blue
I start breathing again"
—Unknown

Breathing

This chapter gives helpful, healthy breathing practices for daily life, meditation, and the martial arts.

Simplicity in Breathing

Much is made of breathing. In this nostril. Out that ear. Four times slowly this way, eight hundred times quickly that way. Instead, remain simple. In. Out. This is often more than many people do. Check yourself when at work, opening mail, putting things away. Are you hunching your shoulders and holding your breath just to hurry through and get it done? Keep breathing normally in and out.

Make Household Activities Your Breathing Meditation

When chopping vegetable for dinner, do you hunch your shoulders and hold your breath during the knife stroke? Make the rhythmic chopping a meditation. When you hang up laundry, do you tense up and hold your breath? When you move during any action, check to see if you tighten muscles and hold your breath, trying to get it done. Lower the shoulders. Lengthen the muscles. Enjoy the task. Breathe.

Make Routine Exercises Your Breathing Meditation

Gardening. Stretching. Stances. Sparring. These are things to do with meditative healthy breathing. Long ago only the idle rich and assisted monks had the luxury of time to sit for hours. The rest had jobs and children to raise.

It's easy to be calm and focused in a quiet room staring at a candle. What about real life when the kids are screaming in the back seat and you need to stay safe and in charge? The original meditations used martial arts techniques of the warriors. They used meditative focus while training the body. Later meditation specialized in certain parts—only to breathe, or count, but kept the original claims of making the body strong, straight, and focused in difficult circumstances. The martial arts keeps the original and more complete tradition of breathing while doing. Mind and body, not one at a time.

Helpful Breathing Techniques

For healthy breathing during life activities, remember to expand your belly to breathe in, not just raise your shoulders and chest. Don't pull your belly inward when breathing in. Let the belly come outward as air fills your lungs. Take a full breath in now and try it.

It used to be thought by some in exercise science that respiratory muscles could not be trained, or that the highest amount of air moving in and out with exercise would not change except to diminish with aging. Now it is established that the breathing muscles are muscles like any other. Train them. This has been long practiced in the martial arts in exercises of sanchin and some chi kung breathing. Purse your lips and breathe in against the resistance. Breathe out without resistance and repeat. There are expensive respiratory muscle trainers to do this. You can get a similar effect yourself by breathing in with pursed lips or trying to breathe through your sleeve. Periodically see how much air you can breathe in and out in one breath, both with and without resistance. See how quickly you can inhale fully. Then how fast you can exhale fully. Regularly exercise heavily so that you need to breathe hard for extended periods.

In martial arts, and arts of war dances and drumming in several countries, a concentrated exhalation coordinated with effort is variously called kiah, kiai, hihap, battle cry, and other terms. Translations vary with interpretation. Beliefs and usage vary with schools. It can be vocalized in a short yell, a loud breath, or silent. One of the purposes, when used with quick, focused physical effort is to increase acceleration at specific points of the move to increase power. For heavy moves, it can help lessen increases of pressure in the chest cavity and blood vessels. Done either quickly or slowly, it can be used to strengthen the move by including expiratory muscles. Often, it is done to remind students to breathe at all. In groups, it helps unify mood or keep cadence. Sometimes it is used just to sound scary. Done without coordinating effort, it is called yelling, and sometimes it is just vocalizing in corny ways.

More than any breathing practice, keep breathing normally in and out for daily life. Don't hold your breath during activities. For hard efforts like throws and strikes, breathe out on effort. When fear or pain control your breathing, get control back by breathing in a deep breath and thinking to yourself, "I can do this," while breathing out. Then breathe in for two counts and out for four counts. Slow down the counts to slow the breathing back to normal.

Foods and Environments That Help and Hurt Breathing

Open a window if it is stuffy. Avoid overuse of incense in closed spaces. Even incense is secondhand smoke. Keep houseplants. They breathe in your exhaled carbon dioxide and give off oxygen. They are natural air filters. Get outside in clean environments if you spend time indoors. Don't smoke. Avoid eating cured meats, which are associated with decreased lung function and increased incidence of obstructive pulmonary disease.

Spiritual Breathing Out

To breathe out and let your sorrows go, here is the story of two boxes. A long time ago, a Master gave two of her students, two boxes each. She told them, "Put all your sorrows in the gray box. Put all your joys in the gold. Now go."

Weeks later, the two students came back. One dragged his gray box, it was so heavy. He struggled into the door and sat down heavily with his filled, oppressive, gray box.

The Master asked him, "Where is your gold box? Your box of joy?"

The student sputtered, "Master, how can I carry anything else but this impossible box of sorrow? It is so heavy and large. Life is full of sorrow. Everyone knows that. It takes all my energy just to carry this one box, how can I do both?"

The other student came in with two boxes. He sat down easily with them. The gray box was light and easy to carry. The Master asked him why his gray box was so light. Didn't he have sorry and tragedy in his life?

"Oh, yes." said the student. Everyone does. Life is full of sorrow. Everyone knows that." He held up the bottom of his gray box. "But I put a hole in the bottom in my gray box. By which I have let my sorrows go. That way I had my energy and arms open to carry the joy. That way, I could put so much more in my gold box of joy."

Breathe in. Breathe out. Let your sorrows go.

"The wise man should consider that
health is the greatest of human blessings. Let food be your medicine."
—Hippocrates, Greek physician (ca. 460–377 B.C.)
who pioneered scientific medicine

Healthy Nutrition

You don't need expensive supplements or special formulas to be healthy and strong. This chapter tells about foods, simple preparation, and recipes that are good for body and spirit.

Foods That Work Against You

Someone who works against you is not a friend. Some foods increase inflammatory process in the body, and are produced in ways that strip nutrition and create new products that do harm: You don't need them: Refined sugar, sweetened fruit punch drinks, refined white flour products, packaged breakfast cereal, dairy, candy, soda, artificial sweeteners, hydrogenated oil, and trans-fats. Trans-fat is a processed fat used in convenience foods like crackers, cookies, and fast food like French fries and doughnuts. Foods like dairy mix problems and benefit. There is no need to take in harmful substances to get some good. Much calcium and protein is available without dairy. Many good tasting foods help your health and strength. You don't need to eat junk. A dedicated martial artist will not do harm with food that works against the body.

Foods That Help You

Good foods, like good people, help you improve yourself and have qualities that discourage harmful things. Eat healthy food for snacks, both raw and lightly cooked in healthy combinations, and mixed in the blender to make your own sport drinks:

Fruit. Eat several different fruit every day. Apples, pears, grapes, kiwi, and others. Wash the skins and eat fruit with the skins, where possible, and seeds. Pulp, skins, and seeds have complex carbohydrates, vitamins, many beneficial nutrients, and fiber. Fiber helps keeps blood sugar stable. Peels and skins of many fruits and vegetables have healthy components.

Grape skins have anti-inflammatory chemicals, as do the seeds, without the side effects of commercial painkillers. Cherry skins have high benefit. Instead of spitting watermelon seeds, gain the nutrition of eating them. Throw some well-washed orange peel in the blender when making blender drinks. Throw in the orange seeds too. Grate in lemon rind for healthy flavoring.

Berries. Strawberries, blueberries, cranberries, blackberries, many others. Eat fresh, with nuts, and in blender drinks. Freeze and crush to make sweet frozen desserts that don't need sugar for sweetening.

Fresh Vegetables. Eat vegetables every day. All colors. Different nutritional compounds produce each color. Add spices instead of sugar, cornstarch, or cream. Steam in soy sauce, balsamic vinegar, and vegetable broth, or lightly sauté instead of frying. Top cooked vegetables with fresh raw tomato, raw crushed garlic, and fresh green scallions for flavor, crunch, and to preserve nutrients that diminish with cooking.

Nuts. Eat raw nuts for small snacks, sprinkled over vegetables, with grains like rice and barley, in salads, and thrown in the blender with fruit and cinnamon. Try walnuts, almonds, pecans, macadamia, and others.

Seeds. Flax seeds, pumpkin seeds, squash seeds, watermelon seeds, basil seeds, pomegranate seeds, sunflower seeds, sesame seeds, and others. Use raw, not roasted, honeyed, coated, or sugared. If you want flax oil, it is healthier and less expensive to use the seeds, not commercial oil already pressed. Oils become rancid, and change chemical makeup into unhealthy products. Put seeds into blender drinks, on salads, vegetables, and sandwiches. Mix into whole grains like rice, corn, and millet after cooking. When preparing pumpkin and squash, scoop the seeds and fresh bake them, seasoned with spices like chili, curry, cinnamon, garlic, wasabi, and pepper.

Grains/Grasses. Use brown rice and other whole color rice instead of refined, hulled, white rice (polished rice). The outer covering that gives color has important fiber and nutrients. Use whole oats and whole barley, millet, and amaranth to make hot cereal instead of sugared, refined packaged cereal. Add nuts and fruit after cooking for crunch and sweetness without losing nutrients to the cooking process. Bake your own bread from fresh whole grains of all kinds. Add raisins, nuts, seeds, or spices like cinnamon, cardamon, curry, and coriander (dhania). Enjoy the meditative and arm-training aspect of kneading the dough, and nature at work as it rises. Share the bread at your training center.

Legumes. Peas, beans, lentils are high protein, antioxidants, many nutrients, and fiber. Good alone, spiced, and mixed with vegetables, seeds, and nuts. Lentils add meaty taste to tomato sauce. Cook lentils for about 30 minutes. Briefly sauté onions with mustard seeds, sesame seeds, and spices over low heat. Add chunked tomatoes, cooked peas, and lentils. Top with sunflower seeds and crushed garlic.

Anti-Inflammatory Food. Ginger, turmeric (spice giving a yellow color to curry), dark grapes with the skins, green tea, uncooked pineapple, pineapple core which contains bromelain. Grate or cut ginger root and small amounts of turmeric root into blender drinks, soups, and for healthy seasoning in food.

Change Unbeneficial Food to Good Food

Juice, Blender Drinks, Sport Drinks. Commercial juice and juice with removed pulp is little more than sugar water. Many sports drinks are a lot of simple sugar. They may fuel exertion over the short run, but sugar water is not health food over the long run. Make your own healthier juice and drinks by throwing fruit in a blender or low speed grinder with clean water. Try apples with the skins, grapes, pears, blueberries, orange slices with clean peels, apricots, and other fruit, and vegetables like beetroot and carrots. Add sweet fresh persimmon juice by scooping seeds out with a spoon into the blender. If you don't have a machine, use martial arts patience and meditative arm movement to mash ingredients in a bowl. If you use a juicer, add back the pulp. Add combinations of healthy foods: uncooked oats, raw nuts, seeds like sunflower seeds, unhulled sesame seeds, basil seeds, poppy seeds, whole flax seeds, pumpkin seeds. Add a piece of fresh ginger root and turmeric root. For protein, sweet beans and rice are surprisingly good tasting mixed in a sweet blender drink. For flavor, try unsweetened vanilla bean, fresh or powdered cinnamon, nutmeg, cloves, grated orange peel, mint leaves, or unsweetened cocoa Use real cocoa, not milk chocolate. Avoid chocolate priducts processed with refined sugar, chemicals, dyes, fillers, and additives. Plain cocoa powder and unsweetened baking chocolate is cheaper, healthier, and has fewer calories. For light hot teas, try cinnamon, clove, grated orange peel, and ginger in hot water.

Figure 12-1. Ginger root (left) turmeric roots (right)

Sweetening. Adding sugar to anything you bake or cook is not necessary. Instead of sugar, use a little fruit like cubed or mashed apples or banana to sweeten. Add cooked sweet potato to cake batter instead of sugar and oil for sweet creamy taste. Add soft prunes for thick sweet taste. Instead of adding cream and shortening to rice, cook in a little pineapple juice then add fresh cubed pineapple after cooking. Cooking kills helpful nutritional enzymes in pineapple, so add after cooking. If you use honey, use raw honey and wait until after cooking the food to add a little. Heat destroys many nutrients in honey. Processed honey is heat-killed. Jaggery is a sweet, aromatic sap of sugar cane or palm, usually available as a sugary lump or a spreadable "gur." It retains mineral content when unrefined and processed without heat or chemicals. Don't overdo.

Oils. High heat changes vegetable oils like peanut, safflower, and corn oil to unhealthy compounds, one of several reasons why it is better not to fry food. Instead, use a high smoke-point oil like grape seed oil to sauté, or cook lightly in olive oil. To cook without oil, steam in soy sauce, balsamic vinegar, or vegetable stock. If you still want oil, add grape seed oil or olive oil after cooking as a light topping.

Seasoning. Check your spices. Healthier without additives for coloring, artificial flavoring, to allow pouring, or added MSG. Table salt is processed with several chemicals that prevent caking and change the nature of the salt. Instead, grind whole, plain sea salt fresh from a grinder. Use fresh ground spices and fresh greens like scallions and oregano.

Applesauce. Commercial applesauce is made without the fiber and vitamins of the apple skins, with sugar and syrups added, and cooked until little nutrition is left. Long cooking and high heat reduces the vitamin content of food. Instead, make your own. Mash apples with the well-washed skins in a blender, grinder, food processor, or by hand in a mortar. Mix well. No cooking, just sweet fresh applesauce. The skins give a natural reddish tint. Add cinnamon or small amount of clove or nutmeg. Eat the applesauce fresh before it browns from exposure to air. Add a little lemon juice if you want to prevent browning. Lemon juice has antioxidants that act against oxidation from exposure to the oxygen in air. Use as pancake and waffle topping instead of syrup, and icing for cake. Make easy fruit sauce from strawberries, pears, and other fruits that you like.

Breakfast. Commercial breakfast cereal is often processed, refined flour and sugar. Healthier breakfast includes many other foods like tempeh, seeds, fruit, brown rice, and vegetables. If you want cereal, try sweet grains like millet, amaranth, and quinoa. Cook whole, or crush in a grinder, blender, or mortar. Simmer in water until soft. Add raisins, cubes of apple or sweet potato with skins, berries, or other fruit while cooling. Add sunflower and pumpkin seeds, cinnamon, and other spices.

Soy. Use soy that is fermented—miso, tempeh, natto, soy sauce, and tamari. Fermentation increases nutritional benefit and protein content, and removes unhealthy components of unfermented soy products. Examples of unfermented soy are mass-produced, heat-processed soy powders, bars, drinks, textured vegetable protein products, flours, and cereals.

In ancient Asia, soy was considered animal food, and used for crop rotation to put nitrogen back in the soil. Soy for eating was not used until fermentation processes developed to remove the enzyme inhibitors that block digestion, goitrogens, which inhibit thyroid function, and phytic acid, which blocks minerals like zinc and calcium. Don't load up on unfermented soy, as it can slow the thyroid and may have estrogen-promoting qualities. Too much of this is not healthy for adults or children. Those with tendency to estrogen-dependent migraine, tumors, fibroids, cystic ovary and breast, or endometriosis may want to look into avoiding unfermented soy and other estrogen promoters like primrose oil, damiana, chasteberry, kudzu, black cohosh, St. John's Wort, dong quai, pennyroyal, burdock root, lavender, clary sage, high amounts of tea tree oil, and others, along with hair products and shampoos with hormone containing placenta and estrogen or its precursors.

Nuts and Nut Butter. Use fresh raw nuts to make your own nut butters. The oil in pressed peanut and other nut butters quickly goes rancid. Put raw nuts in a blender, food processor, grinder, or use martial arts meditation and arm strength with a mortar and pestle. Grind raw almonds, sunflower seeds, walnuts, and others into powder. Mash with fresh fruit slices to make a sweet paste. Find combinations you enjoy, for example, sunflower-pear, walnut-banana, or apple-almond. Eat fresh raw nuts, not roasted, honeyed, or those long-stored out of the shell. Commercial roasted nuts quickly go rancid. Rancidity occurs with exposure to oxygen, which changes the oil to unhealthy compounds. Instead of roasted, sugared nuts, squeeze a lime in a bag of raw nuts, like peanuts, and shake in chili power, cinnamon, or other spices.

Flax Seeds. To get healthy flax seed oil, eat the whole flax seed, not pressed oil. By the time the oil is packaged and sold, it is often already rancid and not as useful nutritionally. Rancidity is a problem with many oil products, including fish oil capsules. Chew flax seeds whole, or crush them in a blender, grinder, or mortar and pestle. Eat crushed seeds fresh each time. Don't store for later, as they will go rancid. Flax seeds are sold in bulk in stores that sell bulk nuts, and are inexpensive compared to extracted oil. Whole seeds have fiber and many nutrients not present in the oil.

Spouted Seeds, Nuts, Beans. Sprouting increases nutritional value. Sunflower, clover, broccoli, radish, and mung bean sprouts taste good, and have many vitamins and disease-fighting phytochemicals. Lentil and pea sprouts are 26 percent protein. Soybean sprouts have 28 percent protein, twice the protein of eggs and more than some meats. Sprouting grains reduces the phytate level, which in turn, increases mineral absorption. Cook lightly.

Rice Milk. Make your own fresh rice milk by crushing uncooked whole grain rice in a blender, mortar, or grinder. Add clean water. Some people prefer lightly cooked rice to make rice milk, so experiment. Use brown rice, black rice, red rice, or all the other many rices that have not had the outer bran removed to make polished (white) rice. If you want a sweeter rice milk, add unsweetened coconut, corn, or fruit.

Fries. French fries and potato chips strip the fiber and benefits of the potato skin, and add unhealthy compounds from the oils and frying in high heat. Bake and eat potatoes with the skin. In the baking container, add soy sauce or balsamic vinegar to help steam in seasonings. To make crunchy snacks, slice potatoes thinly with the skins, season with spices like pepper, chili, cinnamon, curry, wasabi, lemon pepper, and others. Bake until crisp.

Baking. Use whole grains for cereal and baking and choose brown rice over polished white. What is the benefit of brown rice and whole grain? Brown rice and whole wheat are hulled, but the outer light brown bran remains. The outer bran has minerals, fiber, and vitamins. The taste after cooking is more chewy and nutty than white varieties.

Peels. To get the benefit of the nutrients in fruit and vegetables, eat them with the peels, where edible. Wash thoroughly to try to remove pesticides and germs. Make vegetable wash inexpensively yourself. Mix a non-toxic liquid soap with water and white vinegar.

Lotions. Instead of commercial skin lotions with preservatives, dyes, and chemicals, make your own. Try combinations of grape seed oil, tea tree oil, vitamins C and E, ginger, honey, tea, fresh aloe, and fragrances from oils, fruit, flowers like lavender, or leaves like mint. Don't wear citrus oils like lime out in the sun. They can make skin sensitive. For quick, clean skin, instead of using commercial soaps, rub coarse salt briskly, and rinse.

Why Brown Rice and Whole Flour?

Resistance to eating brown rice and other whole rices and grains arose for many reasons. Historically, the softer, expensive processed and hulled white grains were affordable only to the rich. The coarser dark grain of brown, black, and red rices, whole wheat, and millet were left to the worker class and animals. In times of war in Japan, China, and other nations, people who were used to white rice had none. Brown rice became additionally associated with war, the indignity of eating what was considered animal food, and loss of autonomy and social standing. Many people retained the emotional recoil against brown rice and other whole grains, even though healthier.

The nutritional benefits of whole, unpolished grains were rediscovered in modern times by Dutch physician Christaan Eijkman, looking for a cure for beriberi. Beriberi is a Sri Lankese word meaning "very weak." Beriberi was striking sailors on long voyages, damaging their nerves, and in some cases, killing them. It affected thousands on land. No one knew why. Eijkman thought it was an infection and tried to transmit the disease to healthy chickens by exposing them to chickens with beriberi. That didn't work, until suddenly one day, the chickens became sick. Eijkman now couldn't figure how to cure them. Four months later, the chickens were suddenly well. It turned out that four months before, the cook decided to feed the chickens scraps of hospital food, mostly white rice. The chickens got sick. Four months later, the cook left. The new cook didn't want to "waste" human food on chickens, so gave them brown rice, considered animal food. The chickens got well. It was the first recognition that lack of a specific nutrient could cause disease, and that restoring levels could cure, in this case lack of Vitamin B-1 found in the hull but not in white rice and polished grains. Eijkman received the Nobel Prize for Physiology and Medicine in 1929.

Use whole, instead of white flour and white polished rice. Refined flour products are the many biscuits, crackers, cookies, pies, cakes, and cereals. The fiber and most nutrients are stripped out to soften the texture and taste. Check labeling. Products are allowed to call themselves whole grain, even if only a small percentage is whole. Some are refined with caramel coloring added to appear like whole food. Some products state they are enriched. That means that the many original nutrients were stripped out in processing. A few isolated ones were put back in, leaving a more impoverished product than the whole grain. Without the fiber of the outer bran, they remain little more than refined sugar products.

Keep Simple

It is not true that you must avoid eating protein with starch (carbohydrate), or not eat one food group in combination with others. Nutrients usually work better together. It is another food myth that you need to carefully mix specific foods in each meal to get complete proteins from vegetables, grains, and legumes. Proteins combine on their own in the body over the day of eating a variety.

"What some call health, if purchased by perpetual anxiety about diet, isn't much better than tedious disease."
—George Dennison Prentice

Nutrition for Energy

Get energy from complex carbohydrate when you exercise. High amounts of refined simple sugar are unhealthy for your heart, blood vessels, blood sugar, even your skin and eyes. Don't be fooled by "natural sugar" or "no sugar added." Many products labeled as "no sugar" can contain fructose, corn syrup, rice syrup, galactose, and high fructose corn syrup. Commercial brown sugar is refined white sugar with molasses, or sometimes just coloring. Refined sugar is like distilling alcohol until you have an unhealthy "proof." Sugar may taste good, but so does anti-freeze, which is sweet but toxic. Don't put unhealthy things into your body, only because they taste good. Instead, eat complex carbohydrates of whole vegetables, fruit, legumes, whole grains. There is a difference between unhealthy refined, processed sugar, and healthier complex carbohydrate. Both are commonly called "carbs" or carbohydrate, but sources of complex carbohydrate have fiber and nutrients needed for health and to keep blood sugar stable. Don't overdo any food. Eat less carbohydrate when not exercising.

Stress, worry, and anger rob energy. Eating junk food will not restore this. Using drinks that concentrate stimulating compounds can produce a cycle of dependence and fatigue. You can be too stimulated to sleep well at night. If you are tired and want chemicals to increase energy, find out why you are not healthy and energetic without them. Don't put junk in your body or mind. Then you can be energetic and peaceful. Get rest and exercise. They are important to energy.

Nutrition for Aerobic Ability

No food builds muscles and stamina without exercise. Train aerobic capacity regularly with long, continuous efforts. Work the non-aerobic, or <u>an</u>aerobic systems with intense, fast efforts. Keep muscles, blood vessels, heart, and liver healthy for exercise by avoiding alcohol, cigarettes, drugs, and junk food. Don't fry food. Drink water, and juice you make yourself, not soda. You don't need expensive supplements. Complex carbohydrate in amounts needed for the activity fuels the activity and does not hurt your system, make you gain weight, or make blood sugar unstable. Eat complex carbohydrates like vegetables, fruit, good fats like raw almonds and walnuts, seeds like flax, sunflower, and pumpkin, and whole grains, not junk sugar, white flour, white rice, and chips.

PreGame Nutrition for a Competition or Fight

What you eat over the long run has more influence on your health and capacity for exertion than anything you can eat the day before or pack for a meet. Eating junk food all year is not undone with special nutrition for a day. Before a fight or competition, avoid junk food and high fat food like lunchmeats and mayonnaise. Eat a light meal with complex carbohydrates from fruit and light vegetables. Before and between events, foods that work well for some are foods like sweet potato and apple. Right after hard exercise, eat fruit to restock muscle glycogen—a special carbohydrate that is stored in muscles and the liver, and used up with hard exercise. Restoring glycogen improves performance and reduces fatigue in the next hard bout of exercise.

Many commercial "replacer" and "'workout recovery" drinks are mostly processed sugar. Check the label. Instead, get crucial carbohydrate replacement in healthier ways. Make your own drinks with whole fruit. Foods seem to give better nutrition and fuel exercise better when combining carbohydrate and protein. Add easy protein with a snack of rice and peas or other light protein. Remember that health store "workout" and "energy" foods have calories like any other food. You will gain weight if you replace a four hundred calorie training hour with several hundred calories of drinks and energy bars, then eat dinner.

Eating for Cardiovascular Health

Food is more than fuel. Food influences health. Cardiovascular disease has a large nutrition component. Change your risk with what you eat and don't eat. Refined sugar and fat are unhealthy for blood vessels. For sweets, eat fruit instead of junk food. Avoid trans-fats and hydrogenated fat, found in many packaged and fast foods. Many meats create an inflammatory fat called arachidonic acid, unhealthy for blood vessels. Eat complex carbohydrate, found in vegetables, to keep blood sugar more stable—a factor in cardiovascular health. Instead of milk chocolate and candy chocolate, have unsweetened cocoa and chocolate, healthy for blood pressure and the heart. Don't use a lot of acetaminophen and other nonsteroidal anti-inflammatory drugs (NSAIDS) over long periods. They are linked to high blood pressure and other problems, affecting some people more than others. If you have joint or muscle pain, treat the cause of pain by changing unhealthy joint mechanics and exercises using the information in these chapters, rather than trying to hide symptoms with unhealthy medicines. Eat less of inflammation-causing foods.

A daily aspirin is sometimes prescribed for blood thinning effects to protect again a second heart attack. Aspirin can contribute to ongoing stomach pain, often mistaken for an acid problem. Antacids do not treat this pain, but can continue it. Talk to your doctor about using blood-thinning foods instead, like ginko, vitamin E, garlic, and others, under supervision. Overdosing or combining too many thinners—whether by aspirin, drugs, or herbal products—can increase risk of a brain bleed (stroke) and dangerous bleeds from injury, sparring, or dental and medical surgery.

Foods to Diminish Stomach and Digestive Trouble

Several medicines have the side effect of stomach pain, such as allergy medicines, muscle relaxants, some antidepressants, some sleep medicines, and some medicines for nerve pain. Statin medicines for cholesterol are a common cause of gas, heartburn, and painful upset stomach. Many prescription and over the counter anti-inflammatory medicines hurt, even ulcerate the stomach lining and cause ongoing damage and pain. Anti-inflammatories deplete Vitamin C and zinc needed for healing. Pain from anti-inflammatory medicine may feel like burning hunger in high in the stomach. Many people mistake this for hunger. They eat, which temporarily coats the stomach and halts burning. The "hunger" comes back a short time later. The person starts to eat often and may gain weight. Reduce or stop the need for inflammatories for joint pain by learning healthy joint mechanics throughout this book. Stop stomach-damaging anti-inflammatories so the stomach can heal. Antacids and stomach preparations do not solve this problem, are proven to cause rebound high acid, even in people with no history of acid problems, and can add several new health problems.

Check the vitamins and supplements you take. They are an overlooked source of stomach upset. Take them with food, not just with coffee in the morning. Check all the medicines you take to see if they are the underlying causes of stomach problems. Look to solve the original problem in healthier ways than medicines which hurt the stomach, then require other medicines for the stomach, all with their own side effects.

Look to solve the cause of the problems so you don't need medicines that work against your overall health. Health care is supposed to be healthy.

Stomach pills and acid medicines are not meant to be taken for more than a short course. They can cause more problems than the reason they are taken. Reducing normal stomach acid stops good bacteria that normally live in the digestive tract to help digestion. Acid-reflux medicines and antacids also deplete vitamin B-12 and calcium. Some, called proton pump inhibitors, greatly increase osteoporotic fracture rate. If acid is a problem, reduce sources of acid, for example, soda, coffee, alcohol, and antacids themselves, which cause high rebound levels, rather than hurting the body with antacids. To relieve pain and restore natural stomach chemicals, try cabbage, cabbage juice, and fresh sauerkraut. Use fresh-made, not in jars or cans. The packaging process deliberately removes nutrients and living cultures created through fermentation so that the lids don't blow off.

Stomach acid is not always the cause of "acid-related" pain and "heartburn." Normal stomach acid is necessary to kill unhealthy germs and food-borne infection. Taking antacids allows these germs to grow and cause trouble. Helicobacter pylori is involved in many cases of peptic ulcer (ulcer of the stomach and duodenum). Although antibiotics are sometimes prescribed, they reduce good bacteria needed for healthy stomach and intestinal function. It is healthier and more effective to use food. Broccoli sprouts have been found to reduce helicobacter pylori. Seasoning food with raw crushed garlic and fresh ginger root inhibits many strains of helicobacter and bad intestinal bacteria, including like E. coli, Staphylococcus, and Streptococcus, without harming beneficial digestive bacteria.

Low stomach acid inhibits digestion, making pain, frequent burping, and gas from undigested food. These symptoms of low acid are frequently mistaken for acid indigestion or reflux, and made worse with antacids. Adding acid often solves this pain. Try apple cider vinegar diluted in a little water. Squeeze lemons and limes on fruit and vegetables, and add to drinks and blender shakes. Add balsamic vinegar to salads. Soothe the uncomfortable stomach with fresh ginger. Look for ginger root in the vegetable section of the market. Cut a piece to steep in tea, or grate in food and drinks.

For inflammatory bowel and gastrointestinal pain, eat less refined sugar and more vegetables. It was sometimes previously thought that vegetables and fiber made an irritable or inflamed bowel. It is now known that more vegetable fiber and less fat and junk food reduces bowel discomfort. Inflamed intestinal tract problems like diverticulitis are almost unknown in vegetarians. Watch for inflammation-promoting food like dairy, refined sugar, refined wheat flour, hydrogenated and trans-fat in packaged foods, and meat. Substitute complex carbohydrate of vegetables, fruit, and legumes, and anti-inflammatory foods like ginger. They provide energy, sweetness, and fiber, and solve many stomach troubles. Check to make sure you are not taking antibiotics or antacids that interfere with healthy bacteria that normally live in the digestive tract and function in digestion.

The practice of drinking oil, like flax seed or grape seed oil, often leads to uncomfortable, urgent effects. Drinking oil prevents your body from absorbing the minerals in food. Get flax seed oil by eating fresh flax seeds, either whole or crushed in a grinder, blender, or by hand. Chew grape seeds with the grapes. It is cheaper and healthier to have the entire food with all the other benefits.

For pressure, bloating, and gas, see if you eat unfermented soy in products like protein powders, pills, drinks, and bars. Products made with whey and dairy add to bloated uncomfortable stomachs. Many "health" bars, sugar free candies, and gums are made with sweeteners like sorbital and corn syrup, which produce gas. Some people get tight uncomfortable stomach after eating wheat. Instead of buying expensive processed protein and 'energy' products, make your own fun, healthy food. Chapter 15 (Performance Enhancement) gives ideas. Relive gas by chewing fennel seeds, eating cardamom spice, or ginger, or drinking ginger or peppermint in water or tea.

Lack of exercise and fiber, and too much modern processed food often leads to slow, dry, uncomfortable bowels. Medications add to the slowness problem, such as narcotics, tranquilizers, muscle relaxants, some antidepressants, antacids, diuretics (water pills), iron supplements, and some drugs for Parkinson's disease and seizures.

Avoid drinking oils for laxatives. They interfere with vitamin absorption. Avoid stimulant laxatives. They disrupt healthy gut function and the elimination process stops working well without them. Instead, eat less of low-fiber foods, like refined sugar, white flour, white rice, cheese, white bread, meat, dairy, fish, poultry, and ice cream. When you want cereal and grains, use whole fresh grains, not boxed cereal or crackers. Eat legumes like lentils.

Eat more fermented vegetables like sauerkraut (fermented cabbage), fermented chutney, tempeh, oncham, and kim-chi. Fermenting is different from pickling. Fermented food provides good-bacteria to the digestive tract. Although expensively sold as "probiotics" you can have the benefits from these inexpensive simple foods. The natural probiotics in fermented food seem to spur the digestive tract to directly secrete antimicrobial substances. In these ways, fermented foods are thought to be effective against digestive problems, and may reduce diarrhea caused by use of antibiotics. Fermenting grains like tempeh reduces phytic acid content, which increases absorption of calcium, phosphorus, iron and zinc. Look for fermented food with live cultures. Many products kill the cultures through heating, processing, and packaging. Eat fruit and vegetables every day for the fiber and many components helping ease and speed bowel transit. Add a peeled chunk of aloe vera stalk to a blender drink. Unsweetened chocolate also helps. Then there is no need to buy commercial fiber supplements or bowel medicines.

"Avoid fried meats which angry up the blood. If your stomach disputes you, lie down and pacify it with cool thoughts. Keep the juices flowing by jangling around gently as you move. Go very light on the vices, such as carrying on in society. The social ramble ain't restful."
—From *How to Stay Young* by Satchell Paige, American baseball pitcher, first African-American in National Baseball Hall of Fame

Food to Reduce Congestion

Sinus and upper respiratory congestion can be made worse with decongestants. After the decongestant wears off, a rebound occurs of more congestion. Taking more decongestant perpetuates a negative cycle, and can raise blood pressure. Regularly irrigating the nose and sinuses with salt-water sprays and neti pots removes important protective mucosal layers and natural disease-fighting compounds. Rebound congestion and increased risk of infections and discomfort follow in an addictive cycle. Another contributor to rebound congestion is regular use of camphor inhalers. Camphor irritates membranes. Some people develop a habit of inhaling camphor, thinking it is for their congestion, not realizing they have a substance inhalation addiction called "huffing." Cough syrups and pills that contain dexomethorphan (DXM) to block coughing may not be effective for coughs and are commonly abused ("rhobotripping") with unhealthy physical and psychoactive effects.

Instead of relying on decongestants, stop congestion by first finding out what is causing it. For some, it is decongestants and irrigations. For some it is the allergic potential of dairy foods. If it is dust, clean the home of old dust-catching things. Sometimes it is allergy-provoking supplements like bee pollen. If it is cigarettes or inhaled street drugs, you are already doing enough harm without adding unhealthy things to counter the effects. For allergies to things that cannot be avoided, look into methods that stop the allergy process without decongestants. Cook hot chili peppers with favorite food for a quick easy way to clear congestion. Get physical exercise to work the respiratory tract, and try inverted moves as tolerated to help drainage, like headstands, handstands, cartwheels, and downward dog, a stretch with weight on hands. Take a hot shower. To quiet a cough, use chocolate from unsweetened cocoa. Simmer peppermint and eucalyptus oils in water and inhale the steam. If you grow yarrow in your garden or can get some yarrow leaves and flowers, simmer them.

Nutrition For Bones

A young person can lose bone density though bad habits until they are as brittle as someone of ninety. Several habits contribute. A main factor in osteoporosis is lack of exercise. The physical stress of muscle pulling bone during exercise stimulates bone to thicken. Lack of mechanical stress from inactivity or being in a cast leads to bone loss no matter how much calcium you eat. Calcium won't stick on your bones unless you give it a reason with exercise. The physical pulling of muscle where it attaches to the bone, thickens the bone. Without vitamin D, calcium is not well used. Smoking and drinking alcohol are both directly toxic to bone cells. Wheat intolerance (celiac disease) reduces bone density. People with celiac should avoid wheat and related products. Several medicines reduce calcium absorption and increase fracture rate, including SSRI anti-anxiety medicines and proton pump inhibitors for heartburn. Stomach acid drugs themselves cause rebound stomach acid, even in people with no previous acid problem. Reflux "disease" is often from the drugs. Antacids that contain aluminum also increase calcium excretion. Cola drinks and soda have high phosphorus content, bad for bones. Another source of excessive dietary phosphorous is meat. Animal protein, including animal protein in dairy, increases urinary calcium loss. Reducing the many avenues of calcium loss reduces risk of fracture and dietary need for calcium.

Get protein from vegetables as much as possible. If you use protein powder, use vegetable powder without dairy or whey. Dairy is not the only or best source of calcium. Dairy is a potent cause of allergy. The heat process to kill germs in dairy products kills the bulk of the nutrients, making the resulting products diminished in benefit. The milk sugar galactose may be associated with cataracts, and ovarian and prostate cancers. Dairy cows are given various hormones to increase milk production. These hormones pass into the milk, with health effects still to be understood.

Getting enough calcium without dairy is not difficult. A cup of navy beans and two corn tortillas has more calcium and twice the protein of a cup of milk. Broccoli has more calcium per calorie than any food. Spinach and beet greens are high calcium. Spinach calcium is not poorly absorbed, as previously thought. Tofu has much calcium, depending how it is processed. Seaweed is a frequently overlooked source, as is molasses. Fruit has calcium. So do almonds, sesame seeds, and sunflower seeds. Fruit, vegetables, nuts, and legumes have the elements copper and boron, which may be needed to work together with calcium in preventing osteoporosis. Get sunlight for Vitamin D and other healthy effects to improve mood and fight disease. Vitamin D is necessary for calcium to work for bone building. A good workout outdoors is healthy in many ways. Don't overdo sunbathing. It's a balance.

Eating For Weight Loss

You do not lose weight by the act of eating. You lose weight by eating less and exercising more. No supplement has magic chemicals to remove fat cells, no matter how much we wish, or pay, or believe the marketing. Diet food is still food; you don't lose weight by eating more of it. The various diets "work" primarily from having fewer calories, portion control, and reducing junk food, not from changing any zone or body chemistry. Even in stomach surgery, the way it "works" is to eat less food. The choice is, are you being healthy?

For better health and weight loss, stop eating junk refined sugar and flour, corn syrup, and hydrogenated and trans-fats. Overly restricting healthy complex carbohydrate from fruit and vegetable sources is not healthy. Choose healthy food and don't overdo. Eating less does not cause weight gain from "starvation mode." The poor of the world who really starve lose body fat. Rebound eating from hunger is poor discipline and planning, your choice.

It is not a mysterious choice between eating low fat or low carbohydrate. A block of butter is sugar-free. A bag is sugar is fat-free. Both are high calorie. Use common sense. Packaged foods labeled as low fat or low sugar may not be healthy or help weight loss. They can be as much junk food as any other. What does it mean to be a low-carbohydrate food? Foods can be labeled without a real definition. A plate of fruit vegetables has a high percentage of carbohydrate compared percentage of fat and protein contained, so can be labeled high carbohydrate, or it can be measured by actual grams of carbohydrate, which is low, far healthier than packaged "low-carb" cakes and candy.

The calories from eating at certain hours are not greatly different from calories the rest of the day. The key is if you have already eaten all you need by 4pm, 8pm, or any other hour, then eating more will add extra calories and extra weight. It is extra eating that adds weight. A benefit of not eating too late is better sleep. When does timing meals help control weight? Eat closer to times when you exercise to fuel the effort, and less when you don't exercise. Ignoring your family at dinner because it is after a certain hour is not health. Eat less at other times and make healthful choices, rather than believe you can't have healthy family time.

Losing weight by restricting healthy food like fruit and vegetables is missing the point. You can be unhealthy, weak, slow, and malnourished at any weight. To lose weight and have a healthier life, stop eating the junk of refined sugar and flour, trans-fat, and extra fat. Eat more slowly to remember food is a gift. Don't blame weight gain on decreased metabolism with aging. Are you exercising less than in younger years? Remember that children can't wait to run from the table to play, but are trained to have the bad habit of eating too much. Don't give them junk food, little different than putting cigarettes in their mouth. Don't make them eat everything on the plate. Don't make them sit when they can run. If you eat when not hungry, find out why. Address that need. Move and be active for real life every day, not just in artificial movement in a gym or training hall.

"To lengthen thy life, lessen thy meals."
—Benjamin Franklin

Nutrition in the Heat

Drink when thirsty. Don't overdo. Drinking too much water while exercising for long hot hours without eating can dilute the blood, dropping sodium to dangerous levels. An illness called hyponatremia can result. Men lose a higher percentage of body weight in sweat than women during long exercise, increasing risk of dehydration and electrolyte loss. There is no need to drink too many glasses a day, or force drinking when not thirsty. Eat and drink when exercising in the heat to replace fluids and salts.

Disease Fighting Food

Ideally, it is better to get nutrients from food than supplements. Drying, heating, and processing destroys benefits of many nutrients sold as supplements. Many vitamin and supplement pills contain fillers and preservatives. Some pass unused and unchanged through the digestive tract. Many nutrients need to work in the original food containing other components that make each part work better. One example is the B vitamins, which seem to work better together than when taken in single supplements. Another is bioflavonoids. Bioflavonoids are compounds needed for vitamin C to work, and that exert their own benefits. Bioflavonoids are found in foods with Vitamin C, but are not in many vitamin C pills and supplements. Some nutrients do not increase benefit when you take more of them. From three wheels, you can still make only one bicycle.

Eat whole foods, like an apple with the skin, which contain combinations of hundreds of disease fighting chemicals that are not available in supplements. Soil depletion in modern times reduces nutritional content of many foods, depleted further over shipping, storage, and long cooking. Try to find fresh whole foods grown with healthy farming, to reduce dependence on supplementing with commercial vitamin pills. Don't ruin the value of originally healthy food by frying, covering in batter, and adding sugar. Here are some top healthy nutrient sources, among many:

Alpha Carotene. Pumpkin, carrot, squash, orange peppers.
Antioxidants. Blueberries, pomegranate, kiwifruit, strawberries, cranberries, oregano, seaweed (laver, wakame, nori, kombu kelp), brewed green tea, wasabi, most fresh fruits and vegetables.
Beta Carotene. Sweet potato, carrot, seaweed, pumpkin, kale, squash, collard greens, red chard, apricots, mango, papaya, persimmon, wasabi, cantaloupe.
Bioflavonoids. Green peppers, buckwheat, citrus, the white "strings" and material inside citrus peels, currants, cherries, apricots, rose hips (the fleshy part under the rose flower, and other fruit and vegetables with vitamin C.
Bromelain. Anti-inflammatory and wound healing. Bromelain is an enzyme found in high amounts in pineapple, especially the core. Heat processing destroys bromelain, for example, canned pineapple and pineapple juice. Eat pineapple fresh.
Cancer-Preventive Phytonutrients. Cruciferous vegetables: cauliflower, broccoli, mustard greens, cabbage, broccoli sprouts, brussels sprouts, wasabi, kohlrabi, bok choi. Allium vegetables: Onion, leeks, chives, shallots, raw crushed garlic. Phenolic acids: Turmeric spice, curry, mustard greens. Flavonols: onions, apples, berries, kale, and broccoli. Capsaicin: hot peppers. General diet with many fruits and vegetables daily.
Chromium. For glucose and insulin control, and possibly, depression control. Broccoli, apples, bran cereals, white potatoes, tea, cocoa, black pepper, seaweed, mushrooms, oatmeal, prunes, nuts, asparagus, brewer's yeast, whole grains. Sugar depletes chromium.
Fiber. Black beans, pinto beans, garbanzo beans, lentils, raspberries, strawberries, oatmeal, walnuts, fruit, vegetables, beetroot, nuts and seeds of all kinds.
Folic Acid. A vitamin of the B complex. For red blood cells, memory, and reducing heart disease and spinal birth defect. Kidney beans, asparagus, beetroot, soybeans, broccoli, jicama (yambean), cucumber, green leafy vegetables.

Glutathione. Asparagus, watermelon, avocado, walnuts, grapefruit, peanuts, broccoli, oranges, spinach.

Iron. Pomegranate, dried fruit like raisins, figs, and apricots. An ounce of sesame seeds has three times more iron than an ounce of beef liver. Tahini, tomatoes, beet greens, apples, bananas, seaweed, oranges, strawberries, avocado, dandelions, blackberries, lentils, dried peas, beans, quinoa grain, molasses, spirulina, dark leafy vegetables like spinach, chard and kale. The vitamin C in fruit increases iron absorption. Coffee, tea, and dairy products with meals decrease iron absorption from non-heme (fruit and vegetable) iron.

Lauric Acid. Medium chain fatty acid with antibacterial, antifungal, and antiviral properties. Mother's milk, coconut.

Lutein. Kale, spinach, collard greens, turnip greens, bell peppers, green peas, broccoli.

Lycopene. Tomatoes, red pepper, watermelon, pink grapefruit. Anti-cancer effects of Lycopene are thought to work in conjunction with other nutrients in the fruit, not isolated in supplements.

Omega-3. Fatty acid (alpha-linolenic acid). Flax seeds, hemp seeds, pumpkin seeds, raw walnuts, spinach, wheat germ. Eat nuts raw; high heat destroys the omega-3 benefit.

Protein. Oats, brown rice, baked beans, lentils, sesame seeds, nuts, chickpeas, muesli, fermented soy, tempeh, peas, seaweed, kelp, brewers yeast, hummus, tahini, spirulina.

Policosanol. Reduce cholesterol. Citrus peels. Grate the insides and outsides of rinds into blender drinks, salads, baked goods, and cooked vegetables. Other cholesterol reducing foods include almonds, oats, red yeast rice, and cinnamon.

Polyphenols. Anti-oxidant, anti-inflammatory, and other benefits. Berries, figs, dates, prunes (dried plums), citrus, unsweetened cocoa, fresh dark grape skins, apple skins.

Quercetin. Anti-inflammatory plant pigments called flavonoids. Found in most fruit and vegetables. Highest in leafy greens, cherries, blueberries, apples, onions, black tea.

Resveratrol. Anti-inflammatory. Grape skins, cranberries.

Pycnogenol. Anti-inflammatory. Grape seeds.

Other Demonstrated Anti-inflammatory Foods. Ginger, curcumin (turmeric spice, which gives color to curry), brown seaweed (kelp), pineapple especially the core, and boswellia.

Salicylates. Pain reducing compounds (the best known is acetylsalicylic acid, or aspirin). Salicylates occur naturally in many plants like willow bark, strawberries, almonds, and tomatoes.

Selenium. Brazil nuts, mushrooms. Don't overdo selenium through supplements. It is a heavy metal, toxic in high amounts.

Vitamin C. Red and yellow peppers, guava, oranges with pulp, lemons, roses, rose hips, marigolds, pomegranate, strawberries, jicama, beetroot, and broccoli.

Vitamin E. Wheat germ, flax seeds, almonds, dandelions, sunflower seeds, blueberries, olive oil.

Vitamin K. For healthy blood clotting and bone strength. Cabbage, cauliflower, fermented soybeans, red peppers, green leafy vegetables like spinach, red chard, and Swiss chard. Made by the bacteria lining the gastrointestinal tract. Prolonged antibiotic use depletes this layer and vitamin production. Also depleted by aspirin and anticonvulsant drugs.

Sunshine. The body needs sunshine to make vitamin D, necessary for calcium to work to strengthen bones. Sunlight seems to improve immune function to possibly alleviate rheumatoid arthritis and other illnesses. Sunshine in the eyes and skin can stimulate good mood. It is a balance between getting enough sun and too much, which can lead to skin cancers and cataracts. Get outside every day. If you go from house to car to workplace, stop a moment and appreciate the scenery.

What are Omega-3 and 6?

Omega 3 and 6 are both essential fatty acids. "Essential" means you need to eat them because the body does not make them. Omega-3 converts to anti-inflammatory compounds in the body, which is one way that good nutrition helps combat diseases and injuries. Omega-6 can supply fat and convert to anti-inflammatory compounds but only when there is enough Omega-3. Omega-3 reduces the amounts of an enzyme in the body. Without reducing this enzyme, Omega-6 becomes inflammatory.

If you eat far more Omega-6 than 3, you can produce many inflammatory compounds in the body. This problem is common. It is thought to relate to diseases like heart disease, arthritis, and pain syndromes. Omega-6 is found in meat, poultry, corn and safflower oil, primrose oil, and processed food. Trans-fats in packaged food is thought to drive down Omega-3 levels. Food containing saturated fat of animal fat is also inflammatory. Inflammatory diseases are now known to include heart disease. If you eat too much Omega-6, reduce Omega-6 and increase Omega-3.

What is a Natural Diet?

Is it natural to eat meat, or only eat food from the land of your ancestors? The issue is not what is natural. It is natural to hit people and wet your pants too. That is why we discipline ourselves, and evolve the mind to create peace, cleanliness, and health in ourselves. It may be natural to kill and steal for something you want, but we learn control. It may be natural to shout and become angry, but we learn we can be heard without shouting, by learning adult communication. It may be natural to be a coward, but we learn to raise ourselves to face the world with a smile every day. These are arts practiced by the evolved person.

It is the same with nutrition. It may be natural for a child to demand only cookies, if that is what they are used to. We must teach them that there are more wonderful things waiting, and they can't eat anything they want, any time they want. Then it won't be natural to be fat.

Children are often taught to eat when not hungry, and to eat more than they want—forcing them to finish everything on their plate. They are made to eat and prevented from running away from food to go play. They are wheeled in carriages, the equivalent of wheelchairs, when they should walk and run. Look at what you are teaching your children, and yourselves. Are you making it natural to eat too much and be sedentary? Or are you teaching a higher way, until it becomes natural to eat only when hungry, make healthy choices, then stop and go out for healthy activity.

For a Better Earth

Why add to litter and waste with disposable containers? Wrap food in leaves like banana leaves, grape leaves, or spinach. This is common outside the Western world. Get fresh leaves inexpensively from Asian markets. Seal with a toothpick. Seaweed sheets (nori) make handy wraps, easily sealed with a little moisture to roll vegetable, grain, and nut sandwiches.

Nutrition as a Martial Arts Lifestyle

You may train hard. Then go out after training for cigarettes and doughnuts. You say that martial arts gives discipline, but can't turn away from having a soda, or yet another beer. Bring the discipline of the martial arts to how you live outside the gym or training center. You don't have to do everything. But don't be unable to turn away from things you want to turn away from.

A long time ago, two wizards met on the mountaintop to see who was the greater wizard. The first one shouted, "I control the seas. I control the oceans. At my bidding, I destroy whole cities. I control the sun. At the wave of my hand the sun burns away all that I see. I control the moon. I control the rivers and the beasts of all the worlds." He looked at the other wizard and said, "So, what do you do?" The second wizard said, "I eat only when I am hungry. I drink only when I am thirsty. I don't take in anything harmful." It was clear that the second wizard was the true master—the one who is master of himself.

Emotional Nutrition

Like the food you put in your body, thoughts you put in your mind fuel your emotional state. Thoughts of bitterness like, "I hate her." Thoughts of despair like, "I'll never be happy." Thoughts of fear; "I could never do that!" A diet of destructive thought harms as much as a poison. Negative thoughts are unhealthy, just like unhealthy foods. Thinking in negative ways is a bad habit, just like eating junk food. To stop thinking in negative ways, put yourself on a "diet of the mind."

The Navajo believe that how they fill their mind shapes their life. They work to fill their mind only with good, harmonious, and edifying thought. They call this, "Thinking in the Beauty Way" What are you feeding your emotional self? Fill your mind with life-affirming thought and walk along the Beauty Way.

Spiritual Nutrition

A farmer grew wonderful corn. Every year he entered his corn in the fair where. Every year it won the prize as the best corn.

The villagers came to him and asked if he would tell them how he grew such strong, high, bountiful corn. He said, "I will tell you. Every year, I grow the corn. I work to make the best conditions for it. When I harvest the corn, I look for the best kernels. When I find the best, I give them to my neighbors." The villagers were surprised. "How can you give the best corn to others? They can enter the contest against you."

The farmer told them, "I give my neighbors the best of the crop. The wind spreads pollen from field to field. If my neighbors grow poor corn, it will bring down my corn. To grow good corn, I help my neighbors grow good corn."

Life is the same. To live with rewards, we give our neighbors rewards. To live in peace, we must help our neighbors to live in peace. To live in happiness and strength, give happiness and strength. If we are to grow good corn, we must help our neighbors grow good corn.

'Ow' is not a Kempo word
—Jonathan Vance

Injuries

The Eightfold Path sought to stop pain and suffering through understanding. With understanding, right action occurs. When you are injured, your job is to do healthy mental and physical action to get better. This chapter gives understanding of how injuries start and continue so you can take the right actions to avoid and stop them.

Aching Joints

Some of the martial arts concentrate on the sport aspect of physical training with the usual bumps and bruises. Some concentrate on light to full contact fighting with a variety of impressive injuries. Yet the most common aches and injuries from all of them are the same back, knee, shoulder, and neck pain of non-martial artists.

More than strengthening, positioning is key in injury and pain prevention. Low back pain is common from letting the lower back sway inward when standing, moving, and lifting overhead. Knee pain is common from allowing the knee and ankle to tilt medially (to the inner side) under body weight. Neck pain and headache are common from craning the neck forward during sparring, raising arms overhead, and looking upward. Lack of shock absorption—not using muscles to land softly when moving and jumping—adds wear and tear on all the joints. Healthy positioning and ergonomics to stop these problems is covered in the strength, flexibility, and balance chapters, and throughout this chapter.

Nosebleeds

Use direct pressure to stop bleeding. Gently squeeze the nose shut at and below the place it becomes soft below the bony bridge. Keep breathing through the mouth. Don't tip head back, so that blood does not run into the throat. If you are attending an event with medical staff, they may apply adrenaline on a cotton swab, or a clotting agent like thrombin mixed with Vaseline to stop bleeding. If you are on your own, don't disrupt clotting with constant checking and bandage changing. Hold it closed and let the bleeding stop on its own. You don't need Vaseline, which contains petroleum products. If you have a sun garden, maintain the common and colorful yarrow plant. Yarrow is helpful to stop bleeds of all kinds, including nosebleeds. American Indians used yarrow for cuts and after childbirth. The Latin name of yarrow is *"Achillea."* It is named for the Greek warrior Achilles, because stories say he stopped bleeding on the battlefield with yarrow poultices. No stories mention if he tried it for his own heel. Aspirin, anti-inflammatory medicine, and many common health food supplements reduce blood-clotting ability. If you get many nosebleeds, have your blood pressure checked to make sure it is not high, and if your blood clotting ability is normal.

Broken Nose

A broken nose is not enough for a fight to be called in a boxing match, so don't be too alarmed. Straighten the area gently. Control bleeding. Check with a doctor for head, neck, or other injury.

Cuts

Check for and remove foreign matter like pieces of protective gear, fingernails, or splinters flown from breaking boards or other objects. Sterile saline solution is helpful to flush the area. If particles are not easily removed, leave them for the doctor. Stop bleeding with smooth, even, gentle pressure with a clean bandage. Powdered cinnamon works like styptic to stop bleeding in minor cuts. Apply ice to reduce pain and swelling. Cuts usually heal faster when covered and kept moist. During a match, if the cut is around the eye or lid, or inside the ear, see the event doctor. If there is no medical staff, leave the event or training hall for medical attention. For eye cuts, tell the doctor if you wear contact lenses. If you are continuing the event, the medical staff may apply adrenaline to stop bleeding and may use a keeper like Vaseline to hold it in place. Sweat has natural antibiotics and antioxidants. Get back out and train to help healing.

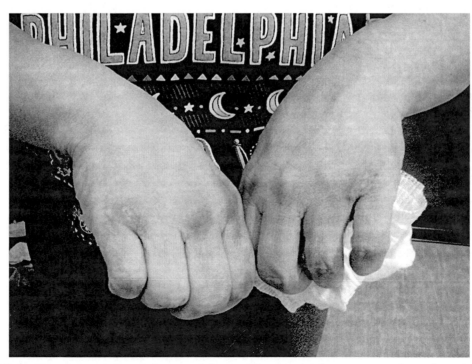

Figure 13-1. Cuts are common in martial arts. Keep cuts clean, covered, and moist for best healing.

Swellings

Don't use brute strength to force swelling away from an injured area. You will do more harm than the opponent. Press ice firmly to areas swelling from a blow, or to painful areas after training. A metal tool called "Endswell" is a common first aid device in martial arts and boxing. The tool is kept cold. The smooth end is pressed over small swollen areas. Don't use it with force. Endswell is used in the same way as a cold coin used to be used, to compress and apply cold to a swollen area. For large areas of body swelling after pummeling in a contact match, get a good medical check to rule out internal damage. Sitting in tub baths helps move out extra fluid.

Figure 13-2. Bruises are common, even prized as evidence of good hard work in some of the contact arts. In Japan, the bruises are called "omiyage," which means "gifts."

Neck Pain, Upper Back Pain

Letting the neck tilt forward instead of holding upright position over the shoulders is called a forward head. A forward head is the cause of much neck, shoulder, and upper back pain, and headache. It also puts the head and neck in an injurious position for fighting. It is closer for the opponent to hit, and increases likelihood of a knockout when a punch connects. Jutting the chin out does not look tough. It is the mark of someone who does not know how to fight. Unhealthy chin posture is so well known in combat, in business, and in life, that someone who invites a bad outcome is said to be "leading with the chin."

Tucked neutral chin position reduces upper back pain during daily life, and the angle of the neck and jaw is safer for the brain if struck. Positioning and healthy movement are the same for martial arts as every day life. Do not let the head and neck hang forward over your computer, desk, and steering wheel, or in the gym or training hall. Keep your shoulders straight, not rounded, and chin in, in loose, relaxed manner when sitting, working, driving. Pull back from the head, neck and shoulder, not by arching the lower back or bending back at the neck, bending it like a straw. The idea is to make posture healthier, not more strained.

Figure 13-3. Left—Tilting the neck and head forward in martial arts and daily life is a common source of neck and shoulder pain, headaches, is an easier target to hit, and is more likely to result in serious injury when hit. Right—Keep head and neck upright.

Figure 13-4. Left—Check for all the times you let the neck and chin jut forward in martial arts and daily activities, particularly when looking upward. Right—Keep your chin in and neck upright, not jutting forward.

To see if your head is forward in bad position, or upright in good position, stand with your back against a wall for a position check. If you cannot stand with your heels, hips, upper back, and the back of your head touching the wall without arching your back or raising your chin, your head is probably forward, and you are too tight to stand upright or protect yourself from neck pain and injury in life and when sparring.

Chapter 5 on flexibility gives two important stretches to restore healthy resting muscle length to make straight standing comfortable: the pectoral stretch, Figure 5-5, and the trapezius stretch, Figure 5-7. It is not necessary to stretch your neck forward, as a forward tilt is already an over-practiced bad habit. When you stretch to the side using the trapezius stretch, do not pull your head to the side with your hands. Stand with your back against the wall (wall posture test above) often to check your body and head position.

Brain Injury

Getting hit in the head can injure the brain. This is no joke. Brain injury can kill, can result in life-long decrease in function, or predispose to depression and neurologic problems later in life. The pituitary gland may decrease ability to produce growth hormone. If you lose too many brain cells now, you may not have enough later while losing more to the normal processes of a long life.

When the head is hit, the soft brain shifts inside the hard skull. Two main brain injuries can result. A moving strike or kick can contact a non-moving head. This causes injury at or near the site of impact. This is a "coup injury." The second way injury results is when a moving head contacts a still object, when falling to the canvas, or hitting a knee or elbow on the way down. The brain gets yanked away from the area opposite the impact. This is a contrecoup injury. In this way, falling flat on your face can leave a brain injury in front from the fall, and in back from the contrecoup. Falling backward, hitting the back of the head on the mat can injure both the back and the front of the brain. This can be in addition to the original coup injury that resulted in the knockout, fall, or throw to the mat. The inside of the skull is not entirely smooth and the brain can abrade against rough areas when it sloshes from blows, adding to injuries.

The biggest danger to the brain is change in velocity with rotation from suddenly moving or stopping. The head never needs to be struck. Snapping the head back when receiving a blow, or being shaken or whipped around can result in great damage. Almost all hits to the face, jaw, or skull result in rotation. The more rotation to the head and brain, the greater the chance of injury and loss of consciousness.

Taking drugs, alcohol, and steroids can increase likelihood of the brain bleeding too much when hit. Avoid combining too many supplements that reduce blood clotting. Common "blood thinners" are ginko biloba, vitamin E, policosanol, many antidepressants, fish oil, GLA oil, selenium, lemon balm, primrose oil, garlic, devil's claw herb, bromelain, aspirin (and medicines that contain aspirin like cold medicine and stomach and cramp remedies), ibuprofen (and many over-the-counter and prescription anti-inflammatories for pain), alcoholic drinks, St. John's Wort, which augments prescription blood thinners (and may make the contraceptive pill less effective), ginger, and others. If you have been knocked out, or are going into medical or dental surgery tell all doctors and anesthesiologists every supplement you take. You don't want to bleed out in surgery.

Don't "take a hit." Slip it, roll it, duck it, parry it, block it, and "don't be there." The concept of aiding survival by reducing the power of a punch is popularized in the common expression, "roll with the punches." Strong neck muscles counter the blows and rotation of the head. Keep the chin in, not jutting, neck strong and straight, not tilted forward. The strength chapter tells about healthy neck strengthening. When rolling, falling, and being thrown, keep your head off the mat and chin tucked, but not bent far forward.

Second Impact Syndrome

A serious injury can occur when a second concussion occurs before the symptoms of a previous concussion have cleared. Not all medical authorities accept that there is a specific second impact syndrome, however, serious injury and sometimes fatalities result from a second head trauma, even following a concussion not known about.

Injury changes the brain's ability to regulate blood flow. A second blow, even if minor, whether in the same fight or weeks later from a previous unhealed injury, is more likely to cause brain swelling and widespread damage. The blow can be a minor strike to the head, or a strike to another part of the body that causes the head to jerk suddenly.

After any blow to the head, with or without loss of consciousness, full evaluation is needed. Check for headache, light-headedness, vision change, and any neurologic symptoms. All symptoms of head injury should be cleared completely before resuming training and matches.

The Fighter Who Can Take a Punch: High Risk of Brain Injury

Be careful. The romance of the scrappy fighter with the iron jaw, who keeps on coming, is a setting for long-term brain injury. A high-risk fighter has had many fights, many head strikes, and been knocked out in the ring, dojo, kwoon, dojang, street, or gym. Check for deteriorating skills and change in reflexes, balance, memory, emotion, and speech. History of drugs and alcohol adds to risk. Even full medical evaluations with blood tests, CAT, and MRI scans after an injury can't identify everything. For contact fighters or someone who might get hit at some point, a good baseline set of scans can help for later comparison. One baseline test is neurocognitive testing—a set of written tests that assess visual and verbal memory, reaction, problem solving, ability to tell similarities and differences, and other important higher functions. History of head strikes has also been associated with decrease in pituitary growth hormone production. Check with your coach or doctor for testing. Before long-term problems result from head injury, you can make a better life with other skills and professional interests developed over your career.

"Boards—don't hit back."
—Bruce Lee

Protective Head and Face Gear

Do you believe wearing a cup is important but don't wear headgear? Headgear reduces chance of cuts, cheek fracture, facial injuries, an ear deformed and swollen by repeated blows called cauliflower ear, and protects your opponent's hands. Headgear helps disperse force from a blow to the head, but it is not known if headgear protects against brain injury. Don't take blows to the head thinking the headgear will prevent all injury.

A mouthpiece protects the hands of your opponent against being cut on your teeth. It absorbs force from blows to the head that otherwise may be transmitted to your brain. A mouthpiece reminds to keep the jaw closed at the same time that it holds the teeth separated enough to prevent dental injury from a blow to the jaw. Keeping the mouth open loosely allows more impact from a hit, which can injure the jaw and brain. Jaw positioning is so important to health that the idea of preparing mental strength in anticipation of a hard event is known by the common expression, "Set your jaw."

Hand Injury

Knuckles. Hands can become injured through both good and bad technique, wearing gloves or fighting bare fisted. A properly done punch directs force through the first two knuckles. It is not uncommon for martial artists to partly or completely rupture the tendon that goes over the first, or more commonly, second knuckle. The hand bones are called metacarpals. The finger bones are phalanges. The knuckle is where a hand bone joins a finger bone, so is called the metacarpophalangeal joint. The tendon that goes over the knuckle pulls the finger back, (extends it). The injury is called metacarpophalangeal extensor tendon injury. The knuckle remains mushy and enlarged. Reduce force on the knuckle by keeping the front of the fist flat, hitting with the entire surface, not the point of the knuckles. Save phoenix fist, or "noogie-fist," for when you have hardened the knuckles through training.

Thumbs. In both gloved and open-handed fighters, strong punches often catch and yank a slack thumb, spraining, breaking, or dislocating it. Keep the thumb curled over the fist, not over or inside the knuckles.

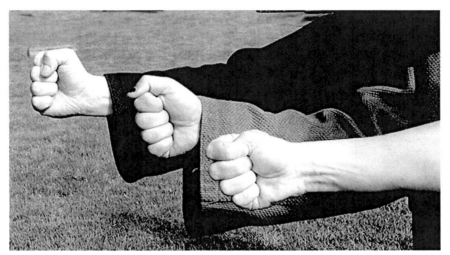

Figure 13-5. For most punches, keep thumb curled over the fingers (left), not the top of the fist (middle) or inside the fist (right)

Hand Bones. Tilting the wrist during a straight punch, so that contact is against the side of the hand, can fracture the last bone, the fifth metacarpal. This is sometimes called "sloppy punch injury" and "drinkers injury" for prevalence in bar fights. Avoid this by keeping hand and wrist straight, directing force through the first two knuckles, whether wearing gloves or fighting bare handed.

Open and Bare Hand Styles. In barehanded styles, injuries include the usual closed fist injuries, plus jammed, dislocated, and broken fingers. Open-handed techniques reduce the common knuckle and wrist injuries of closed fist punches. Some personnel of the Thai Army and police use an open hand style, sometimes called Lerdrit (Lerdlit) for effective close combat with reduced fist injury. Lerdlit is like Muay Thai with open hands instead of fists. For open hand techniques, keep good hand and finger position. Avoid punches to the mouth that tear your hand on your opponent's teeth, and introduce their body germs into your system. The bad habit of not keeping the thumb firmly against the side of the hand for knife-hand techniques can fracture, sprain, or dislocate the thumb. Keep thumb in close position.

How to Toughen Hands. Boxers wrap, tape, and wear padded gloves. Students of karate and other styles deliberately bash their hands and fists repeatedly into rocks, sand, beans, boards, shot pellets, even glass over years to toughen them. Both kinds of fighters suffer hand injuries with high frequencies. Why? Because they punch things. If the hand is weaker than what it hits or blocks, it may be injured. According to Russian proverb, "If a stone falls on the pitcher, woe to the pitcher. But, if the pitcher falls on the stone, woe to the pitcher." You need to train to be the stone.

Should you injure your hands using repeated strikes to toughen them to prevent injury? The answer is simple. Toughen, don't injure. It is a balance. Joints need frequent exercise to avoid arthritis. At the same time, a frequent consequence of joint trauma is arthritis. Your hands must be tough enough not to be injured when striking things or being struck. Use your hands. Open jars. Strengthen hands with pushups, handstands, and pull-ups or hanging from a bar. Improve wrist positioning and stability with pushups on fists. The strengthening chapter gives many ways to strengthen hands.

Figure 13-6. Strengthen hands until they can withstand strong blows

Practice punching, with intelligent judgment, against bags, boards, carpets, and other objects to progressively strengthen and toughen the hands until they withstand hard strikes without injury. Learn good hand wrapping technique to reduce repeated hand trauma. Remember not to use a hand against a stronger target, which can injure the hand, not the target. Instead, use leg and elbow strikes, handy objects, evasive defenses, and non-striking submission moves like throws, locks, holds, and chokes. When the issue is sudden self-defense in the street, use open hand techniques to protect the hands while meeting the need of the occasion.

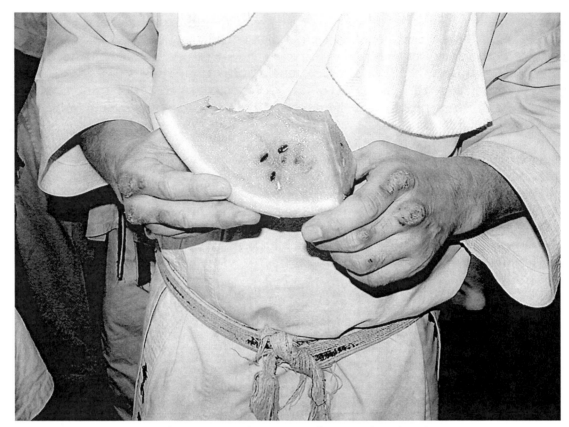

Figure 13-7. Master martial artists spend years toughening their hands

Wrist Injuries

An interesting wrist injury is a metacarpal boss. A boss is a knob-like protuberance. When the first or second hand bone buckles upward at the wrist, it makes a painful bump. A boss is different from the squishy bump of a ganglion cyst that also sometimes follows wrist trauma. A ganglion cyst can be drained or may open and drain on its own through vigorous exercise. Don't bang it deliberately to burst it.

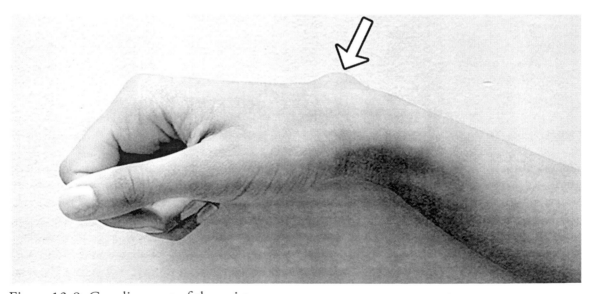

Figure 13-8. Ganglion cyst of the wrist

Striking with the wrist bent can forcibly bend the wrist on impact, breaking, jamming, or spraining it. Hold wrists straight for strikes.

Figure 13-9. Keep straight wrist position (upper left). Don't let the wrist bend (below, right) when striking.

If you have wrist pain, check the cause. Taking growth hormone is sometimes a hidden cause of wrist pain. Weak wrists are more likely to hurt and don't function properly in activities that use hand strength. Most common is not using muscles of the arm and hand to power moves, and let the force compress the wrist joint. The carpal tunnel is the passageway through the wrist for the median nerve and tendons supplying part of the thumb and first two fingers. The muscles of the hand and arm are supposed to be used to distribute forces. With poor technique and lack of muscle use, the carpal tunnel can become strained and compressed.

The way to reduce carpal tunnel symptoms is not to further weaken the wrist in an immobilizing splint. Movement is important for all joints to get oxygen in and wastes out, and to strengthen and heal. Pushups, done properly can strengthen and retrain use of the wrist. For pushups, planks, handstands, and other arm balancing moves, keep weight distributed over the entire hand, not mashing the wrist, which compresses the carpal tunnel. Push and balance with fingers and hand muscles, don't let weight concentrate on the wrists. When using hands for typing, opening jars, preparing food, and driving, don't angulate wrists backward, compressing the joint. Bend the wrist for normal movement, but use muscles to position the wrist, don't just fold the joint under the load. When lifting hand weights, keep the weight on the hand and arm muscles, not compressing the wrist backward.

Foot Injuries

Like hand injuries, foot injuries occur with good and bad technique, with protective gear and barefooted. Toughening the feet and learning healthy positioning with repeated kicking practice is needed. Common foot injuries from kicks are jammed, dislocated, and broken toes, broken foot bones, torn nails, bruises, cuts, sprained ankles from kicking or landing on a bent ankle.

Part of the training system for Thai fighting is to bash the shins against trees, pipes, heavy bags, and opponents. Toughen the feet and shins through progressive training. Don't damage with the toughening exercises. Damage doesn't toughen. Breaking a bone does not make it grow back stronger.

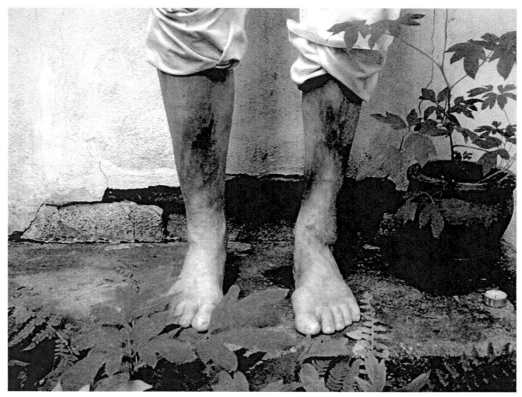

Figure 13-10. Result of years of conditioning the shins by hitting them with pipes, bo staff, and partners' shins

The most common foot pain comes from tight, weak feet and ankles, and poor positioning during ordinary daily life. Keep feet facing straight ahead for walking and moving. Standing toe-in strains the foot, knee, and hip, and affects gait. Standing with feet turned out contributes to hip and knee pain, bunion formation, and is often mistaken for "flat-foot" because it weights the inside edge of the foot, flattening the arches. Turning the foot toe-out changes gait to press each step off the side of the big toe, rather than the ball of the entire foot and all toes. This reduces speed and jumping ability, and reduces shock absorption.

Use your hands to stretch the toes apart, side-to-side. Make sure the big toe can move up and down, forward and back. When the big toe joint gets stiff, it does not bend enough when walking. A stuck big toe alters gait and posture, reduces the normal stretch on the bottom of the foot from walking, and promotes bunion.

Use good shock absorption from leg and foot muscles to land lightly when jumping, sparring, and for everyday movement. Walk softly; heel first, rolling to your toes. Keep foot straight, not turning in or out. Bend at the toe knuckles and push off the ball of the foot, not the side of the toes. When descending stairs, come down toe first, then bring the heel down. Don't crash down on heels. Bend knees for shock absorption with each step down. Walk softly, without a sound. Practice until you can leap, jump, and step through all martial arts practice and daily movement without a sound.

Support for feet and ankles should come from your own muscles, not the shoes you wear. Allowing your feet to slump so that the arches flatten is no different than allowing yourself to sit and stand round-shouldered. Use your own foot and leg muscles to hold and position feet and ankles in healthy position for all movement, both wearing shoes and barefoot. Avoid tight shoes. They deform the feet, allow foot muscles to atrophy, and reduce balance and positioning. Walk and move barefoot daily with proper positioning.

Plantar Fasciitis

The word "plantar" means the bottom part of the foot that you "plant" on the ground. Fascia is strong tissue that connects and wraps soft body structures. The suffix "-itis" means inflammation. Plantar fasciitis is when the fascia at the bottom of the foot gets inflamed. It usually occurs from tight feet.

Walking with the feet parallel, not turned out, gives a natural stretch during daily movement across the bottom of the foot. When the feet turn out, the normal stretch of the bottom of the foot is lost. Turning the feet toe-out (duck-foot) when walking is a common bad habit. Wearing hard shoes also prevents normal stretch on the bottom of the foot. The fascia of the bottom of the foot becomes tight from lack of daily stretch during walking and moving. The plantar fascia attaches to the heel. Every step on a tight plantar fascia yanks the fascia and the heel. Eventually the heel and bottom of the foot become irritated and painful from the yanking.

Often people with plantar fasciitis stop stretching or walking straight because their tightness makes the normal stretch of walking hurt, preventing the very stretch they need. Stretching is needed to stop the cycle. It is a balance. Easy foot stretching and straight positioning when walking prevents and treats fasciitis. The strength and flexibility chapters explain good foot exercises, positioning, and stretches.

Ankle Sprain, Weak Ankles, Fallen Arches

Sprains and Weakness. Training good foot and ankle placement more effectively prevents ankle sprain than taping and special shoes.

One drill to reduce chance of sprains is to practice ankle positioning and stability by standing on toes. Keep body weight over the big toe and second toe when rising up on toes during stances, moves, jumps, and landings. Don't let the ankle roll, letting body weight shift outward over the small toes. Rolling outward is the motion in most ankle sprains. Train the ankles to resist this motion during activity.

Once you understand and can maintain standing placement, try jumps, landing with feet and ankles in good placement, not rolling outward.

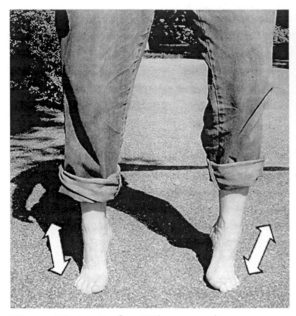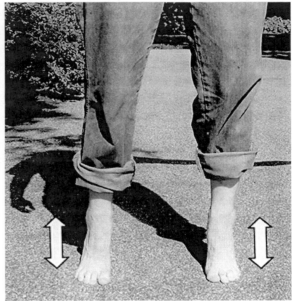

Figure 13-11. Left—When standing on toes and landing from jumps, don't let body weight roll outward to the small toes, tilting the ankle into sprain-prone position. Right—Train healthy placement by standing with weight over the big and second toe.

Avoiding overstretching the side of the ankle is important to preventing ankle pain and injury. Ligaments hold the side of the ankle in place. Ligaments are not supposed to stretch much. When ligaments are injured through overstretching, the joint becomes unstable and more likely to turn sideways and sprain.

When sitting cross-legged or when stretching, do not bend your ankles sideways. Stretching the side of the ankle can makes ligaments loose enough to let the foot turn and sprain during activity.

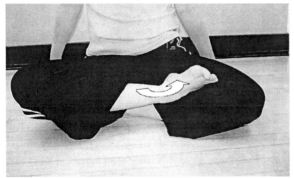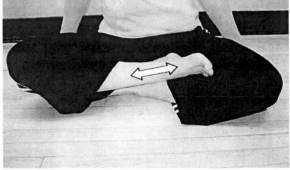

Figure 13-12. Left—When sitting, don't let the ankle turn inward, overstretching ligaments, predisposing to ankle laxity and sprain. Right—Practice ankle stabilization by keeping ankle straight. Straight position gives better stretch from the hip.

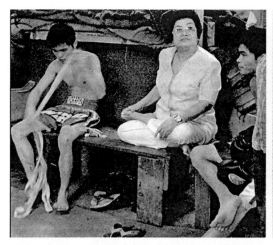

Figure 13-13. Hold ankles straight and sit up straight when sitting cross-legged (left) and stretching (right)

Flat Feet, Fallen Arches. During daily walking and movement, don't let your body weight sink inward onto your arches. Use muscles of the side of your leg to reposition your weight over the sole of the foot, not the arch. The arch will no longer flatten under your weight. With proper use of leg muscles, you do not need orthotics and arch supports. Your own foot and ankle muscles are the supports, reducing ankle and knee load and twisting.

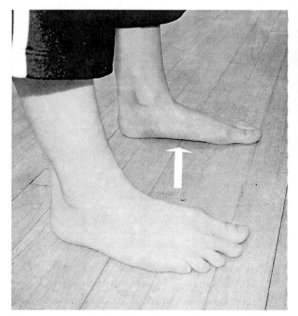
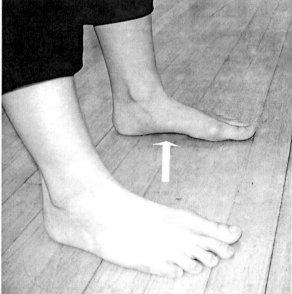

Figure 13-14. Left—Flat arches are often just a bad posture. Don't let body weight shift downward onto your arches, which flattens them. Right—Use leg muscles to stand with weight distributed around the sole, off the arches.

When walking and moving, keep feet facing straight ahead. Don't turn feet toe-in (pigeon toe) or toe-out (duck-foot). Crooked positions create uneven and unhealthy forces that gradually injure and deform feet, ankles, and knees.

Elbow Injury

A common mistake by beginners is hyperextending the elbow during punches. Hyperextension means to go beyond a straight position. Hyperextension can damage the joint and cartilage. Keep your elbow slightly bent at the end of all strikes and weapons moves, whether contact or non-contact. When holding arms straight for planks, handstands, and hand balancing moves in styles like capoeira, keep elbows slightly bent, with your weight on your muscles, not the elbow joint. When practicing joint locks, don't overdo.

Figure 13-15. Elbow hyperextension during strikes (student at right) is injurious, even without contact. Keep elbow slightly bent (teacher at left) at the end of the strike. The student is also allowing the wrist to bend and the low back to overarch, instead of holding them straight.

In throws and overhead weapons use, the pivot should come from the hip and torso muscles, not the elbow. Keep your hip tucked under to use core muscles in overhead movements. Effort should be felt in the muscles of the torso and arm, not the elbow joint.

Strengthen elbows with pushups, handstands with bent elbows, weapons practice like bo staff and other weighted objects, and pull-ups with hands facing both in and out.

Knee Injury

Overpressure. Several common exercises injure the knee and are not helpful to the martial arts. One is walking in a full squat on the toes called the duck walk. Similar traditional gym exercises also put body weight forward onto the knee joint, like heel-up full squats on the toes, sometimes called Hindu squats, and low side lunges with the knee forward, heel up, and body weight resting on the ball of one foot. The physical pushing of the thigh against the calf muscle can pry open the knee joint, particularly if you have heavy legs.

Preventing knee injury when bending is easy. Bending properly can also strengthen the knee, helping injuries heal. When bending the knees for lunges, squats, stances, and to bend to pick up any item, keep your heels down, knees positioned over your feet, and body weight back over the heel. Good positioning takes body weight off the knee and shifts effort to the thigh and hip muscles. Good bending with the heel down also gives a healthy stretch to the Achilles tendon. All over the world, people sit on their heels in full squat for many daily events from eating to waiting for a bus to going to the bathroom without knee injury. People who use squatting on their toes with their heels up, like baseball catchers, have a higher rate of knee cartilage tears. Chapter 3 on strength shows how to strengthen legs and improve martial arts skills without using moves that may be traditional, and may train to an extent, but add wear on the knees.

Figure 13-16. Left—For side lunges, don't lift the heel and shift weight forward to the toes. Body weight shifts to the knee joint. Right—Keep the heel down and torso upright. Keep the knee over the foot with weight back over the heel to keep weight on the muscles.

Hyperextension. A common source of knee pain is hyperextending the knee during standing and during kicks, both contact and non-contact. Don't fully straighten the knee at the end of kicks. Keep a slight bend to prevent banging the joint against itself with each kick. Keep the standing knee slightly bent. Standing hyperextended hurts the knee by itself, and a straight leg is an invitation for an opponent to kick it, pushing the joint backward into hyperextention injury.

Some people try to strengthen the thigh and hamstring in specific ratios to prevent knee hyperextension. It was previously thought that a stronger thigh would force too much straightening when kicking, and the weaker hamstring could not counter it. After strengthening in physical therapy for their knee pain, the same people would go back to kicking with overextended knee joints, reinjuring their knee. It is kicking technique not muscle ratio that creates knee hyperextension injury.

Inward Sway. Don't let the knee sway inward of the feet in stances, running, and moving in everyday life. Inward pressure scrapes the kneecap (patella) and twists and pressures the inner side of the knee joint. For hour-glass and sanchen stances, turn inward from the hip, not the knee. Use leg and foot muscles to keep weight from falling inward on the knee joint.

Figure 13-17. In low stances, don't let body weight fall inward on the knee. Turning inward twists and grinds knee cartilage.

Figure 13-18. Left—In high stances, don't let the knee sway inward. Right—Use muscles on the outside of the thigh to pull knee straight over the foot.

Figure 13-19. Healthy knee position of both kicker (middle) and receiver (right). The knee is in line with the foot, not swaying inward. Kneecap faces same direction as foot. Knee not forward of toes on the weight bearing leg.

Use Shock Absorption. Step lightly when walking and running. When walking downstairs, bend the knee upon landing. Use thigh muscles to absorb the landing force, not the knee joint. When walking down steep hills, maintain heel to toe rolling. Don't let body weight shift forward through the knee.

Back Pain

The major causes of back pain in martial artists are the same as for non-martial artists; letting the lower back overarch backward when standing and moving, and letting the upper and lower back round forward when sitting, bending, moving, and lifting.

Allowing the lower back to increase the arch under body weight when standing is called hyperlordosis (often used interchangeably with lordosis). Lordosis creates a larger than normal inward curve to the low back and pinches the spine under body weight. Lordosis is not a structural condition or something you are born to have. It is a bad posture. Lordosis can come from tilting the hip to stick out your behind in back. It can also come from letting your upper body slouch backward. In both cases, the low back pinches and folds backward under your upper body weight. Hyperlordosis is a major hidden cause of low back pain in the vertebral joints called facets, and soft tissues.

Figure 13-20. Left—Allowing the low back to arch in hyperlordosis compresses the low back joints on impact. It also produces a weaker strike. Right—Tuck hip under to reduce the arch to neutral. Then core muscles hold the spine in position and absorb the blow, instead of transmitting force to the lower back. Do not curl so much that you impact with a rigidly straight or rounded forward spine, another source of back injury.

Figure 13-21. The boxer is allowing his low back to arch backward too much while standing to be taped. Allowing the arch compresses the low back under the weight of the upper body, and accounts for much low back pain. Tuck the hip and pull the upper body forward, to stand upright and shift upper body weight to the torso muscles and off the low back.

Keep the hip from tilting downward in front. Don't let the upper body angle backward in bad slouching posture. The chapter on core and abdominal strengthening shows how to use muscles to prevent lordosis. The chapter on strength shows many exercises that retrain healthy back positioning.

Figure 13-22. Left—Slouching with a rounded back pushes discs outward and is a common cause of achy back muscles. Right—Use muscles to hold yourself straight to reduce back pain from poor ergonomics during movement

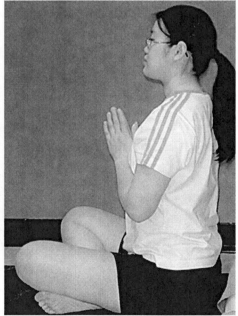

Figure 13-23. Left—Sitting rounded pushes the discs of the neck and low back outward, and practices overstretched, pain-producing posture. Right—Sit straight.

A tight hip pulls you backward when sitting, making sitting straight difficult. Tight hamstrings make it difficult to sit with legs out without rounding your back. Sitting rounded is hard on the discs. Many people stretch rounded because they are too tight to stretch with healthy back position, with the result that many stretches contribute to back pain. Avoid stretches and exercises where you sit or stand with your weight pressing on a rounded back. Chapter 5 on flexibility shows healthy hip, back, and hamstring stretches.

Figure 13-24. Left—The student kicking the bag is arching the lower back too much and rounding the upper back too much. Right—Hold straighter back position. Lean from hip, not spine.

Herniated and Degenerating Discs, Sciatica, Impingement

Discs are tough cushions between each of your spine bones (vertebrae). Over years of letting your low back or neck round in bad posture, and wrong lifting bent over, a disc can be slowly squeezed outward toward the back, like squeezing toothpaste. A bad disc is an injury, not a lifelong condition. It is not something you inherit, get from aging, or have to live with. It has a simple cause and can usually be simply healed without surgery by stopping bad positioning and using healthy movement.

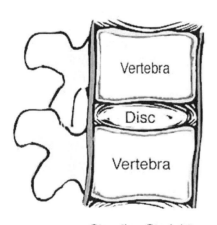

Figure 13-25. Spine section in side view, forward is to the right. The bumpy parts pointing left are the back of each vertebra that you can feel in your own back. When you stand and sit straight (left), pressure is even on the discs. After years of bad bending forward, discs may break down and degenerate, and eventually squeeze backward, becoming a bulging or herniated disc (right).

It takes years of squeezing to break down a disk so that it degenerates. It may begin to ache. With continued bad bending and slouching, it can finally squeeze enough to hurt a great deal. It may start to hurt suddenly one day, or pain may finally occur with one more throw with bad technique, or one more fall. However, it was injured over years, no differently than if after 20 years of smoking, you cough, or after unhealthy eating for 20 years, you feel tightness in your chest. If you continue bad habits, the herniation can get bigger and the pain worse. If you stop the cause of the outward pressure, the herniation can heal, get smaller, and the pain can stop and not come back.

A tough ligament down the back of the spine prevents discs from squeezing straight back toward the spinal cord. For that reason, a disc that is in the process of herniating usually squeezes out to the side, and can bulge against the nerves that exit the side of the spine and go down the leg. When the disc pushes on the nerve, it is called impingement. Impingement on the sciatica nerve that goes down the back of the leg is called sciatica. Discs can impinge other nerves that go down the front and side of the leg too. When a disc in the neck herniates from bad slouching posture and repeated forced neck bending, the pain can go down the arm. If you overstretch the ligament, the disc can bulge centrally, and impinge on the spinal cord itself.

Disc pain and herniation almost never honestly requires surgery to fix, even though many people have surgery. Surgery often causes more pain and injury, deconditioning, and loss of function. After surgery that removes the shock absorbing disc, and spinal fusion, the vertebra above and below are subjected to double load with each movement, resulting in a high incidence of recurring pain and herniation in those areas next, especially when continuing the same poor habits that caused the first herniation. Sciatica and disc pain do not require bed rest. With rest, often people begin to feel too weak to stand. They lie down again, furthering the cycle. More important, bed rest and surgery do not treat the cause of the herniation.

It does not take long to heal a herniated disc and stop sciatica and impingement without drugs or surgery. Stop the repeated rounded posture and bad techniques that cause it. Lie face down and prop on elbows often to reverse the pressure on the discs that forward bending causes. Don't sit rounded on the bed first thing in the morning. Turn face down in bed and prop on elbows to unload the discs and practice straightening out. Don't sit rounded at your desk and in the car, or to stretch. Do back extension exercises, explained in Chapter 3 on strength, and extension stretches shown in the flexibility chapter.

Use a lunge or squat for all bending, instead of bending over forward, pressuring the discs outward. Healthy bending gives leg strengthening while letting your discs repair themselves, and trains how to not hurt them in the first place. Tight muscles can impinge spinal nerves mimicking disc pain. Good stretches, done without injurious rounded posture prevent painful tightness, and restore muscle length needed for healthy back positioning (Chapter 5, Flexibility).

Shoulder Pain
Hunching. Tightening and hunching the shoulder when punching is common. Hunching is sometimes taught as a way to block or protect the neck. Hunching and tightening can injure the neck and shoulder muscles and result in tight, aching neck and shoulders. You can protect your chin and neck without injuring your shoulder. Keep your shoulder relaxed, not tight.

Figure 13-26. Left—Hunched, tight shoulder is a common source of shoulder pain and interferes with arm motion. Right—Prevent your shoulder from raising tightly.

Neck Position. Don't let your neck slouch forward during sitting, driving, standing, and exercising. Tilting the neck so that the chin comes forward is a bad posture called a forward head. The tension that a forward head produces on the neck and upper back muscles often makes the shoulder area ache. Keep the chin in and shoulder from rounding forward to prevent muscle aches from the forward head.

Rotator Cuff. The rotator cuff is a set of four muscles and their tendons that circle the shoulder socket like a cuff. The rotator cuff helps rotate your arm to reach and throw. The unhealthy neck position of the forward head rotates and tilts the shoulder bones forward. When your raise your arm with bad forward neck position, nerves can become squeezed (impinged) between your arm and shoulder bones, making pain down your arm. The soft tissue of your rotator cuff can be squeezed until it eventually tears. Keep your chin in and shoulders back, not rounding forward, to prevent rotator cuff tears from the forward head.

Another bad habit that strains the rotator cuff is making the shoulder joint the pivot of overhead throws and weapons moves, instead of the torso muscles. The rotator cuff only contributes a small part of arm power. The torso and legs should provide the bulk of motion involving the shoulder. In throws, don't let your arm be pulled back by the weight of your opponent. The pivot point should be your hip and torso muscles, not your shoulder. Make sure that shoulder rehabilitation exercises start with hip and abdominal repositioning exercises like the lunge, before moving to shoulder exercises. Feel how tucking your hip under shifts the fulcrum of throwing away from the shoulder to your torso and legs.

Hip Pain

Hip pain in the martial arts that does not come from direct blows is often from tightness in the front of the hip. The front hip is usually kept bent in sitting for most of the day. When standing, the hip often is held in a bent position, particularly when the low back is allowed to arch. Most common exercises bend the hip forward. Exercise that straightens and extends the hip is often ignored. The hip is often kept bent for relaxing in an easy chair, then all night in sleep. The resulting tight hip restricts straight standing, and pulls and yanks during movement. The flexibility and strength chapters explain important hip extension stretches and exercise. Add these exercises to reduce pain and injury to the hip.

Another contributor to hip pain is pushing the hip out to the side when putting weight on that leg. The tilted, side-pushed pelvic position drops body weight on the side of the hip joint while compressing it. Hip pain, and sometimes knee pain can result. This weak posture is commonly seen when shifting weight ascending stairs, running and walking, doing forms, sweep kicks, cross kicks, and in aerobic exercise and "box-aerobics." The tilting is called a "Trendelenberg" sign. The common remedy is to give strengthening exercises for the side hip muscles, called the medius muscles, by lying on the floor and opening and closing the legs in "clam" exercises. But, someone with strong medius muscles can still let their weight sag sideways if they do not know it is a simple matter of just correcting this bad habit. The medius muscle only prevents hip sway when you use it, whether strong or not. Don't allow the hip to sway to the side. Use muscles to keep level hip positioning during all activities and you will get the functional strengthening the muscles need.

Figure 13-27. Left—Allowing the hip to slide to the side under body weight is a common cause of hip pain and weak stances, as body weight drops on the side of the hip joint. Right—Keep hips level and weight on the hip and leg muscles.

Groin Pulls

A common habit predisposing to groin muscle pulls is keeping the front of the hip bent at the crease where the body meets the leg. This is the most often missed cause of groin muscle tightness.

When standing, the angle of the hip crease in front should be flat, without inward bend (hip stuck out in back, back arched). When walking and running, the hip should be able to extend to a greater angle than straight. Long sitting, and the common habit of standing and exercising bent at the hip, often create a hip too tight to lengthen for healthy movement, or even healthy standing. Look for standing posture with the belt line tilted down in front, indicating standing with the hip bent forward. When stretching the hamstring by lying on the back with one leg up, check if the other leg rises too, indicating a tight anterior hip. Look for hip tightness that pulls the standing leg forward and under during front kicks. This is a sign of tightness enough to cause sudden pulls of back and groin muscles, and impede kicking ability. Tightness in the front of the hip is a common reason for the standing leg being pulled forward in kicks until it slips, causing a comic fall.

The common groin stretches of sitting with feet apart, and sitting with feet together and knees out, promote, rather than reverse the bent hip position and do not retrain healthy hip mechanics for standing and movement. People are often puzzled why they get a pull even though they stretch. They were not getting the needed stretch.

Use the hip stretches in Figure 5-10, and 5-12 to 5-16. In the lunge stretch, keep the back foot straight, not turned out, and tuck the hip under to stretch the groin and anterior hip muscles. When stretching the quadriceps with one foot in hand behind you, tuck the hip or there is little or no stretch in the intended muscles. When lying on the back with one leg up to stretch the hamstrings, keep the other leg flat and straight on the floor, without bending the hip. When sitting with legs apart to stretch inner leg muscles, do not round the back and hip forward. Sit up, lifting the chest to reposition the hip straight, not rounded. When lying on your back stretching legs apart in the air, keep the head, back, and hip on the floor without rounding or lifting them. Chapter 5 on flexibility gives many more good stretches.

More important to preventing pulls than doing isolated stretches, is to retrain standing hip position. If you stand, run, move, and exercise with the behind stuck out in back, tuck the hip under to reduce the low back arch and straighten the front of the hip. You may feel a stretch in the front of the hip. Retrain kicking positioning. For front kicks, do not round the hip and back forward or let the standing leg be pulled forward when lifting the kicking leg. These bad habits don't allow the front of the hip to lengthen normally. Rounding the back with each kick also pushes the discs outward, increasing herniating forces. For side kicks, do not stick the behind out in back, a common unattractive habit in beginners and box-aerobics moves. Figure 5-47 shows a wall stretch to retrain side kick positioning.

Tapping Out
In grappling and submission arts that apply chokes, joint locks, and painful holds, the uke (receiver) can control a practice session with the tap out. When you are tori (the giver) respond immediately. When you are uke, remember that taps on the mat or against your own body often can't be felt or heard. Make an effort to tap the tori, who is giving the move to you. Be willing to tap before something snaps, or a choke continues until your brain runs out of oxygen.

Falls and Throws
Reduce injury when being thrown or when using a controlled fall for a takedown. Use good rolling technique to avoid landing on bony joints. Roll over your shoulder, not neck, and don't let your neck bend forward under your body weight. Distribute your weight. Use shock absorption.

Avoid techniques that prevent controlling the fall. In a falling break or cross body arm bar like juji gatami, don't step over your opponent with both legs. You will fall on your spine without hands free to disperse the force.

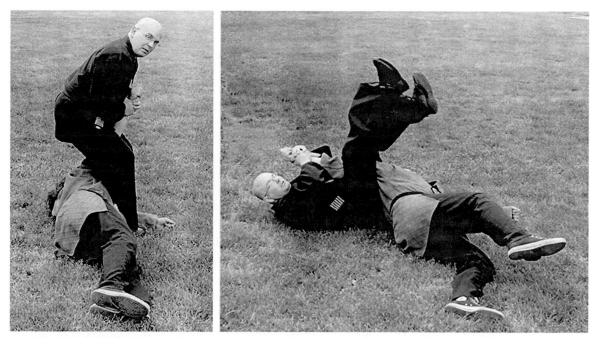

Figure 13-28. Don't injure yourself by falling on your back doing locks, bars, breaks, and takedowns. Don't step over with both legs.

Figure 13-29. For arm locks, step over with one leg not both, to prevent injury during your own fall, and allow more kicking technique during the controlling move.

Wounds

Large cuts and wounds should been seen by a doctor to rule out foreign body, tendon trauma, and infection. For home care, some long-used preparations have proven effective to prevent infection and reduce inflammation. Topical honey was used by many cultures including the Egyptians at least as far back as 1500 B.C. Raw honey patted over an open wound stops growth of bacteria, has anti-inflammatory action, creates a moist environment that promotes wound healing, and helps preventing scarring. Do not heat the honey. Heating destroys antibacterial ability. Australian Aboriginals historically crushed and applied tea tree leaves for cuts and skin infections. Use crushed tea tree leaves or tea tree oil of at least 70 to 100 percent. Don't use tea oil on burns. Native Americans applied poultices of witch hazel leaves and willow bark for wounds, insect bites, and skin ulcers. Witch hazel is an astringent that helps draw together torn tissue. Willow bark is one of the original sources of the chemical from which aspirin is made. Calendula flower applications, already approved in Europe, speeds skin wound healing and reduce infection and inflammation. Steep a tablespoon of calendula flower in hot water for fifteen minutes. Apply as a compress for fifteen minutes, several times a day, tapering as the wound improves. Aloe seems to have mixed results. Processing into commercial products may remove or destroy the active component. If you want aloe, get a living aloe leaf from the supermarket or keep a living aloe plant. Cut a section and squeeze the gel directly. Keep wounds covered and moist for better healing. Watch for increase in redness, swelling, pain, or heat in the area, which could mean infection.

Wound healing has a nutritional component. Large wounds may need more protein in the meals than usual, with additional vitamin C, zinc, and possibly magnesium. Several foods might aid healing though their anti-inflammatory effect—ginger root, turmeric root, blueberries, grape skins, pineapple particularly the stem, and others. Chapter 12 on nutrition tells about healthy food. Nutritional healing is summarized in this truism of unknown origin:

2000 BC: Here, eat this root.
1000 AD: That root is heathen. Here, say this prayer.
1850 AD: That prayer is superstition. Here, drink this potion.
1940 AD: That potion is snake oil. Here, swallow this pill.
1985 AD: That pill is ineffective. Here, take this antibiotic.
2000 AD: That antibiotic doesn't work anymore. Here, eat this root.

Tendon and Ligament Tears, Reduced Bone Healing

If an otherwise ordinary activity results in tears or injuries to joints, check to see if you are using anything that weakens them. Anabolic steroids are a major contributor. Long use of fluroquinolone-type antibiotics like Cipro, Floxin, and Noroxin increases risk of tendon or ligament tear or rupture. Fluroquinolone overuse is also linked to otherwise unexplained nerve pain. Instead of taking systemic antibiotics for traveler's diarrhea, try a version like rifaximin that works in the digestive tract while being poorly absorbed elsewhere. For broken bones, avoid smoking, a big factor in reduced healing. Avoid long term use of non-steroidal anti-inflammatories like ibuprofen (Advil, Motrin, Nuprin), naproxen (Aleve, Naprosyn), and COX-2 inhibitors (brand names such as Bextra, Celebrex). Studies are mixed but evidence suggests they reduce bone healing.

Unexplained Weak Aching Joints and Muscles

In cases of unexplainable aches in joints or muscles, check that it is not something like Lyme disease from a tick bite. More commonly, several medicines cause joint pain and tender weak muscles. These include statin drugs for cholesterol and lipid lowering drugs, stomach acid prescriptions, allergy medicine like Allegra, some antifungal drugs, the calcium channel blocker drug verapamil, Lisinopril, the antibiotics erythromycin and clarithromycin, some HIV medications, and several antidepressants. Large doses of some B-vitamins, including niacin (nicotinic acid), can lead to nerve pain. Surprisingly, some prescription medicines for joint pain list muscle aches as a common side effect. Check for low Vitamin D, involved with pain commonly confused for fibromyalgia.

Many people take several medicines together and have much pain. They may be diagnosed with pain syndromes they do not have, but are from the medicines. These people may reduce physical activity from the pain. Reducing activity leads to more pain, misery, and weakness. They may be given increased dosage for the increased pain, plus medicines for the side effect of stomach pain, leading to more pain. Doing a few stretches does not treat the cause of all this pain. Choose other medicines that do not have the side effect of body aches. Most important is to treat the cause of the original problems and break the cycle of pain and medicine, so that, in a majority of cases, you do not need the medicines.

Antibiotic Resistance

Overuse of antibiotics has led to a world problem of infections resistant to antibiotics. A growing number of infections are becoming more deadly and unable to be treated by usual means. These are the "superbugs." Sources of antibiotic overuse are misuse for small or non-bacterial problems, overuse prophylactically (just in case), long term use for illnesses, added to daily hand, body, and household cleaners, and in factory farming. Antibiotics are fed in large amounts to many animals grown for meat, eggs, and dairy. Antibiotics enter the sewage system from the animals, and your system if you eat the animals. Antibiotics reduce the number of weaker germs, leaving the strong ones to grow and learn more resistance.

Resistant germs can live in your system, especially digestive tract, unnoticed for long periods. Trouble comes when your own resistance to disease lowers through poor health, or the germs are spilled or introduced to surrounding tissue through injury or a surprising variety of medical procedures. Antibiotic resistant germs are more common in hospitals than anywhere else. An example of resistant germs is methicillin-resistant Staphylococcus aureus, abbreviated MRSA. The term has come to mean any of at least 17 strains of Staphylococcus bacteria, resistant to one or more antibiotics. Infections no longer responding to methicillin are treated with vancomycin, a drug considered the "last line of defence" when all other antibiotics fail. The increase in vancomycin use has resulted in vancomycin-resistant Staphylococcus aureus (VRSA).

Hospitals are a main source of resistant infections because Staphylococcus strains are concentrated there, with staff invasively touching patient after patient, with many doses of antibiotics, accelerating development of resistance.

Don't take antibiotics for non-bacterial problems. Antibiotics are for bacterial infection. They do nothing against viral activity like colds or flu. Instead of using antibiotic creams for every cut, try tea tree oil for disinfecting. Reduce the amount of antibiotics introduced to the food chain and water sources by reducing dependence on factory farming and animal food.

Use cleaners without such antibiotic agents as Triclosan. Don't overly-worry if children get dirty. Exposure to germs is necessary to develop natural resistance. Reduce your need for antibiotics by raising your resistance to infection with healthy habits of exercise, nutrition, sleep. Wash your hands. Wash fruit and vegetables well. Wash hand wraps, gloves, and practice pads after use. Wipe boxing gloves before and after use, and in between sparring partners. Keep your uniform (gi, dobak) or workout clothes clean. Use vinegar for kitchen cleaning instead of antibiotic hand gels and soaps.

Leg and Foot Cramps

A cramp happens when a muscle tightens painfully (spasm) and will not untighten. Since muscle shortening is what makes the cramp, you can stop the cramp by lengthening the muscle. When the cramp is at the bottom of your foot, stretch the bottom of the foot by pulling the toes and ankle back. When the cramp is in the calf muscle, stretch the calf by pulling the ankle back and straightening the knee. When the cramp is in the hamstring in back of the thigh, stretch the muscle by straightening the knee. Don't rub or hit a cramp. That is not what lengthens the muscle to release the cramp. Stretch it. Leg cramps are more often from overly tightening and clenching muscles when training or turning over in bed, than from lack of a particular vitamins or nutrients.

Over-supplementation of single vitamins can unbalance contractile function. Beta blocking drugs and statin drugs for cholesterol increase leg cramps. Check with your doctor. Healthy changes can make the cause of the medicines unnecessary. For cramping from disease or medicine, sometimes a short course of tonic water (which contains quinine) may stop one of the causes of cramping. Stretch the contracted muscle right away to release the cramp. Stretch legs and feet before bed to reduce night cramps. Use the wall hamstring stretch, wall Achilles stretch, downward dog, described in Chapter 5 on flexibility, and standing lunges with good knee positioning. Prevent cramps through lifestyle stretches. Keep feet parallel, not turned out when walking and running for built-in stretch for the back of the leg with each step. Keep heels on the ground for all squatting, bending, and ascending stairs. Don't clench toes when walking and exercising. Push off toes with easy, straight function.

Skin Herpes—Gladiator's Herpes

Skin herpes is herpes simplex I. It is a virus spread mostly through skin-to-skin contact. It has been reported in a small number of wrestlers, grapplers, rugby players, and other athletes involved in close skin and mat contact. Lesions occur most often on the head and neck and can spread to the eyes. There may be fever and generally feeling not well. There is no immunization yet available. Antiviral drugs are available to lessen severity, but no cure yet. All grappling arts participants should have routine skin examinations before contact training and bouts. Don't wrestle with suspicious skin lesions.

Hepatitis, HIV, and AIDS

Hepatitis means inflammation ("-itis") of the liver. Hepatitis can be caused by exposure to toxic agents (like too much alcohol), and through a virus. The hepatitis virus has been identified in strains called A, B, C, D, and E. Hepatitis A, B, and C are most common. All are contagious. Hepatitis A comes from food or water contaminated with infected human feces but can also be spread by blood and sexual contact, even if the person does not seem to have symptoms. Wash your hands after the bathroom, changing diapers, and before preparing and sharing food. In travel to developing countries, drink and prepare food with purified water.

Hepatitis B and C can be spread by blood or sexual contact with an infected person, and possibly saliva, even if they do not have symptoms at the time. Symptoms take one to six months to appear. You may feel flu-like aches and weakness, tenderness over the liver in the upper right abdomen, have dark urine and light feces. Hepatitis can seriously damage the liver. It affects millions worldwide, and is more infectious than AIDS. You may become seriously ill for a long time. You can die. You cannot drink any alcohol if you have hepatitis.

Reduce infection risk by not sharing razors or toothbrushes. Don't reuse or share needles for tattoos, piercings, or injected street drugs, insulin, steroids, or epinephrine. Don't spit. Wash your hands after using the bathroom and before eating. Don't share hand wraps or mouthpieces. Do not strike, head-butt, or kick shared bloodied equipment. Use gloves, goggles, and mask to clean blood spills. Dispose cleaning materials in hazardous waste receptacles.

HIV is the retrovirus that causes AIDS. AIDS is a communicable viral disease that severely suppresses the immune system. Reduced immune ability leaves you open to serious infection and other problems that can become fatal. The HIV virus that causes AIDS is spread mostly from sexual contact, blood, and body fluids of an infected person. Use the same precautions as for hepatitis. There are no vaccines yet against HIV or cure for AIDS. Effective immunizations are available for hepatitis A and B. Ask your doctor.

Athlete's Foot
Athlete's foot is called tinea pedis. "Tinea" means fungus. "Pedis" means foot. Athlete's foot is a contagious fungus. It makes the toes, toenails, and sometimes hands itch, blister, crack, and scale. The fungus that causes athlete's foot is usually present on the skin and floor surfaces. Just walking on shower surfaces does not cause infection. Like the irritating people of the world, fungus germs are always around. They only irritate you when you let them under your skin. You make yourself open to infection when you change healthy foot environment to one that supports fungus. You encourage athlete's foot when you keep toes squeezed together, in the dark, and moist.

To prevent athlete's foot, dry your feet after showering. Powder with baking soda. If you wear closed shoes, wear socks. Clean socks. Don't spend long periods in tight, sweaty foot covering. If your toes fit together, your shoes are too tight. Regularly stretch toes apart to restore space between them. Shower shoes usually are not necessary inside the shower. Germs wash from and to your feet with or without shoes. Sometimes shower shoe-straps help grind fungus into water-softened skin. Throw out infected shoes and socks. Use flip-flops or slippers to walk to and from communal bathroom areas so that you do not spread your infection on shared surfaces. In courtesy to others, don't use public showers if you have open sores or foot infections. If you use antifungal creams, use them for the entire prescribed time. Try 100 percent tea tree oil for irritated skin.

Hookworm
Hookworms are small round parasitic worms. They usually enter your body through your feet. The feet may itch and get a rash at the site of entry. Symptoms are sometimes mistaken for athlete's foot. After entering the body, the worms go first to the lungs where they may cause asthma-like symptoms. From there they make their way up to the throat where they are swallowed and go to their home in the intestines to live, eat blood, and lay eggs. Some people get hookworm from swallowing dirt that contains worms. This can occur with not

fully washed food or from sparring in the dirt. Intestinal worms cause diarrhea, gas, blood loss, even malnutrition. Hookworms can be serious, especially for children. Infection is diagnosed by searching the stools for worm eggs.

Treatment is by oral anti-worm medication. The World Health Organization reports that eating crushed garlic, curry, the clove spice, and coconut help through specific anti-worm properties. In developing countries you may not want to train barefoot outdoors, and may need foot covering in washrooms. Don't walk barefoot or swim in areas with untreated sewage. Many places drain bathroom wastewater directly to the surrounding beach and ground area.

Too Much Water—Hyponatremia

Drinking large amounts of water in a short time without eating can dilute the blood. An illness may occur called water intoxication or hyponatremia, which means low salt in the blood. There is no need to drink when not thirsty, as sometimes thought. Replace fluids lost through hard exercise, but do not force yourself to drink. Do not force anyone else to drink, in well-meaning help or for hazing or initiation. Effects of hyponatremia range from weakness and dizziness to convulsion, water in the lungs, and occasionally death. When exercising in the heat, eat and drink. If someone seems to be heat-sick, but is not hot to the touch and has been drinking water, do not make them drink water. Give food or electrolyte drinks. With long exercise, drink when you are thirsty and eat food to restore minerals lost. Between bouts of competition or training, eat fruit, sweet potatoes, and other easy foods to restore mineral and carbohydrate.

Revival from Chokes (Kappo) and Knockout Punches

The aim of choke holds is to put the opponent unconscious. All the many chokes work in a period of seconds to do the same things—close off the breathing tube called the trachea, the blood flow to the brain, or both. In all cases, not enough oxygen goes to the brain.

The moment unconsciousness begins or the opponent taps out, release your hold. Do not continue a choke hold. Chokes are supposed to be temporary.

Most of the time, people wake quickly from chokes. Still, several ineffective remedies have become known in training halls. Do not strike or hit the unconscious person. Do not pour water on him. Do not put medicine, water, ice, or anything in the mouth. Do not hit or knee them in the spine. Do not massage the side of the neck. Receptors in the neck can lower heart rate when stimulated. Do not stand or sit the unconscious or recovering person up. Blood is trying to get back to the brain. Upright position will drain it away. During a match, if your opponent goes unconscious from a choke, immediately lower them to the ground.

The same principles hold for someone unconscious from a blow, with added concerns of brain and neck injury. Do not shake the person or tip back the head if spinal trauma at the neck is suspected.

Learn rescue breathing and CPR. Various techniques called 'katsu' sit the person up to manually press air in and out or stimulate functions. Do not sit the person up. Lie them flat. Make sure their airway is open by gently tilting their head back if there is no neck injury. Check for breathing, watching the chest and abdomen, and listening and feeling for breathing with your cheek over their mouth. If they are not breathing, call emergency services and begin rescue breathing and CPR, according to your training. If they begin convulsing, do not restrain them or put anything in the mouth. Move objects they may accidentally hit. Note the precise time and their actions for later reporting. Don't volunteer too often for choke holds. Keep your hands up and protect your head from blows. The long-term effect of being without oxygen to the brain one or more times is not known.

Smoking

Your opponent will not injure you as much as you injure yourself. Smoking hurts your mind and body as a martial artist. Smoking is used because it has qualities to calm nerves, digestion, and hunger. At one time, smoking was prescribed by doctors for those effects, and thought of as a tonic. Smoking causes serious injuries that outweigh the benefits. Don't start smoking. It will be miserable to quit. If you smoke, quit. It will be even more miserable not to quit.

"Now that I'm gone, I tell you: don't smoke, whatever you do, don't smoke."
—Yul Brynner, Russian-Mongolian actor, in a television public service announcement that aired after his death from lung cancer

Cardiovascular Disease

Cardiovascular disease lowers capacity for exertion, and increases risk of illness or sudden death during exercise. Cardiovascular disease increases tendency to abnormal heart beats called arrhythmias. Many people dying a sudden death during physical activity have been found to have underlying heart disease.

Top risk factors for cardiovascular disease are cigarette smoking, high blood pressure, high cholesterol, and lack of exercise. Cardiovascular disease has a large nutrition and fitness component. Reduce your risk by changing what you eat and how much you exercise. Exercising regularly reduces stress, blood pressure, bad cholesterol, and your risk of diabetes, which is a risk factor for heart disease. Exercise helps your body regulate blood levels of insulin, which controls blood sugar. You can prevent or control most kinds of diabetes with exercise and not eating junk. Cut back on simple sugar and trans-fat in your diet, both unhealthy for the blood vessels. Are you dependent on steroids for bodybuilding? Steroids can raise cholesterol, and change your brain and other important parts. Get your muscles through honest training and save your money and health. Even with no other risk factors you may have a sudden heart attack if you use cocaine. Stimulants like amphetamines, ephedra, and Ritalin raise risk of heart trouble. Don't smoke. Unhealthy habits injure you more than any opponent could. Get enough sleep. Sleep deprivation is tough on the heart. Don't take a lot of acetaminophen and other nonsteroidal anti-inflammatory drugs (NSAIDS), cold medicines, ginseng, and licorice herb over long periods. They are linked to high blood pressure. Constant use of acetaminophen (paracetamol outside the US) is a factor in liver damage. Long use of other anti-inflammatories can make problems from stomach damage to irreversible ringing in the ears. If you have joint or muscle pain, treat the cause, not the symptoms with pills. When working out or sparring, warm up first and build up your capacity for work through regular exercise.

Clogged and injured blood vessels don't just affect the heart: Reduced blood flow to the brain can hurt mental processes. Senile behavior used to be called "hardening of the arteries." Another warning of cardiovascular disease is reduced blood flow to the genitalia. The

Achilles tendon, the cord that attaches the fleshy calf muscle to your heel, is also hurt by narrowed and hardened blood vessels. People with Achilles pulls and tears, and reduced vascular response of the genitalia should be checked for cholesterol and other indicators of heart health.

Herbal Medicines

Herbal and botanical medicines are medicines like any other. They have side effects like any other medicine. Being natural does not automatically mean they are healthy or safe. Anthrax is natural and tobacco is an herbal product. Dependence on Eastern medicine is no different than dependence on Western pills. For example, some ancient remedies to increase energy and reduce pain contain a stimulant and a plant sterol, making them the equivalent of taking a cup of coffee and a Motrin.

Herbs may be grown using pesticides, fungicides, and other chemicals that transmit to the final product. Mixing herbs can cause unhealthy interactions. Herbal medicines are not regulated, meaning anyone can make any claim of cures, true or not. Use them intelligently. Use the lowest dose needed for the problem. Do not take them for extended periods. Avoid casual use or for small things your body can heal on its own. Use food, exercise, and good health practices as medicine wherever you can, instead of dependence on medicine. Keep your common sense and don't fall for fantasy claims.

"Let us be as real people. Let us be genuine people who don't require doctors, medicine, aspirin, codeine, all the rest of it. Let us just be basic human beings."
—Chögyam Trungpa of Tibet

Making Weight

Fighters sometimes do unhealthy things meet weight requirements for wrestling, boxing, and physical appearance. Losing many pounds of water in a short time is not losing fat. Some fighters restrict fruit and vegetables to lose water, and eat meat because meat helps dehydrate the body. Remember that water is helpful in your body to win a fight and be healthy. Carbohydrate is so important to fueling exercise that the body stores it in the muscles and liver in a form called glycogen. The larger the stores, the longer you can exercise before fatigue. Glycogen holds water in the muscles. Muscle water is needed for good muscle contractility, strength, and a healthy muscular look. Depleting carbohydrate through low carbohydrate diet depletes body stores of water, making you smaller. This is not fat loss, and does not help your martial arts. A dehydrated, carbohydrate-deprived athlete is more likely to have an injury or loss in a fight. Plan ahead if you need to "make weight." Exercise and eat healthy food without overeating to lose weight.

Eating Disorder

Both male and female athletes can have an eating disorder. Eating disorders are not always identified by low body weight. Body weight may be normal or above normal. Hidden problems are malnutrition, reduced bone density and increased risk of osteoporosis, impaired reproductive function in both males and females from malnutrition, bad teeth and cramps from intentional vomiting, and dehydration. Disordered eating may not be as obvious as vomiting food. It can be fixation on fad diets, restricting food, and overeating. Eating disorders are unhealthy for martial arts. Find out why you have problems with food. Sometimes it is no more than bad habits. Then don't use those problems as an excuse. Don't take pain out on yourself. Being a continuing victim is not the way of the martial arts. Don't fall for fad diets to solve weight problems. Use knowledge of healthy nutrition. Eating disorders are not all psychological. Eating refined sugar can produce craving for more in a continuing cycle.

It is not true that eating a low fat diet causes insulin problems and hunger. Salty, fatty, fast food also contributes. All food stimulates insulin, because insulin is needed to move both carbohydrate and protein into cells. Healthy low fat eating includes complex carbohydrates from fruit and vegetables, which keep blood sugar steady, not a junk food diet of sugar. Check if there is monosodium glutamate in food. It makes the desire for the taste of food stronger. Don't fall for fad diets. Keep your wits and make a pledge that health comes first.

Take Action to Stop Injury

With understanding and knowledge, right thought and conduct follow. Right thought, right action, right speech is all ahimsa. Ahimsa is the Hindu, Jainist, and Buddhist principle of non-injury. Ahimsa was reintroduced to the West by the Mahatma Gandhi, and applied by leaders like Martin Luther King Jr. The vow of ahimsa, the ahimsa-vrata, is the foremost of all the maha-vratas, the great vows. When you understand and live ahimsa, then arokaya, or non-illness follows.

Don't harm yourself. Don't harm others. Don't cause others to do harm. Don't harm yourself through destructive thoughts and bad company. Don't harm others through destructive words and actions. Keep your word. Don't harm property with littering and stealing. Don't harm animals or the weak. Don't harm yourself through unhealthy eating. Don't harm yourself through unhealthy exercise.

Mental Injury

What can you do when something injures your psyche by gnawing at you, keeping you from focusing, and keeping you awake at night? You must learn to put it down and walk away. Here is the story of the Two Monks and the River.

Two monks walked in silence. It was their custom, and silence their vow. They walked far. They came to a river. The only way across was to walk through the high water. There at the riverbank was a fine woman, wearing good clothes. She could not get across the river.

The first monk asked her, "May I?" He picked her up and carried her across the river. Then set her down.

The two monks walked miles until the second one couldn't control himself. He broke the silence. "First Brother Monk! How could you have done this terrible thing? You broke our vow of silence. You touched a woman. You saw her fine clothes. Spoke to her! It is not our way. How could you have done such a terrible thing? I can't meditate. I can't see the beauty of the path. I can only think of the terrible thing you did."

The first monk looked at his friend and said, "Second Brother Monk, I carried her across the river. You are still carrying her."

Don't be injured by past negative thoughts. Put them down and walk away.

"Pain is the best instructor,
but no one wants to go to his class."
—Choi Hong Hi, founder of Tae Kwon Do

Soreness

Soreness can develop in the days after hard activity. The type of soreness that develops after, rather than during activity, is called delayed onset muscle soreness (DOMS). This chapter tells how the interesting process of delayed soreness develops, and healthy ways to deal with it.

How Muscles Get Sore

Anyone can be sore following hard activity, whether out-of-shape or highly conditioned. Delayed soreness is not from lactic acid produced during hard activity, and is not just muscle fatigue. In brief, stress to muscle fibers starts a chain of events that releases inflammatory chemicals that begin the healing process. The inflammatory response attracts white blood cells and other healing cells and chemicals. Your body regulates healing with a balance of pro-inflammatory and anti-inflammatory components. The result of this balance is that you are stiff, sore, and weak for one to five days.

It is sometimes said that soreness mostly comes from lengthening muscles under load, called an eccentric contraction. However, soreness can result from all the different ways that muscles work. When muscles shorten to do their job, it is called concentric muscular contraction. Contracting the quadriceps muscles in the thigh for kicks, and biceps in the arm for throws are concentric muscle contractions. Isometric contraction maintains the muscle at one length while under tension, for example, chokes, holds, locks, and for holding good posture and joint position when standing. Eccentric muscular contraction is when the muscle works while getting longer. You work muscles eccentrically when lowering yourself or weights, going down hills, and many controlled motions. When going to low stances, leg muscles lengthen while in high contractile state, to lower your body at your chosen speed and direction. You can be sore after working hard at any of these activities.

Preventing Muscle Soreness

Soreness in muscles usually means a good workout. Do not fear it. If you are not sore, are you really working at any new or harder things?

"I was unable to walk for a whole week after that, so much did the race take out of me. But it was the most pleasant exhaustion I have ever known."
—Emil Zatopek describing his marathon win at the 1952 Helsinki Olympics

Not much reduces incidence of soreness from hard efforts. Still, work out regularly. Vary training. Eat healthful food before physical training to fuel exertion. Eat soon after exercise to restock the muscle carbohydrate needed for energy, and ability to exercise. Muscles should be sore after hard exercise, but not joints, which indicates injurious form or practices.

Check if pain is not soreness or fatigue, but injury from strained muscle fibers from poor posture, or joints twisted into harmful positions. If pain, tearing, or pinching is felt in a joint, or a feeling like electricity radiates down a limb, that is likely an injury process. Note if joints feel hot or swollen following efforts.

Soreness from training with poor body ergonomics, such as forward head and rounded shoulders and upper back, will often be later felt in the neck, upper back and shoulders, or in a headache. Pain from keeping too much inward curve in the lumbar spine (hyperlordotic posture, also called swayback, arch, or too much lordosis) will often be felt in the lower back and posterior hip after long standing and running. Pain from rounding the low back forward for sitting, stretching, exercising, and lifting contributes to lower back and disc pain.

Identify and change injurious movements to healthy ones. If you have hyperlordosis from arching the lower back and tilting your pelvis out in back, tuck hips under enough to stand straight without pushing the hip forward. If you have hyperlordosis from leaning the upper body backward, don't move the hip, but bring the upper body forward until upright. Don't tighten abdominal muscles, just use them to change vertebral and pelvic angle, similar to changing any other posture. Tight muscles reduce shock absorption and ability to breathe and move properly. Keep your body in healthy positioning so that your exercise and all daily movement becomes your built-in health promoter and injury prevention.

Eat as soon following hard exercise as practical, to restock the muscle glycogen to reduce fatigue on subsequent exertions. Eating within the first 30 minutes restocks the most glycogen, but eating in the first two hours is also helpful. Not eating after exercise results in lowered glycogen for many days after, reducing exercise capacity. Take a hot bath, where available. Reward yourself for the grand effort. After resting, return to activity to become better accustomed to the activity and induce less soreness on subsequent efforts.

Treating Muscle Soreness

Movement. No specific warm-up or stretching before activity prevents soreness from exertion. Several expensive devices make claims of healing by introducing specific energy wavelengths, light waves, or vibrational energy and "chi" to the area. These are mostly heat lamps. Hot cloths are hot baths are as good. To reduce soreness after activity, keep sore areas warm and moving. To reduce stiffness, stretch the areas.

Anti-inflammatory Food. Eat food with anti-inflammatory components to help soothe inflammation: leafy green vegetables, cherries, dark grapes with seeds, blueberries, flax seeds, hemp seeds, pumpkin seeds, olive oil, fermented soy, and the spices curcumin (turmeric) and ginger. These are light and easily carried as snacks.

Eating fruit and vegetables with the peels seems to give more helpful nutrition. Plants have to protect themselves from bugs and infections. Many natural compounds are present in their peels, because the peel is their defense. Salicylic acid is the anti-inflammatory chemical in aspirin. Plants produce it to protect themselves. Organic vegetables have higher concentrations of salicylic acid than non-organic vegetables because they were less likely to be sprayed with pesticides and had to produce their own natural defense. Willow bark is high in salicylic acid and was an original source of aspirin. Good amounts are found in strawberries, almonds, and tomatoes.

Some foods convert into inflammatory compounds when eaten in excess. Avoid foods that convert omega-6 fatty acids into pro-inflammatory compounds: beef, chicken, cooking oils like corn oil, and possibly refined sugar.

Muscle Balms. Traditional injury medicine was called Dit Da (tieh ta), variously translated as "fall and hit medicine." This early trauma medicine included bone setting, massage, exercise, medicinals, and compassionate guidance for mental wound healing. The variety of liniments and potions developed were the dit da jow (tieh ta jiu), translated as "hit wine" or "iron wine," referring both to the injury and the high proof vodka and other strong spirits they are made from.

Preparations have varied ingredients depending on desired effect. Those for aches from blows and exertion may give a feeling of cold with menthol, or heat with ingredients like allspice or eugenol, which is extracted from clove oil and cinnamon. Some add local numbing to make it seem like it hurts less, with clove oil, methyl salicylates, either in direct form or as naturally occurring in wintergreen (gautheria), sweet birch, and betulia oil from Russian birch. Remedies for cuts may add an astringent like witch hazel, antibacterial and antifungal agents like wormwood; antiseptics like goldenseal, garlic, myrrh, tea tree oil, cloves, honey, or modern equivalents, and a styptic to stop or slow bleeding.

Many traditional and modern muscle rubs use a principle called "counter-irritant." They make a new irritation to counter the original uncomfortable feeling. This works like shaking or rubbing your hand after painfully hitting it. Examples are capsaicin, derived from the hot pepper (capsicum), benzoic acid (component of Russian church incense), camphor, cajuput oil, and turpentine, which are strong irritants to the skin and mucous membranes.

Some compounds add fever reducers, or agents to toughen the skin, like tannic acid. Some ancient potions added fragrance to hide the smell of infected or healing areas, or give a medicinal character to enhance perceived benefit. Compounds brewed for internal use may add ingredients to speed wound healing and reduce inflammation like comfrey, ginger, and turmeric. Some may dull the senses (sometimes dangerously), like absinth made from one of the components of wormwood. Some balms and salves have a large base of petroleum jelly. Petroleum products are unhealthy for the body. Modern products are often menthol and methyl salicylate with preservatives, dyes, fragrances, and thickeners.

Not all preparations do what they say or imply. Soreness usually passes with time, regardless. Some have little of the advertised active ingredient. Some add more injury with toxic ingredients than the original injury. High skin absorption makes several of these compounds dangerous for children. Because of the high alcohol content and the teaching that you must help your opponent after a fight by sharing your medicine, the healing perception of many traditional jows may be more related to the shared drinking.

Reducing Mental Pain and Soreness

What can you do about mental pain? How can you be free of the pain of regret and unforgiveness? What can you do about the pains that are too great to forgive?

The Master told the students to take a potato and write the name of a person they could not forgive. Then take another potato and write the next pain. Then the next. They put each potato into a bag. Some of the students' bags were heavy. The master told them to carry this bag with them everywhere, to put it beside their bed at night, next to their desk, everywhere they went. Over time, the bag of pain and potatoes began to smell. It became slimy. Still, the students were told to carry their pain and potatoes everywhere. Eventually they did not want their pain any more. What a weight they were carrying spiritually. This was the price for keeping pain. What was once too hard to let go of, was now something they didn't want to hold on to. The students wanted to let go of their pain and potatoes and wash themselves from the smell. Too often we think of forgiveness as a gift to the other person. It is for ourselves. Don't keep pain until it stinks. Throw away your pain. Let it wash away.

"Leave your drugs in the chemist's pot
if you can heal the patient with food."
—Hippocrates

Performance Enhancement

Hundreds of products are advertised to give energy, cause weight loss, or make you faster and stronger. Some may do those things, but are unhealthy. Some are banned in athletics or are illegal because they are unhealthy. Some don't work. Some are simple, good nutrition that you can make yourself. This chapter tells how different products and substances work and don't work in your body, so you can make wise, healthy choices.

Performance Food is Not New

Substances to alter physical and mental state have been used in many places around the world. Mountain people have long used stimulant plants like coffee, kola, khat, betel nut, and coca to withstand cold, thin air, hunger, and fatigue. Aztec warriors ate the hearts of brave enemies, believing it would increase their own bravery. Before the first Olympics in 776 B.C., athletes tried to enhance performance by drinking wine to dull pain. Soldiers widely used amphetamines to delay fatigue. Authorities in warfare and medical practice distributed amphetamines until recent times when the dangers became known, some even after. Australian Aborigines used the nicotine-rich plant *pituri* to help them endure desert travel without food. Indigenous animals chew various parts of stimulant plants, while others know when fruit ferments and seek it for the drunken effects.

Performance Food Has Moved Away From Original Use

Modern products often concentrate, distill, and combine products to intensify effects. Some previously mild and useful substances became used in ways that are unhealthy or addictive. Mass production may add unhealthy components, and diminish beneficial ingredients through heating, drying, chemically enhancing, and processing.

Performance Food Can Have Conflicting Effects

Smoking cigarettes "works" to lose weight. It "works" and feels good, but it is still not good for you. You can use wine to dull pain to prepare for a fight, but also dull your body enough to lose a fight or know when to fight and when not to. Many performance-enhancing products have mixed effects. There is no need to take the bad with the good. By learning how they work, you can discard unhealthy practices and get healthy effects in healthy ways.

Caffeine

Caffeine is the main stimulating compound in coffee and kola nut. Kola nuts are nutlike seeds containing caffeine and other substances used in sodas and pharmaceuticals. Caffeine was probably discovered in the Stone Age and widely used ever since. Goats in the Middle East are credited with showing the effects of eating coffee seeds to humans. Although popularly called "coffee beans," coffee seeds look like, but are not real beans.

Many people drink caffeine drinks for socializing, for energy, for dieting, and for staying awake, never realizing it is something that the body accustoms to, or that there is a down side. Negative cycles build of need and use. Some people start using caffeine because they heard it helps endurance in long athletic events. Those who drink coffee every day do not get the benefits of this effect. They do worse without it and are stuck in a negative cycle. Others drink coffee because they think it gives them energy for staying awake for deskwork. Energy is for moving the body. Without exercise, the stimulating effects can be unhealthy and agitating.

Unhealthy effects come with mixing caffeine and cold medications, ephedra, ginseng, stimulants, and some prescription drugs. Phenylpropanolamine (PPA) is a decongestant and weight control drug. Mixing caffeine with PPA increases risk of hemorrhagic stroke. The FDA banned the combination in 1983.

Dependence and withdrawal from not getting the accustomed amount of caffeine from soda and coffee can be severe. Withdrawal rebound headaches, tiredness, moodiness, inability to function without it, and other effects are common. The solution lies in using less not more.

Guarana

Guarana is commonly found in supplements and drinks for "energy" and headache relief. It works for headache relief by supplying the caffeine-like substance craved in a caffeine-withdrawal headache. Guarana is made from the crushed seeds of *Paullinia cupana*, a South American vine. The active chemical in Guarana may be guaranine. Guaranine is like caffeine, with similar effects. Coffee contains between one and four percent caffeine. Guaranine is reported to either contain, or be the equivalent of, five percent caffeine. It also has smaller amounts of the other substances in tea and chocolate. Like using caffeine, get insight into why you use it. See if you are dependent, get headaches, or don't feel well without it.

Yerba Mate

Yerba mate (pronounced MOT-tay) is a South American tea-like beverage made from mate. Mate is an evergreen holly called *flex paraguariensis*. It contains plant substances, vitamins, small amounts of the main chemicals in tea and chocolate, and a small amount of a chemical like caffeine called mateine. These chemicals attract much speculation about possible benefit. One claim is that people with caffeine sensitivities can drink mate for stimulation without insomnia and irritability.

Like other substances processed for sale, the yerba mate in stores may be far from the effects from the original plant. At least three studies link mate consumption with cancer but there are too many variables to know if this is an effect from the plant, the processing, or mixing it with other foods and habits. Like other comfort drinks, the less you depend on external substances to increase your activity and ability to control mood, the less the effects of these substances will control you.

Nicotine

Nicotine's stimulant effects have been long used to decrease hunger and fatigue. Nicotine is usually chewed or smoked, although nicotine patches and gum have been used to try to boost alertness. Mostly people use nicotine because it has become a habit.

Nicotine can increase alertness, but does not enhance physical ability. Nicotine is an addictive, poisonous alkaloid. The negative effects on health make smoking something that martial artists would shun. If your peers require smoking for coolness, they are not cool or healthy. You do not have to follow them by smoking. They can follow you by not smoking. If you are addicted, that is still no reason to smoke.

Amphetamines

Amphetamines are addictive stimulants. Methedrine (methamphetamine or meth), benzedrine (laevoamphetamine, benzie, or bennies), and dexedrine (dextroamphetamine, dex, or dexies) are all amphetamines. Street names are speed, uppers, amp, road dope, diet pills, sparkle plenty, and others that describe the effects or appearance.

Amphetamines are not new. Amphetamines were first synthesized in the United States as a substitute for Chinese ephedra, when the Chinese supply was cut off after World War I. Amphetamines were widely distributed to World War II soldiers, sailors, and airmen to reduce their regard for rest or conscience. A tremendous post-war epidemic followed in several countries.

Amphetamines are used by dieters and exercisers to stop hunger and fatigue, and by self-medicators trying to feel happy. Withdrawal brings fatigue, rebound appetite, and intense withdrawal depression. Users purchase more, or do things they would not previously do to get more to stop the uncomfortable symptoms. Higher doses are needed for the same effect. This is addiction. Addiction builds in the first weeks of use. It quickly reaches a level that is uncomfortable to break.

Stimulation causes high or irregular heart rates and raised blood pressure. Abdominal cramps, incoordination, dizziness, dry mouth, nausea, and vomiting may accompany initial use. Along with their high, users can have changes in mental states resembling paranoid schizophrenia. Chronic users have been found to have damage in several brain areas. Increased side effects occur when mixing amphetamines with other common substances like antidepressants, alcohol, cold medicine, ginseng, caffeine, diet pills, diuretics (water pills) and many medications for cardiovascular, respiratory, and other illnesses. Amphetamines increase risk of overheating. Deaths in the heat have been reported in endurance athletes and soldiers taking amphetamines hoping to extend endurance, and dieters taking appetite suppressants then exercising in the heat.

Methamphetamine

"Meth" is an addictive amphetamine. Street names are speed, crystal, ice, glass, crank, tweak, zip, ya ba in Asia (meaning crazy medicine), and others. It is sometimes made from cold medicines containing pseudoephedrine, a main ingredient of methamphetamine. Smoked, snorted, swallowed, or injected, methamphetamine often cause irritability, insomnia, anxiety, hallucinations, paranoia, neglectful behavior, promiscuity, and violence. The user is not always aware of destructive behaviors, or does not care. The extreme dry mouth common with frequent methamphetamine use can result in severe dental rot and tooth loss known as "meth-mouth." Meth is illegal and counterproductive to martial artists who want to be healthy and happy.

Cocaine

Cocaine is a powerful cardiovascular stimulant. Although there are smarter ways to increase physical performance, people take cocaine to increase speed and endurance. Cocaine's effects come from making the nervous system send more chemical signals. The problem is that the intense stimulation uses up the signaling chemicals called catecholamines. Without catecholamines to transmit nerve impulses, the body experiences intense loss of many functions. This is the cocaine crash. Users often have big changes in health, personality, money handling, and ethics. Sudden heart attack may occur, even with no predisposition to heart disease. Combined with alcohol, cocaine becomes cocaethylene, a compound where each ingredient greatly increases the action of the other. Side effects increase when mixed with anti-depressants and many common medicines. Addictive, expensive, illegal, socially and medically unhealthy, cocaine is unsuitable and profoundly unwise for martial artists and any healthy athletic efforts.

Khat

Khat is a plant that grows in East Africa and southern Arabia. The leaves are chewed for amphetamine-like stimulation. Leaves contain the alkaloid cathinone, and a milder form of cathinone called cathine. Cathinone works like amphetamine to increase blood pressure, heart rate, and mental and verbal stimulation. People talk excitedly, thinking their ideas important. Tribal rulers even gave it in social situations to visiting rivals, to encourage them to spill their strategies. Cathine is one of the alkaloids found in Ephedra. Both cathinone and cathine are controlled substances. Cathinone is a Schedule I drug, meaning it is considered the most dangerous class of drug with no recognized medical use. Cathine is also a controlled drug in schedule IV. These can lead to dependence. Don't blow a martial arts career with drugs.

Ephedra, Ma Huang, and Weight Loss Products

Ephedra is used because it has effects similar to amphetamine but to a smaller degree. Many dozens of products that have, or used to have, ephedra in varying amounts and forms, with claims of weight loss or energy increase. Ephedra is a shrub native to Pakistan, China, and northwestern India. The three kinds of ephedra plant are known by their Chinese name, ma huang. Mormons used a variety known to native American Indians, instead of coffee and tea in the 1800's. It is called Mormon Tea and Squaw Tea, but is not ma huang.

The ephedra plant has three active compounds ephedrine, pseudoephedrine, and norspeudoephedrine. They are strong central nervous system stimulants. Ephedrine opens the main airways of the lungs. Its main use is in treating asthma and respiratory problems. The problem is not when ephedra is used as a plant in low, normally occurring concentrations as a breathing medicine for a few doses, but when ephedrine is refined and concentrated as a stimulant and weight loss product and used often. More unhealthy problems occur when it is mixed with other products like caffeine to enhance effects, or used when exerting in the heat.

Effects do not always depend on dose. Nervous system effects like insomnia, tremors, anxiety, and seizures have occurred. Ephedra is associated with a small number of cases of heart trouble, abnormal heart rhythms, heart attack, and sudden death. The effect to increase blood pressure may be one factor in adding to risk of stroke. Ephedrine causes uterine contractions. Don't use if pregnant. The risks show that ephedra is not smart, needed, or helpful for martial artists. There are easier, smarter, healthier, and more fun ways to get energy and work off calories.

Ginseng

Ginseng can be any of several different plant species from different countries, each with different effects. The root of the ginseng plant is usually used. Ginseng is used in candies, pills, and drinks, with claims of energy or well-being. The active compounds vary with species of the plant, age, location, and method and timing of harvest and processing. Main active agents are ginsenosides. Investigations have found that many ginseng preparations contain other stimulating compounds, usually caffeine, which account for some of the claimed effects. Interpretation of claims of the many different products is difficult because ginsenoside content varies, with some preparations containing none at all.

Ginseng may make you feel stimulated, but does not seem to increase true athletic ability. It is one thing to use a small amount in plant form as a pleasant tasting drink with benign effects, and another to continually use concentrated pills and drinks that overstimulate, and mix them with other stimulants and interacting ingredients. Diarrhea, nervousness, blood glucose changes, and insomnia may result. It is unhealthy to mix ginseng with caffeine, the blood thinner warfarin (Coumadin), and an older class of antidepressants called monoamine oxidase inhibitors, which includes Marplan (isocarboxazid) and Nardil (phenelzine). Withdrawal lethargy and depression are another good reason to remember that ginseng is for occasional, not regular use.

Anabolic Steroids

Anabolic steroids are controlled drugs. Anabolic is an abbreviation for ana-metabolic. It means adding an ingredient to build body tissue as part of metabolism. Anabolic steroids build muscles when used with intense training and adequate nutrition. Users may take 10 to 100 times the dose ordinarily used for medical conditions. A large black market exists for prescription medical and veterinary anabolics like trenbolone, which is used to increase weight of cattle. A related steroid is THG (tetrahydrogestrinone), a designer anabolic steroid derived from gestrinone, a European drug for endometriosis, which is abnormal growth of tissue in the uterus.

Anabolic steroids can help grow muscle. They don't improve aerobic conditioning. One problem with anabolic steroids is that long-term use reduces your own body's production of male hormones. Male genitalia can shrink permanently. Several popular steroids increase activity of the female hormone progesterone. Other steroids turn into the female hormone estrogen. Men's breasts can grow. The conversion is called aromatization. Aromatizing steroids include boldenone (Equipoise), methandrostenolone sold as Dbol, Dronabol,

Dianabol, and Danabol, and to a lesser extent fluoxymesterone (Halotestin). Users trying to avoid estrogenic side effects, or trying to recover depressed testosterone production after a "cycle" of use, have to purchase and "stack" or combine anti-estrogens like Cytadren (aminoglutethimide) and Clomid (clomiphene). These have their own side effects. The pattern of increasing a dose through a cycle is called "pyramiding." Pyramiding has its own problems. Taking steroids preferentially raises only some hormone levels, changing how they interact with others in the body.

Tendons and ligaments do not strengthen as quickly as muscle from steroid use. They may tear in competition or training. Emotional changes, dependency, night sweats, bloated swollen "moon-roid" face, and other unhealthy effects may take time to occur, lulling users into thinking they will not get problems. Withdrawal depression can occur. Acne is common. There are reports of afflicted users taking prescription acne medications that have serious depression as a side effect. In women, genitalia and facial and body hair may grow irreversibly, but head hair can thin. Infection and abscess are not uncommon at sites of repeated injection. Drinking alcohol while taking steroids increases risks to the heart and liver. Mixing anabolic steroids with common substances like antidepressants, coffee, stimulants, cold medicines, ephedrine (ephedra stacking), and street drugs adds unhealthy interactions.

Instead of taking steroids, you can raise your own levels of hormones for strength and growth naturally and in healthy arrangement with other body chemicals by regular exercise. Some steroid users state that they do not care if it kills them as long as they put a muscular corpse in the coffin. Martial arts is mind and body. So don't lose your mind. Steroids do not give you martial arts skill or ability. Bigger muscles alone are a bigger target to hit. Training without steroids gives you healthier, wiser, less expensive, and legal muscle. Training without steroids trains judgment, discipline, and ability to be a role model. Give the money to worthy projects. You will be more looked up to that way, than by being a drug user.

Anabolic Non-Steroids, Muscle Builders, Weight Gainers

Not all steroids are anabolic. Vitamin D and adrenal hormones are steroids, for example, but they do not build muscles. Not everything that is anabolic is a steroid either. Substances that add body weight and help build body tissue are considered anabolic. This includes regular food. Many products that call themselves anabolic and give the perception of being something that will build muscle. All they have to do is supply calories to let you gain weight— even fat weight—whether the ingredients are healthy or not, to truthfully sell themselves as anabolic or bodybuilding. Check the labels for refined sugar, stimulants, trans and hydrogenated fat, artificial flavors and other unhealthy things. Don't be fooled by a few vitamins thrown in. Healthy nutrition with good training will build your body just as well, and more cheaply.

Growth Hormone

Growth hormone is naturally made in the pituitary gland. It does several things, including stimulating protein to make muscle. Aging alone does not cause deficiency. Levels diminish with lack of exercise, high dietary blood sugar, certain anti-inflammatory medicines, and lack of sleep. Injecting synthetic forms reduces natural production but does not (as far as known) cause the serious damage of steroids. Problems are joint pain, wrist pain, carpal tunnel syndrome, joint swelling, facial swelling, facial elongation, increased blood pressure, decreased thyroid function, and increase risk of diabetes. It can increase tumor growth in existing cancer. Hormone doping is expensive and lengthy before results occur. For bigger results, users combine, or "stack," growth hormone with anabolic steroids. Some add the dangerous practice of injecting insulin for a leaner look. Insulin doping can cause serious, long-term illnesses. There is more to growth, metabolizing fat, or building muscle than taking hormones. You can be younger, leaner, and stronger without injections through the three main things that stimulate human growth hormone—healthy exercise, sleep, and eating right.

DHEA

DHEA is a weak intermediate or non-steroid, the most abundant one naturally made in the body. The initials stand for dehydro-3-epiandrosterone. DHEA is manufactured mostly in the adrenal glands from cholesterol, and to a smaller extent in the ovaries and testes. People buy it hoping it will convert only to testosterone. But DHEA converts to dozens of hormones including both estrogen and testosterone in both men and women.

DHEA levels wane with age and some illnesses. Some people question if restoring levels will reduce effects of age and disease. It's unknown if lowered DHEA causes the problems or just happens along with them. Many substances decrease in the body for good reasons, because they are not needed or even healthy to have after a certain time. Restoring them may not reverse aging, raise testosterone level, or do any good. Before taking DHEA, have blood levels checked for deficiency. Because of the several different possible hormone effects and many effects still unknown, people with a family history of breast or prostate cancer should not take DHEA.

Androstenedione

Androstenedione, or "andro" is made in the body from DHEA. This occurs naturally without supplementation. Androstenedione is a precursor molecule to both testosterone and estrogen. Which hormone androstenedione becomes depends on several factors. For example, high percentage of body fat increases the tendency of going to estrogen, the female hormone, not testosterone. Popularity of use seems to come from people hearing that it is a precursor molecule to testosterone. For perspective, cholesterol is also a precursor molecule to testosterone, but eating more cholesterol does not increase testosterone. Reports from gyms and andro manufacturers state that athletic ability is always greatly helped. Controlled studies don't find that it helps. Some studies show increased strength, but the same as control groups with matched exercise without andro. Supplementation may suppress your own production. Over-the-counter androstenedione supplements have sometimes been found to have other elements not on the label that can cause a positive drug test for other banned substances.

You do not have to choose between health and muscles. Regular training naturally raises your own hormone levels to those that build a fitter healthier body. Androstenedione will not give you the technique and experience needed to improve your martial arts. You can build plenty of muscle and physical ability without androstenedione.

Protein

Advertising for protein products wants you to believe that eating more protein builds muscle and loses fat. Protein has many functions in the body. Eating more protein does not automatically increase these functions. One function of protein is making skin pigment. Another is making skin. Eating more protein does not darken your skin or grow extra skin.

Exercise brings the protein in meals to your muscles. Eating extra protein does not build muscle. Your body does not use all the protein eaten in an average Western diet. When you exercise more, you use a small amount more protein. You may still not use all the protein you eat.

Muscles are not made only of protein. You need more carbohydrate when you exercise to fuel that exercise and build muscle. More water, too. Your body recycles protein from old cells that are being broken down during everyday repair. You need very little extra protein to build new muscles. It is not necessary to eat high amounts of protein to get better training results or lose weight.

Proteins are big molecules made of smaller amino acids. Your body makes some of the amino acids you need. The amino acids you can't make, you need to eat. These are called essential amino acids. All essential amino acids are present in plants in varying amounts. It is not necessary to eat meat to get complete protein, high quality protein, or enough protein. It is not necessary to carefully mix the right amino acids in each meal to get complete protein. Essential amino acids combine in your system over the day of eating varied meals. Avoid fad diets and folk tales to only eat single food items. Protein and other nutrients work better in combination.

Know the big picture, not just the claims. Some studies of supplementing protein show greater performance after their supplement. Sometimes the method of the study is to deplete body protein in subjects first. In these cases, adding protein helps. Some studies are done by the manufacturer, without strong basis in scientific method. Some studies are misinterpreted or results taken out of context of what they actually studied. Avoid the lure of half-facts. It helps to know the real study, not just the marketing. Claims of more digestible protein in meat or designer pills, powders, and dairy foods, does not mean your body will use more of the protein. There are claims that high protein diets reduce the production of insulin that stores fat in the cells. That doesn't tell the rest of how insulin works. Insulin transports both amino acids and fat into cells. That's part of how you digest food.

Keep your diet healthy without overloading on protein. Too much iron in the diet from eating a lot of meat is associated with higher rate of heart disease. Eating meat protein increases loss of calcium from bones. Plant protein does not. Eating a lot of meat can be dehydrating, which can give the illusion of weight loss but is not the same as fat loss. Eating high protein without eating much carbohydrate results on loss of the muscle glycogen that holds water in muscles, resulting in loss in size from loss of water. This is also not fat loss.

Remember that many protein supplements are just food in an expensive wrapper, little more than candy bars with some protein. Remember that things sold in "health food" stores can still be junk food. Check the labels of protein powders and supplements for fillers, artificial flavors, dyes, thickeners, artificial sweeteners, and many hidden simple sugars. Certain sugar substitutes cause a lot of gas, as do protein supplements of soy and whey. Try non-soy, non-whey vegetable protein instead with no added sugar or artificial sweetener. Experiment with making your own protein bars by pressing together raw oats, shredded coconut, cooked brown rice, sticky rice, sesame seeds, sunflower seeds, cooked sweet peas, various nuts, and any of a variety of natural flavoring like cocoa powder, anise, a little honey, cinnamon, mint, various fruits, and vanilla bean. Don't overdo; they are high calorie.

There is much high quality protein in grains, legumes, and vegetables. Don't be fooled by tales of people who got a particular result from highly supplemented protein and fad diets that restrict fruit and vegetables. Their results were from training, which would occur on normal amounts of protein. A healthier diet would have given better long-term benefits. It is tempting to believe that a better body will come from an expensive supplement. Eating supplements will not build your body. They will not make up for deficient nutrition or uninspired training. Give the money to the poor and get protein in healthful, real meals. Build a healthier body for less money from intelligent training and simple good nutrition.

Carbohydrate

Carbohydrate provides fuel and delays fatigue during long-duration exercise, and when doing many short bouts one after the next. Carbohydrate aids recovery after exercise. Carbohydrate is so important to exercise that it is stored in the muscles and liver in the form of glycogen. The larger the stores, the longer exercise can continue, depending on fitness level. Glycogen is stored by doing hard physical training then eating complex carbohydrate right after training. Eating in the first 30 minutes after bouts of exertion seems to store more, but eating within two hours helps. Not restocking glycogen can lead to fatigue during the next bout of exercise. While it is easy to store fat, you can only store enough carbohydrate to last an hour or two. Between events, have a piece of fruit, or a home-made blender drink. Put a whole kiwi fruit in the blender with a whole cucumber. If you can only get commercial cucumbers, the wax and pesticides on the skin makes it better to use them skinned. Blend to make a cool sweet fruit mush to drink. After training, restock carbohydrate from the healthy complex carbohydrate of fruit, whole grain, and vegetables, rather than sugar water. Don't overdo eating. Extra food of any kind can make you gain weight.

Vitamins and Minerals

Supplementation can be useful when nutrition is poor, for athletes in weight-restricted events who restrict food, and travel situations without access to healthy food. Supplementation is not always needed and will not improve physical ability if you have good nutrition. Many nutrients do not work as well in isolation in pills, but need the many other components of the whole food. Supplementing with vitamins and minerals is expensive, and makes the urine smell and become cloudy. It's tempting to put hopes on a small pill to do big things. Remember that the purpose of advertising is to make you want to spend the money for products, not tell you if you can do it in healthier, less expensive ways.

It's hard to know if food or supplements are better to provide certain vitamins. Modern growing and processing depletes many foods of usual nutrients. Chemicals are added to increase production, then food value is further lessened with long periods on the shelf, then the food may be cooked in unhealthy ways. To get better nutrition through food, try to find whole, fresh food from farms that use methods of keeping nutrient value of food. Prepare without unhealthy sugar, fatty sauces, or cooking until little vitamins are left. Many foods concentrate high amounts of nutrients that work together, such as brewer's yeast, kelp, seaweed, and raw wheat germ. Taste raw wheat germ to see if it's fresh. It will be sweet. Pills do not have the related nutrients that many vitamins and minerals need to work well. It can still be is healthier, cheaper, and more fun to get vitamins and minerals through whole food nutrition.

Bee Pollen

Bee pollen claims include various effects, from vague "vitality" to specific athletic improvements. Bee pollen has several nutritional components. It has not been shown to enhance any athletic aspect. It can provoke allergic reactions. Check the cause if you have recurrent itchy, watery, upper respiratory symptoms.

Water

Although water has no work-enhancing chemical or property, it is a needed and easy fluid replacer for healthy exercise and daily activities. You need enough water to help muscles work and to cool your skin. Without enough, ability to work, or keep yourself from overheating, or both, diminishes. Drinking too much will not enhance health or exercise ability. A common result of drinking too much water is overdiluting stomach acid, leading to many digestive complaints. In extreme, it dilutes the blood, a serious condition called hyponatremia. Drink more when you need it—in the heat and when training. Don't force drinking when not thirsty, or drink constantly all day.

Energy Drinks

Packaged "health" and sports drinks may contain stimulants of many kinds, including ginseng, guarana, variations of ephedra, caffeine, and others. Overuse of stimulants is associated with health problems and dependency. Check the label. Check if the drinks contain refined sugar, hydrogenated fat, dyes, artificial flavors, preservatives, and fillers. Some drinks are just sweetened water with various isolated vitamins added. It is cheaper, healthier, and more fun to make your own. Put clean water in a blender and add a kiwi fruit with skin, and a little fresh ginger root. Add a few grapes or berries. Or blend a green pepper. Tea drinkers can steep a tea bag for a few moments in the mix. For healthy effects of a chocolate shake without junk sugar, put water in a blender and add flax seeds, fresh coconut, and unsweetened cocoa powder. Hundreds of healthy combinations of sweet fruit, fresh greens, and spices are quick to make, and easy to take with you. The nutrition chapter gives options to try.

Brewer's Yeast

Brewer's yeast is a by-product of the brewing process. It is not the yeast used for baking. It is a combination of protein, vitamins, and minerals. It does not increase athletic performance, but is an easy aid to nutrition, which can help you exercise. Look for brewer's yeast that is not highly heat processed. Throw a tablespoon-full in cereal and blender drinks. Use in moderation.

Chocolate

Chocolate is made from fermenting the ground, roasted beans of the cacao tree. The primary chemical substance in chocolate is theobromine. Theobromine has two word roots. *"Theo-"* means God and *"broma"* comes from a word meaning food. The theobromine in chocolate was named for "food of the gods." Theobromine is an antioxidant, weak diuretic, stimulant, and mood booster, opens breathing airways, and relieves coughing. Dark chocolate contains higher levels of theobromine than lighter chocolate, along with good amounts of flavonoids and phenolics, plant substances that are good for the heart. Some people who get a kind of headache called migraine do better not eat chocolate. Otherwise, use unsweetened cocoa rather than candy chocolate, which is diluted and sweetened to a more unhealthful form. Unsweetened cocoa powder and baking squares are available inexpensively in the grocery store. Look for cocoa not processed with alkaline (not Dutch, or Dutched, chocolate). Add to blender drinks, baking, and cereal. For a healthy treat that is as creamy and sweet as ice cream, mash a frozen banana with cocoa powder. If you like crunch, add crushed pecans, walnuts, or flax seeds. Add flavor with cinnamon, crushed ginger root, and other spices.

Soda Doping, Soda-Loading

Soda doping involves drinking concentrated sodium bicarbonate, which is baking soda, or sodium citrate before short intense activity, in an attempt to delay muscle fatigue. During hard exercise lactic acid in working muscles builds. It was previously thought that lactic acid only fatigued the muscles. The hope of soda doping was for the alkaline sodium bicarbonate to neutralize the acid of the lactate. But lactic acid has many functions including serving as a fuel, to help increase breathing rate to get oxygen to the muscles, and to reduce the amount of muscle electrical activity it takes to fire the muscles. Common side effects of soda doping are diarrhea, cramps, bloating, and thirst, which can inhibit performance. Regular use of bicarbonate reduces normal stomach acid. Low stomach acid is a common hidden cause of recurring stomach pain, often mistaken for acid stomach, and compounded by a negative cycle of taking more antacids. Soda doping does not seem to have benefit for activities needed in the martial arts. Training gives better gains than any amount of baking soda.

Oxygen

Supplemental oxygen breathing used to be done by football players and other athletes on the sidelines. Unless you are ill or exercising at altitude, breathing extra oxygen does not help exercise or hasten recovery after exercise. In experiments of recovery from exercise, subjects could not tell if they were breathing 100 percent oxygen or regular room air and had no faster recovery with oxygen. In other studies, subjects were told they were breathing oxygen but received room air. Some subjects reported elevated mood. Their mood change was an illusion.

Several commercial drinks advertise oxygen dissolved in the drink. There is no exercise benefit to drinking these drinks. All liquids have dissolved gas because of the normal pressure of the air in the air around us. It may be true and legal to claim that their drinks have dissolved oxygen, but so does tap water. Some drinks are bottled with extra oxygen compressed into them. Most of the oxygen releases into the air upon opening, and the rest does not get absorbed into the blood where it can reach the cells. There is no benefit to drinking them. It is marketing hype.

For extra oxygen to help during exercise, you would have to carry an oxygen tank on a vehicle or your back and breathe it while doing continued activity. Another way to get additional oxygen is through regular physical training. Exercise makes many adaptations in your body to carry more oxygen to cells and extract more oxygen inside the cells. One adaptation is to make your body grow more oxygen-carrying red blood cells. Another way to trigger your body to produce extra red blood cells is to go to higher elevation, such as to the mountains. The percentage of oxygen in the air is still 21 percent at any altitude, but with less total air, the body doesn't get as much oxygen. Over several days to weeks at altitude, the body is stimulated to make more oxygen carrying cells. After days to weeks back at the original elevation, blood levels go back to normal. For sport competitions like short sprints, thin air does not affect performance. Sprinters find they run quickly, and golfers find the ball travels easier through thinner air. If you are competing in a sport needing aerobic effort that is held at a high elevation, go and train there before your event.

Some people get transfusions or take hormones to get more blood cells for training advantage. This is blood doping. The blood can become too concentrated with many unhealthy effects. There have been deaths. Blood doping will get you banned from sports. Get the same blood building effect in a healthy, legal way, plus all the other effects that doping can't give, through normal healthy nutrition and honest training.

Abdominal Exercise Machines, Electric Stimulation, and Metabolism Products

Many exercise machines claim to work the abdominal muscles. They may cite studies showing that using the product activates the muscles. The question is not if it happens to use a muscle. An exercise can work a muscle, but not be the way the muscle works for martial arts or anything else you do. The machines usually promote poor, bent-forward posture. Just like smoking "works" to lose weight, the forward-bending exercise of many machines "works" abdominal muscles but is not a healthy or functional way to exercise. You do not fight curled forward. Or stand up that way. Abdominal muscles do not automatically support the spine or prevent back pain, no matter how strong they are. Abdominal muscles work like all other skeletal muscles; they move your body. They only support your spine when you use them to move your hip and spine into healthy position, and prevent unhealthy position during movement. Simply strengthening abdominal muscles does not automatically change spinal posture. Plenty of muscular people have poor posture, bad movement habits, and back pain. Chapter 4 on abdominal and core training shows how to use your abdominal muscles to change painful spine postures, and gives many exercises to train and strengthen the abdominal muscle in the ways needed for real life and the martial arts.

Some electrical muscle stimulation devices are little more than vibrators with no effect to strengthen muscles. Others are similar to units used in physical therapy to passively contract muscles atrophied from paralysis or wasting diseases. There is muscle contraction, but not enough to produce the results claimed. Devices that wiggle the body through massaging belts or bands claim that moving the body stimulates blood flow. Exaggerated and false claims are made that increasing blood flow will take away fat or strengthen. This does not happen. Increasing blood flow does not strengthen areas. Bringing in oxygen does not make the cells use it. Exercise training does.

Some devices, pills, and patches claim to burn calories or fat while you sleep or watch television. They can claim that because the body always needs to burn calories and fat to stay alive. Even in sleep. It is not because of the pill or the machine, but the natural process of metabolism. Devices and pills claiming to increase metabolism after exercise ends can say that because all exercise does that. Exercise raises levels. It takes time to return to resting level after stopping. Other products claim to increase metabolism without exercise. They may contain stimulants that increase heart rate. That is not something helpful to the body. Exercise would do that more safely and burn more calories without the negative side effects of these products. Many products do nothing at all, but the act of using them encourages some people to remember their goals of eating less and exercising more. It is not the case that weight gain is inevitable with aging because of "lowered metabolism." When you are doing less activity than in earlier years, and eating more, that is not lowered metabolism.

Natural Performance Aids

Put on music if music makes you exercise more vigorously. Music can be your no-cost performance enhancer. Historically, people have sung and chanted during efforts to reduce the perceived exertion, using rhythmically repeated sea chanties, the "Jody Calls" of military training, mantras, hymns, and chants to deities. Thai boxing (Muay Thai) has long been done to the changing rates and pitches of the Pi Muay, the music of drums, flute and cymbals. If you exercise more easily with friends, then friends can be your performance aids. Children can be a great aid to exercise. Don't use your kids as an excuse not to exercise. Exercise with them to give them valuable physical and mental interaction with you. Lift young children and babies up and down instead of lifting weights. Use them (safely) as fun leg and arm weights, and on your back for pushups and pull-ups. Do short repetitions of moves from your martial art with older children. Put up a chinning bar or other safe, inexpensive way to be physical in the house and use it each time you pass. Under your guidance, even infants, who have natural reflex grip, can hang safely. Involve family members in healthy, caring, fun, and educational ways. Make martial arts and all exercise into natural activity.

Do Performance Pills and Supplements Work?

As much as we wish for results, some products don't work. Fortunately, the answer is not so much if specific products work, but that you still don't need most of them. You don't need energy boosting supplements or weight loss pills. Exercise builds body and spirit more than any supplement. Get sunlight, eat greens and nutritious food, and get rest. Keep body and mind clean. Train in healthy ways. These are mainstays of fueling physical ability. Get out and enjoy your life. Cut back on (or eliminate) stimulants. Vicious cycles of dependence, even addiction, build. Look and see why you think you need them. Then live a wise life so you don't need them. Stop unhealthy food, drink, and habits that sap energy. Find the real reason if you eat too much, and work on the cause. It works against you to take pills that are unhealthy on top of a weight problem. If you are working late and exhausted, a five or ten minute break of fast, fun exercise will fuel your physical and thinking ability without pills and coffee. If you are sad, try the same instead of reaching for alcohol, stimulants, or worse. When things are rough, fine. You still don't need pills, drugs, binging on alcohol, or overeating. You're a tough martial artist. Don't forget the art.

Don't be lulled by advertising that claims their pills and products will change your life. It's tempting to buy them when you doubt yourself. But you can succeed without them because you are already good and valuable. Why deprive yourself of untainted accomplishment, or deprive the world of your contributions by hurting yourself? Anyone can fake it. You can be the real thing.

Buying an expensive paintbrush will not make you an artist. Take the money not spent on commercial products, supplements, and excess food. There will be enough to give to the poor and get a vacation. Keep in perspective that supplements increase performance of elite professional athletes by small amounts, while the martial artist can increase abilities to a large extent without side effects by simple healthy habits and exercise. These are the most effective performance aids. Be happy. That is the healthiest thing you can do.

Feeding Good Energy or Bad Is Up To You

You can feed bad habits, traits, and energy, or feed positive ones.

The Indian child went to the town with his father to trade the all the work they had done the past winter. He was happy, because the father said since he had helped with the work, he could get something at the trading post. He chose a beautiful knife. Some town boys gathered outside the post. They called him a dirty and stupid Indian. They pushed him down. They took the knife and ran away laughing.

The child went to his Grandmother to ask her what he should do. "I hate them, I hate them for how they make me feel. They took what is not theirs!"

The Grandmother said, " I too, at times, have felt a great hate for those that have taken so much, with no sorrow for what they do. Hate wears you down and does not hurt your enemy. It is like taking poison and wishing your enemy would die. I have struggled with these feelings many times. It is as if two wolves live inside me, one is gray and one is silver.

"Silver Wolf is good and does no harm. He lives in harmony with all around him and does not take offense when no offense was intended. He will only fight when it is right to do so, and in the right way.

"Grey Wolf is full of anger. Small things set him into a fit of temper. He fights all the time for no reason. He cannot think because his anger and hate are so great. It is helpless anger, for his anger will change nothing. Both these wolves try to dominate my spirit."

The child asked, "Which one wins Grandmother?" The Grandmother said, "The one I feed."

"Uchu-reisei; Have a universal spirit."
—First of the Ten Major Precepts of Aikido

Is Gender an Issue?

The Buddha said that men and women are the same being. Their paths may be different only as the paths of any two men are different from each other. Their qualities thrive when both are used together.

In physiology, women and men are not so different. Gender does not determine ability to fight an attacker, whether it is a dog, a man, woman, or a swarm of bees. Some exercise books have a separate section about women, stating they are smaller and less muscular, with shorter limbs and less iron in the blood, and so on. This chapter explains how these attributes are not disadvantages in women or men.

Physical Size

A common belief is that since women are smaller they will have a disadvantage when trying to defend themselves. If that were true there would be no betting in boxing. The bigger person would always win. Goliath would always beat David, and any Westerner who was larger would have the advantage over any Asian who was smaller and lighter.

Many combinations of speed, strength, agility, training, body weight, endurance, determination, technique, strategy, experience, and dumb luck determine outcomes between any two fighters. Bruce Lee was 5'7" and 135 pounds. Jackie Chan is 5'9" and weighs about 145 pounds. Jet Li is said to be only 5'6" (169 cm) at 145 pounds (66 kg). Jean Claud Van Damm (real name Van Varenberg) is about 5'8". His five years of ballet lessons helped his karate training as a shy, slightly built teenager.

Having higher or lower body weight than your assailant, or longer or shorter arms and legs, does not determine success at defending yourself. Being larger or smaller both have advantages and disadvantages. Ducking punches and grabs can be easier for the shorter person. A shorter person usually has a lower center of gravity, offering leverage in throws. Shorter limbs can have a leverage advantage over longer limbs, which have to generate more torque (force during turning or twisting) to lift the same weight. A short-limbed person may be able to reach as far as a longer-limbed person, by training for speed and technique. A larger, heavier person is more likely to overheat during physical exertion. There is always the idea of, "The bigger they come, the harder they fall," but even that's not true all the time.

Certainly, it is difficult to fight a Sumo, but it is even difficult for a Sumo to fight a Sumo. Characteristics like balance, speed, strength, agility, and reaction time are not determined by physical size or gender. Anyone of any size can develop martial arts skills through training and practice. If you are slow, train for speed with speed drills. If you are weak, strengthen yourself to better defend yourself. If you are afraid, repetition of all your techniques until you know them well builds confidence. None of these attributes are gender-based. You just need to do the work to gain the skills.

Muscles

The muscle cells in men and women are the same cells. Women's muscle cells aren't structurally different or weaker than the muscle cells in a man's body. Several things make one person's muscles stronger than another's. One contributor to strength is how many muscle cells you have. This is mostly determined during developmental years as babies and children. Exercise during these years encourages cell development, making it important to encourage girls to be active. In adulthood, muscle cell size is increased through exercise, the same way people get fatter by increasing the size of each fat cell through overeating. Increasing size of muscle cells determines how big the muscles become. Size is not the only determinant of strength. Just having bigger muscles will not always make you stronger than someone with smaller muscles.

When you start a weight lifting program for strength, your body does several things that make you stronger. Usually the first adaptation is a learning effect in nerves and muscles, and how you coordinate them. This immediately increases the amount you can lift, or how hard you can hit, before any physical changes occur.

Next, changes begin in the nerves serving the muscles. You have many nerves serving each muscle. These nerves do many things. They tell the muscles how fast and how hard to contract. They tell information about the weight and the shape of the thing they are lifting. They tell where they are moving, if they are working quickly or slowly, or if they are getting stretched or torn. When you do physical training, the nerves learn to fire more of your muscle cells at once, making you able to contract your muscle harder. They can fire more, making you more able to sustain the contraction.

A third change is muscle size. Young males increase strength mostly by increasing muscle size. Women and older men increase strength more through neural changes than large size changes, even when they make the same strength increases as a young man. Muscle size is not the only predictor of strength. A tiny bullet can do much if it moves quickly. Strong things may come in small packages.

Not having strong muscles comes from not using them, not primarily from being a woman or being older. Your muscles will be strong only if you train them. Don't sit around. Lift packages. Lift children. Lift any kinds of weights. Practice martial arts skills. Lifting weights is important to keep bones dense. Lift your own body weight by taking the stairs and doing pushups. Bend knees and squat properly to get exercise and save your back during all the many dozens of times you bend and lift every day for normal daily life. Train a variety of ways to be stronger, faster, and more able.

Aerobic Capacity

Aerobic capacity determines how long and fast you can fight, run, bike, skip rope, swim, skate, or move continuously. It is part of how tired you will be after doing things all day. Being female does not necessarily mean a lower aerobic level than being male.

Your body takes oxygen out of the air you breathe to make energy to live, think, do body functions, and exercise. Your body can only use so much oxygen. If you breathe a higher amount of oxygen at rest, your body does not use the excess. You breathe out the extra. You don't use all the oxygen in each breath of regular air. Each breath you exhale is still mostly unused oxygen. Your exhaled breath has so much unused oxygen, you can give mouth-to-mouth resuscitation. When you move around, you need more oxygen, so take more oxygen out of the air with each breath. The better shape you are, the more oxygen your body knows how to take from air and use to make energy. The more you exercise, the more your body makes changes so it can take and use oxygen to make energy to do exercise.

The maximum amount of oxygen your body can extract and use to make energy to do exercise is called VO_2max (pronounced vee-oh-two-max). It determines aerobic capacity, also called cardiovascular endurance. Breathing more oxygen won't make these changes in your body. Exercise training makes these changes.

The more you exercise, the higher you can build aerobic capacity to make energy from oxygen to do things. Having a low aerobic capacity is not determined by gender, but mostly by activity level.

In the early 1900s, it was accepted among Western authorities that women were not physically capable of running farther than 200 yards. Sport events barred women on that assumption, accepted as true. The first women who entered a race did not fare well. They were burdened both by their long heavy skirts, and the fact that they had never been allowed to exercise before.

An average untrained female may have a low aerobic level, which may be lower than an untrained male. Or it may not. It does not mean that her maximum capacity is low, just that she is untrained. A trained female will have a higher aerobic capacity than an average male. A highly trained female will have a higher capacity to make energy than a trained male. Among elite athletes, the performance gap is narrowing with better training opportunities for women. Dr. Christine Wells, exercise physiologist and gender researcher at Arizona State University observed, "It's amazing how closely matched our abilities are, given our basic biology."

There is more to aerobic ability than the highest level your aerobic capacity can reach. Some people with lower aerobic capacities can work at higher percentages of their maximum, with less lactic acid build-up and other markers of high work load. They can run or fight at a faster pace, and endure longer than someone else who has a higher aerobic capacity (higher VO_2max).

Not all martial arts movements are aerobic. Short, intense activity is not aerobic. Activity that is too intense and hard to get all the energy it needs from your aerobic system needs another system to make quicker energy. That system is called your anaerobic system (an-air-RO-bic). Your anaerobic system does not use oxygen to make energy. It gets energy from molecules stored in your muscles, blood, and liver. The more and the harder you exercise, the more of these special molecules you can store. You use this system for activities like hitting hard then running away fast. You have to train this system separately than your aerobic system by training hard and fast enough to gasp and pant within seconds to minutes. Train your aerobic system with longer, less intense efforts, enough to be challenging but at a level you can sustain for 20 and 30 minutes at a time, at minimum. Train both regularly.

Aerobic ability is not as much determined by gender as physical fitness, efficiency, and practice in the skill. To improve aerobic and anaerobic energy systems, exercise regularly with long, continuous movements and intense, fast efforts. Keep muscles, liver, and blood healthy to fuel efforts by avoiding alcohol, cigarettes, drugs, and junk food. For health and energy for workouts, eat complex carbohydrates like vegetables, fruit, raw nuts like almonds and walnuts, seeds like flax, sunflower, and pumpkin, and whole grains. Not junk with sugar, white flour, white rice, and greasy chips. Don't fry food. Drink water not soda. Don't waste money on expensive supplements. Make a few nutrition changes to improve your health and ability, and get out and exercise.

Work Load

Even when a women is smaller than a man and has less musculature, it's not the case that she would not be able to do as much physically. If that were so, a male body builder would beat a female Olympic swimming medalist in a swimming race. Or any larger man would win over any smaller woman. In a real race, after the first few elite males cross the finish, the rest of the race to the last stragglers is checkered with females and males of all shapes, sizes, and abilities, except in cold water marathon swim races where women hold almost every record, and ultramarathon runs where women currently are coming in first more often.

Ability to do physical work depends on your level of conditioning, how efficiently you exercise while doing the activity, and whether the work is external like carrying weights and throwing your attacker around, or internal like moving yourself around. While walking up a hill, for example, a heavy man may work harder and closer to his maximum than a light woman of similar fitness, or even lesser fitness. Internal work like gymnastics and many self defense moves can often favor the smaller, lighter person. In external work, a larger person and a person with high muscular fitness usually has an advantage, male or female. In the shot put, for example, athletes who do well are usually large. It is not gender alone that determines ability to do heavy work, but training.

Cardiovascular Health

Women usually have lower blood pressure and other cardiovascular responses to cold, fear, and pain than men, and a lower tendency to irregular heart beats. Before menopause, women develop cardiovascular disease at a far lower rate than men. Still, cardiovascular disease, including stroke and heart attack, is the major cause of death in both men and women. This is not a gender problem, but lifestyle. For most women living a Western lifestyle, heart disease is a higher risk than breast cancer.

Flexibility and Joint Injury

Women generally have greater joint flexibility than men, although men can attain healthy flexibility with regular stretching. It is not true that musculature or exercise reduce flexibility. Lack of stretching reduces flexibility.

Joint Structure and Injury

A common misconception is that women have more knee and lower body injuries than men, because of anatomy. Some studies have found more lower body joint injury from exercise in women than men, but found that the reason was not gender, but fitness level and leg posture.

Data from the US Army Research Institute of Environmental Medicine on army recruits showed that those of lower physical fitness had consistently higher injury rate. When men and women of equal aerobic fitness were compared, their rate of injury was similar. Confirming data came from a 13-year study of 60,000 high school athletes involved in 18 sports which concluded that injury rate was not a gender issue, but instead a combination of training error and physical fitness.

Legs have posture, just like your back and neck. Don't stand, walk, run, or train, with your knees or the arches of your feet sinking inward or tilting outward. Knee pain can develop from sagging, the same as automobile tire will wear unevenly from tilting tires. Tires need alignment to prevent tilting. So do your legs. Use your leg muscles to keep your knees in the same line as your feet. Don't stand, walk, or run with your toes pointing in (pigeon toe) or pointing out (duck footed). If your legs are so tight and your posture is so poor that bad leg posture feels normal, you need to stretch and retrain leg posture, not allow bad posture.

Overheating

A large pot of water takes longer to boil than a small one, and requires more heat energy to bring it to a boil. But the comparison that a woman will overheat during training more easily than a man because she is smaller is false. Heat production increases with body mass. As people get bigger, a discrepancy grows between how much heat they produce and how much they can lose. Men usually produce more heat than women but can't get rid of it as easily. Women are usually less prone to heat injury than men.

Less serious than heat stroke is simple overheating which is uncomfortable, reduces exercise capacity, and may dehydrate through high sweating. It is common to see larger people sweating and red faced in rooms where the smaller people are training comfortably.

Large body size predisposes to heat buildup in hot conditions, but it does not seem to be as important as physical fitness in susceptibility to heat problems. An out-of-shape woman working at the same intensity as a more in-shape man would also have high core and skin temperatures. Keep your fat weight low and get in good physical shape. Both increase heat tolerance. Hydration and physical condition are major factors in heat tolerance, more than gender.

Sweating and Dehydration

Men and women have the same number of sweat glands. In general, men begin sweating at lower body temperatures but that does not put women at higher risk of overheating. Other heat dissipation pathways compensate. Thermal researcher Wyndham described men as, "wasteful sweaters" when comparing males and females in the heat. In studies of marathon runners, women lose a lower percent of their body weight in sweat than men during long exercise, lowering women's risk of dehydration and electrolyte loss compared to men during long hard exercise.

Remember to drink fluids when training in the heat. Except with running marathons or exercising long hours in the heat without stopping to eat, electrolyte loss is not usually a problem to men or women. Most meals restore needed electrolytes.

Osteoporosis and Bone Density
For throws, falls, being struck, and movement needing strength, your bones need to be dense and strong to reduce chance of fracture, and increase impact on the opponent.

Your bone density in later years depends on what you are doing right now. Unhealthy habits during youth can reduce the bone density of 20 and 30-year-old people to the equivalent of those in their 70s and 80s.

Osteoporosis is bone atrophy. It occurs in both men and women. It occurs when bones lose minerals and become thin and porous. There is no pain or warning of fracture to come. Hip fracture has a high death and disability rate in the year following, without intensive rehab.

The three main sites of osteoporosis are the wrist, upper back, and upper leg bone where it meets the pelvis (hip). Other areas can also have damage from osteoporosis, for example, tooth loss from bone loss in the jaw. Several factors lead to thinning bones and fracture risk: lack of exercise, high meat diet because animal protein leaches calcium, lack of sunshine and Vitamin D, regular use of anti-inflammatories, both steroidal and non-steroidal, alcohol and cigarettes, wheat intolerance (celiac disease), and several prescription medications including stomach acid medicines.

A major contributor to osteoporosis is lack of exercise. The job of bones is to support your body against the pull of gravity and your muscles. Bones thicken and strengthen when they work to resist the physical stress of muscle pulling on bone during exercise. Lack of mechanical stress from lack of exercise, or being in a cast, leads to bone loss no matter how much calcium you eat. Fad diets that severely limit calories and nutrients, and eating high amounts of animal proteins contribute to bone loss Sedentary young people with bad eating habits can be setting themselves up for later bone problems that could easily be prevented. Don't smoke or drink much alcohol. Both are toxic to bone cells. Prescription antacid medicines (PPIs) decrease bone mass, along with SSRI antidepressants, the anti-convulsant phenytoin (Dilantin), the birth control shot Depo Provera, and others. Ask your doctor about precautions and alternatives.

Exercise is crucial in osteoporosis prevention, another reason for women to train regularly and vigorously. To keep wrist bones strong, load wrists through pushups, acrobatic martial arts moves, handstands, and weapons training. Load the upper back vertebrae through pushups, headstands and handstands, acrobatic martial arts moves, and other weight lifting. Load the upper leg and hip through weight lifting, stances, kicks, and training using the lower body.

Get protein from vegetable sources. Animal protein, including animal protein in dairy, directly increases urinary calcium loss. Broccoli has more calcium per calorie than any other food. Spinach, seaweed, tofu, almonds, tahini, sesame seeds, and sunflower seeds are high calcium. A cup of navy beans and two corn tortillas has more calcium than a cup of milk. Fruit has calcium. Fruits, vegetables, nuts, and legumes have the elements copper and boron, which may participate in preventing osteoporosis.

Training and Reproductive Injury

Hard exercise and direct blows are not injurious to female reproductive anatomy, which is better protected than in males. Even a direct kick to the groin is not more injurious or painful than the same kick to other areas. Here is one area where women have a distinct advantage and do not need the protective gear males often must wear. Blows to the chest have not been found to be dangerous to breast tissue or create a risk of later developing any disease or cancer. To reduce pain from blows to the chest and torso, develop the upper body musculature.

Cold and heat both affect male fertility. The testicles reside near the body surface, subject to temperature variation. Infertility is estimated to affect 15 percent of marriages, with a "male factor" in up to one-half of these couples. "Hostile environments" from tight shorts, hot protective cups, constant bicycle riding, and chronic hot or cold exposure have been named as contributors. These conditions do not affect female fertility. A compression injury named "stretcher's scrotum" is documented to occur when a man performing a knee-to-chest leg stretch wore restrictive gym shorts, squeezing the testes between the bent leg and the body. The reporting journal cautioned that males should wear loose, stretchable pants. Females do not need any special considerations.

Training and Pregnancy

An old, unfortunate idea was that pregnant women should not exercise. Exercise is uppermost in preventing several of the discomforts of pregnancy, and maintaining mobility. The old idea was that if a woman was not previously active she should not start new exercise when pregnant. That is now replaced by the recommendation that if you were not active before, pregnancy is an important time to start. The American College of Obstetricians and Gynecologists (ACOG) has recommended that pregnant women should do 30 minutes or more of moderate exercise on most, if not all, days of the week. ACOG reminds not to do activities with risk of abdominal trauma, which can occur with ice hockey, soccer, horseback riding, or contact martial arts. Regular exercise during pregnancy is associated with healthier mothers and healthier babies who are less disposed to high body fat weight later in life.

Iron Levels

An intriguing risk factor for cardiovascular disease is high blood iron level. People with high iron have been found in high rates to develop heart disease. Conversely, premenopausal women who lose small monthly amounts of iron, and vegetarians and athletes who often run a bit low, have lower incidence of heart disease than the rest of the population. High iron levels may also be linked to unusual fatigue and possibly cancer. One of many reasons to cut back on (or eliminate) red meat is high iron content.

The University of Kansas Medical Center recommended that no one, unless a diagnosed iron deficiency exists, should routinely take iron supplements. Even a slightly high iron level may raise cardiac risk, particularly in men who don't have the benefit of monthly blood loss.

Training and Menstruation

Some students have heard they should reduce activity or not exercise during the menstrual phase of the monthly cycle. However, exercise reduces symptoms. Physical activity, both during menstruation and for regular conditioning reduces fatigue and aches, and keeps blood sugar and mood even. Reducing body fat through regular training reduces cramping and helps normalize high hormone levels, keeping a more even and healthy mood. Keep your training regular. You will feel better.

An old belief among some practitioners of yoga is to avoid exercises or postures that turn upside down during menstruation, with the hips higher than the head. The assumption was that flow would reverse or somehow "backwash" into the abdomen with a variety of claims of illness or problems. No real evidence shows a connection to exercise itself or different postures during exercise. Other folk myths about menstruation include that it will attract bears in the woods, that a menstruating women can make wine go sour by standing nearby, as believed in biblical times, and that it will make the wings fall off planes, as believed in the 1930's. None of these stories are true.

It is sometimes stated that premenstrual syndrome (PMS) increases problems dealing with others. There is no evidence that such a tendency is any higher than in the average male throughout the month. Considering the evening news, or any war or action movie, and some aspects of the martial arts, it may be safe to say that tendency to aggression or altercation is more likely in the male than female.

Exercise and Loss of Menstruation

Loss of the menstrual cycle is called amenorrhea (AY-men-oh-REE-uh). It is popular to blame exercise as causal, with some authorities going as far as saying that athletes with amenorrhea should be banned from training. Preventing amenorrheic athletes from exercise is counterproductive to their health and their bones. Physical exercise is crucial to preserving health, reproductive health, and bone mass.

Exercise and reduced body fat alone don't seem to cause amenorrhea. Poor nutrition is key. It seems an obvious and natural safety feature that, in evolutionary times, if conditions were harsh with scarce food, that conditions weren't favorable for reproductive survival. If an athlete stops menstruating, check other contributing factors so the athlete can continue vigorous training with all the benefits to health and well-being. Exercise reduces menstrual symptoms and may be protective against the ill effects of high hormone levels. Long, unbroken years of regular menstruation is thought to be related to ovarian cancer, from the continuous wash of hormones. This is why shorter reproductive span (years between menarche, the start of menstruation, and menopause), longer menstrual cycles (weeks between periods), pregnancies, and use of the contraceptive pill are thought to be protective.

Hormone levels affect bone density in males, too. Testosterone has many functions, including regulating bone mass. The stress of extended periods of extreme exercise on the body seems to send a signal to the brain to decrease levels of two hormones, which stimulate the testes to produce testosterone. As hormone levels decrease, risks of various reproductive and bone density problems go up. Much attention in the literature is paid to the role of hormones, exercise, and bone density in women, but unfortunately little about the phenomenon that occurs, just the same, in men.

Generality Not Gender

Over 2300 years ago Aristotle stated with certainty that women had fewer teeth than men. Until the time of the great anatomist Versalius in the 1500's, it was also dogma that women possessed one rib more than men. Neither is true. Today similar myths about anatomy, gender, and ability persist. Instead of following myths, find knowledge.

The Buddha has many forms in historical iconry—male, female, and combined, representing the many aspects of humanity and life. Everyone is the same kind of person with different abilities to train. Don't be discouraged from learning from martial arts, doing hard exercise, or fighting for sport, competition, or self-defense. With inactivity, inability and possibility of injury grows. Anatomy and gender do not determine ability to fight or risk of injury. Both women and men need regular physical exercise for health, positive mood, discipline, injury prevention, and ability to defend themselves.

Become more active. Make activity a lifetime habit, rather than a chore to endure and avoid. There is no secret in physical conditioning. You must train harder than the next one, and train often. Strengthen yourself, continually practice your techniques, take your lumps, and work to improve all the different skills you need in sports, exercise, martial arts competition, to defend yourself in a fight, and to life a healthy life.

In Thailand there is an expression, "Tai siam mai khom, tai dam nak." It means, "If the sword is not sharp, use a heavy shaft." That means if you are not the strongest at something, work your hardest. If you are weaker than the next person, lift weights diligently and practice techniques that may work better for you. If you are shorter than the next person, practice speed and other aspects to excel over them. Capitalize on skills where you excel. Remember that skills where you are weak are the ones you must train the most. Get in shape. Go train. Develop the physical ability and skills to win.

Two Water Jugs. Neither is the Weaker

This is the story of two water jugs. One was traditionally thought to be the stronger. But they were the same jug. Each watered the world.

A water bearer in India had two large water jugs. They hung on each end of a pole, which he carried across his neck. One of the pots was strong and always delivered a full portion of water at the end of the long walk. The second one dropped water along the way. Every day, from the stream to the master's house, the second pot arrived only half full.

The perfect pot was proud of its accomplishments. The second pot was ashamed of its imperfection, accomplishing only half of what it thought it had to do. After years of what it was told by everyone was bitter failure, it spoke to the water bearer one day by the stream.

"I am ashamed of myself, and I want to apologize to you." "Why?" asked the bearer. "What are you ashamed of?" The second pot continued, "I have been able for these past years, to deliver only half my load. Because of my flaws, you have to do all this work and not get full value for your efforts."

The water bearer said, "Look at the path to Master's house. What do you see?" "Nothing," said the second pot. "I see the path. There is nothing on it. But on one side it is full of flowers."

The bearer said to the pot, "Did you notice there were flowers only on your side of the path. Not on the other pot's side? Every day as we walked home from the stream, you watered them. For years you have made beautiful and nutritious flowers for Master's table. Without you being the way you are, he would not have had this bounty to grace his house."

We are all water jugs. We all carry water. Not being as strong in the same way as another water jug can be the cause of beauty and bounty. In this, see strength.

"Teachers open the door, but you must enter by yourself."
—Chinese proverb

This book teaches many things to make martial arts training and daily life healthier, stronger, faster, more fun, and pain free. You don't need supplements, special weights, machines, or equipment. You don't need to go to a gym.

Instead of separate exercises, train the same way for martial arts, health, and healthy daily function. Use exercise that directly transfers to effective healthy movement for all you do. Discard common stretches and exercises "for body parts" that practice bent-over posture, and movement that isn't healthy for joints or real life. Simplify all you can. Do the most healthy thing you can do—be happy.

Chinese politician Sun Yet-Sen said, "To understand is hard. Once one understand, action is easy."

Go through the door. Use all your martial arts for a healthy, happy lifestyle. Enjoy your training.

Photos

Cover photo and design by Jolie Bookspan Plevakas. Cover model is Paul Plevakas, third degree black belt in Shotokan karate, who uses the techniques in this book without supplements.

Photos by Paul and Jolie Plevakas. Some photos © 2006 Jupiter Images.

Photo production supervision by Steve Kramer, "Photoenvisions" Freelance Photography, Chiang Mai Thailand.

About The Author

Dr. Jolie Bookspan, MEd, PhD, FAWM, is a 4th degree black belt in Shotokan karate and undefeated full contact Muay Thai fighter, earning the title Kruu Muay. She trained with several of the pioneers of martial arts and with the monks of Japan, Nepal, and Thailand. Dr. Bookspan is a former military research physiologist, professor of anatomy, and sports medicine specialist known around the world for developing techniques that change medicine for the better. Her training and injury rehabilitation techniques, used by police, military, athletes, and top rehab centers, are so successful that Harvard Medical School clinicians named her "The St. Jude of the Joints." Paralyzed in a non-fighting accident, she rehabbed herself over years to walk again, and started over as a white belt until earning her black belt a second time. More severely injured in a second non-fighting accident, she again worked years to walk, train, teach, and compete. Jolie and her husband Paul were inducted into the Eastern USA International Black Belt Hall of Fame. Together they teach martial arts at Temple University and at their dojo, and were named Black Belt Man and Woman of the Year 2004 and Instructors of the Year 2009.

LaVergne, TN USA
07 April 2010
178391LV00001B/62/P